English-Spanish
Spanish-English

Word to Word®
Bilingual Dictionary

Compiled and Translated by:
C. Sesma, M.A.

Bilingual Dictionaries, Inc.

Spanish Word to Word® Bilingual Dictionary
4th Edition © Copyright 2010

Published in the United States by:

Bilingual Dictionaries, Inc.
PO Box 1154
Murrieta, CA 92562
T: (951) 461-6893 • F: (951) 461-3092
www.BilingualDictionaries.com

ISBN13: 978-0-933146-99-0
ISBN: 0-933146-99-X
Printed in India

Table of Contents

Preface

Bilingual Dictionaries, Inc. is committed to providing schools, libraries and educators with a great selection of bilingual materials for students. Along with bilingual dictionaries we also provide ESL materials, children's bilingual stories and children's bilingual picture dictionaries.

Sesma's Spanish Word to Word® Bilingual Dictionary was created specifically with students in mind to be used for reference and testing. This dictionary contains approximately 22,000 entries targeting common words used in the English language.

Word to Word®

Bilingual Dictionaries, Inc. has created a new series of over 25 languages, 100% Word to Word®, in order to provide ELL students with standardized bilingual dictionaries approved for state testing. Students with different backgrounds can now use dictionaries from the same series, specifically designed to create an equal resource that strictly adheres to the guidelines set by districts and states.

part of speech

entry ➡ **can** *iv* poder ⬅ translation
can *v* enlatar
can *n* lata,

entry: our selection of English vocabulary includes common words found in school usage and everyday conversation.

part of speech: part of speech is necessary to ensure the translation is appropriate. Entries can be spelled the same but have different translations and meanings depending on the part of speech.

translation: our translation is Word to Word® meaning no definitions or explanations. Purely the most simple common accurate translation.

List of Irregular Verbs

present - past - past participle

arise - arose - arisen
awake - awoke - awoken, awaked
be - was - been
bear - bore - borne
beat - beat - beaten
become - became - become
begin - began - begun
behold - beheld - beheld
bend - bent - bent
beseech - besought - besought
bet - bet - betted
bid - bade (bid) - bidden (bid)
bind - bound - bound
bite - bit - bitten
bleed - bled - bled
blow - blew - blown
break - broke - broken
breed - bred - bred
bring - brought - brought
build - built - built
burn - burnt - burnt *
burst - burst - burst
buy - bought - bought
cast - cast - cast
catch - caught - caught
choose - chose - chosen
cling - clung - clung

come - came - come
cost - cost - cost
creep - crept - crept
cut - cut - cut
deal - dealt - dealt
dig - dug - dug
do - did - done
draw - drew - drawn
dream - dreamt - dreamed
drink - drank - drunk
drive - drove - driven
dwell - dwelt - dwelt
eat - ate - eaten
fall - fell - fallen
feed - fed - fed
feel - felt - felt
fight - fought - fought
find - found - found
flee - fled - fled
fling - flung - flung
fly - flew - flown
forebear - forbore - forborne
forbid - forbade - forbidden
forecast - forecast - forecast
forget - forgot - forgotten
forgive - forgave - forgiven
forego - forewent - foregone
foresee - foresaw - foreseen
foretell - foretold - foretold

forget - forgot - forgotten
forsake - forsook - forsaken
freeze - froze - frozen
get - got - gotten
give - gave - given
go - went - gone
grind - ground - ground
grow - grew - grown
hang - hung * - hung *
have - had - had
hear - heard - heard
hide - hid - hidden
hit - hit - hit
hold - held - held
hurt - hurt - hurt
hit - hit - hit
hold - held - held
keep - kept - kept
kneel - knelt * - knelt *
know - knew - known
lay - laid - laid
lead - led - led
lean - leant * - leant *
leap - lept * - lept *
learn - learnt * - learnt *
leave - left - left
lend - lent - lent
let - let - let
lie - lay - lain

light - lit * - lit *
lose - lost - lost
make - made - made
mean - meant - meant
meet - met - met
mistake - mistook - mistaken
must - had to - had to
pay - paid - paid
plead - pleaded - pled
prove - proved - proven
put - put - put
quit - quit * - quit *
read - read - read
rid - rid - rid
ride - rode - ridden
ring - rang - rung
rise - rose - risen
run - ran - run
saw - sawed - sawn
say - said - said
see - saw - seen
seek - sought - sought
sell - sold - sold
send - sent - sent
set - set - set
sew - sewed - sewn
shake - shook - shaken
shear - sheared - shorn
shed - shed - shed

shine - shone - shone
shoot - shot - shot
show - showed - shown
shrink - shrank - shrunk
shut - shut - shut
sing - sang - sung
sink - sank - sunk
sit - sat - sat
slay - slew - slain
sleep - sleep - slept
slide - slid - slid
sling - slung - slung
smell - smelt * - smelt *
sow - sowed - sown *
speak - spoke - spoken
speed - sped * - sped *
spell - spelt * - spelt *
spend - spent - spent
spill - spilt * - spilt *
spin - spun - spun
spit - spat - spat
split - split - split
spread - spread - spread
spring - sprang - sprung
stand - stood - stood
steal - stole - stolen
stick - stuck - stuck
sting - stung - stung
stink - stank - stunk

stride - strode - stridden
strike - struck - struck (stricken)
strive - strove - striven
swear - swore - sworn
sweep - swept - swept
swell - swelled - swollen *
swim - swam - swum
take - took - taken
teach - taught - taught
tear - tore - torn
tell - told - told
think - thought - thought
throw - threw - thrown
thrust - thrust - thrust
tread - trod - trodden
wake - woke - woken
wear - wore - worn
weave - wove * - woven *
wed - wed * - wed *
weep - wept - wept
win - won - won
wind - wound - wound
wring - wrung - wrung
write - wrote - written

**Those tenses with an * also
have regular forms.**

English-Spanish

Bilingual Dictionaries, Inc.

Abbreviations

a - article
n - noun
e - exclamation
pro - pronoun
adj - adjective
adv - adverb
v - verb
iv - irregular verb
pre - preposition
c - conjunction

A

a *a* un, una
abandon *v* abandonar
abandonment *n* abandono
abbey *n* abadía
abbot *n* abad
abbreviate *v* abreviar
abbreviation *n* abreviatura
abdicate *v* abdicar
abdication *n* abdicación
abdomen *n* abdomen
abduct *v* secuestrar
abduction *n* secuestro
aberration *n* aberración
abhor *v* aborrecer
abide by *v* atenerse a
ability *n* habilidad
ablaze *adj* ardiendo
able *adj* capaz
abnormal *adj* anormal
abnormality *n* anormalidad
aboard *adv* a bordo
abolish *v* abolir, suprimir
abort *v* abortar; cancelar
abortion *n* aborto
abound *v* abundar
about *pre* acerca de
above *pre* encima de
abreast *adv* de frente
abridge *v* abreviar

abroad *adv* en el extranjero
abrogate *v* revocar
abruptly *adv* de repente
absence *n* ausencia
absent *adj* ausente
absolute *adj* absoluto
absolution *n* absolución
absolve *v* absolver
absorb *v* absorber
absorbent *adj* absorvente
abstain *v* abstenerse
abstinence *n* abstinencia
abstract *adj* abstracto
absurd *adj* absurdo
abundance *n* abundancia
abundant *adj* abundante
abuse *v* abusar; maltratar
abuse *n* abuso; maltrato
abusive *adj* ofensivo
abysmal *adj* pésimo
abyss *n* abismo
academic *adj* académico
academy *n* academia
accelerate *v* acelerar
accelerator *n* acelerador
accent *n* acento
accept *v* aceptar
acceptable *adj* aceptable
acceptance *n* aceptación
access *n* acceso
accessible *adj* accesible
accident *n* accidente

accidental *adj* accidental
acclaim *v* aclamar
acclimatize *v* aclimatarse
accommodate *v* alojar; agradar
accompany *v* acompañar
accomplice *n* cómplice
accomplish *v* realizar, lograr
accomplishment *n* logro
accord *n* acuerdo
according to *pre* según
accordion *n* acordeón
account *n* cuenta; relato
account for *v* explicar
accountable *adj* responsable
accountant *n* contable
accumulate *v* acumular
accuracy *n* exactitud
accurate *adj* preciso
accusation *n* acusación
accuse *v* acusar
accustom *v* acostumbrar
ace *n* as
ache *n* dolor
achieve *v* lograr
achievement *n* logro
acid *n* ácido
acidity *n* acidez
acknowledge *v* reconocer
acorn *n* bellota
acoustic *adj* acústico
acquaint *v* informar
acquaintance *n* conocido

acquire *v* adquirir
acquisition *n* adquisición
acquit *v* absolver
acquittal *n* absolución
acre *n* acre
acrobat *n* acróbata
across *pre* a través
act *v* actuar
action *n* acción
activate *v* activar
activation *n* activación
active *adj* activo
activity *n* actividad
actor *n* actor
actress *n* actriz
actual *adj* verdadero
actually *adv* en realidad
acute *adj* agudo, grave
adamant *adj* firme
adapt *v* adaptar(se)
adaptable *adj* adaptable
adaptation *n* adaptación
adapter *n* adaptador
add *v* sumar, añadir
addicted *adj* adicto
addiction *n* adicción
addictive *adj* adictivo
addition *n* suma
additional *adj* adicional
address *n* dirección
address *v* dirigirse a
addressee *n* destinatario

adequate *adj* adecuado	**adrift** *adv* a la deriva
adhere *v* adherirse	**adulation** *n* adulación
adhesive *adj* adhesivo	**adult** *n* adulto
adjacent *adj* junto a	**adulterate** *v* adulterar
adjective *n* adjetivo	**adultery** *n* adulterio
adjoin *v* lindar con	**advance** *v* avanzar
adjoining *adj* contiguo	**advance** *n* avance
adjourn *v* aplazar	**advantage** *n* ventaja
adjust *v* ajustar	**Advent** *n* Adviento
adjustable *adj* ajustable	**adventure** *n* aventura
adjustment *n* ajuste	**adverb** *n* adverbio
administer *v* administrar	**adversary** *n* adversario
admirable *adj* admirable	**adverse** *adj* adverso
admiral *n* almirante	**adversity** *n* adversidad
admiration *n* admiración	**advertise** *v* anunciar
admire *v* admirar	**advertising** *n* publicidad
admirer *n* admirador	**advice** *n* consejo
admissible *adj* admisible	**advisable** *adj* aconsejable
admission *n* entrada; confesión	**advise** *v* aconsejar
admit *v* admitir, confesar	**adviser** *n* consejero
admittance *n* entrada	**advocate** *v* recomendar
admonish *v* reprender	**aeroplane** *n* avión
admonition *n* amonestación	**aesthetic** *adj* estético
adolescence *n* adolescencia	**afar** *adv* lejos
adolescent *n* adolescente	**affable** *adj* afable
adopt *v* adoptar	**affair** *n* asunto; aventura
adoption *n* adopción	**affect** *v* afectar
adoptive *adj* adoptivo	**affection** *n* afecto
adorable *adj* adorable	**affectionate** *adj* cariñoso
adoration *n* adoración	**affiliate** *v* afiliarse
adore *v* adorar	**affiliation** *n* afiliación
adorn *v* adornar	**affinity** *n* afinidad

affirm v afirmar
affirmative adj afirmativo
affix v pegar, fijar
afflict v afligir
affliction n afección, achaque
affluence n riqueza
affluent adj acomodado
afford v tener medios
affordable adj asequible
affront v ofender
affront n ofensa
afloat adv a flote
afraid adj temeroso
afresh adv de nuevo
after pre después
afternoon n tarde
afterwards adv después
again adv de nuevo
against pre contra
age n edad
agency n agencia
agenda n agenda
agent n agente
agglomerate v aglomerarse
aggravate v agravar, irritar
aggravation n agravamiento
aggregate v agregar
aggression n agresión
aggressive adj agresivo
aggressor n agresor
aghast adj horrorizado
agile adj ágil, ligero

agitator n agitador
agnostic n agnóstico
agonize v angustiarse
agonizing adj angustioso
agony n agonía
agree v acordar
agreeable adj agradable
agreement n acuerdo
agricultural adj agrario
agriculture n agricultura
ahead pre adelante
aid n ayuda
aid v ayudar
aide n ayudante
ailing adj débil
ailment n achaque
aim v apuntar
aimless adj a la deriva
air n aire
air v airear; ventilar
aircraft n avión
airfare n billete de avión
airfield n campo de aviación
airline n línea aérea
airliner n avión de pasajeros
airmail n correo aéreo
airplane n avión
airport n aeropuerto
airspace n espacio aéreo
airstrip n pista de aterrizaje
airtight adj hermético
aisle n pasillo

ajar *adj* entreabierto

akin *adj* similar

alarm *n* alarma

alarm clock *n* despertador

alarming *adj* alarmante

alcoholic *adj* alcohólico

alcoholism *n* alcoholismo

alert *n* alerta

alert *v* alertar

algebra *n* algebra

alien *n* extranjero

alight *adv* en llamas

align *v* alinear

alignment *n* alineamiento

alike *adj* parecido, igual

alive *adj* vivo

all *adj* todos

allegation *n* acusación

allege *v* alegar

allegedly *adv* supuestamente

allegiance *n* lealtad

allegory *n* alegoría

allergic *adj* alérgico

allergy *n* alergia

alleviate *v* aliviar

alley *n* callejón

alliance *n* alianza

allied *adj* aliado

alligator *n* caimán

allocate *v* asignar

allot *v* asignar

allotment *n* ración, porción

allow *v* permitir

allowance *n* paga

alloy *n* aleación

allure *n* atractivo

alluring *adj* atractivo

allusion *n* alusión

ally *n* aliado

ally *v* aliarse

almanac *n* almanaque

almighty *adj* poderoso

almond *n* almendra

almost *adv* casi

alms *n* limosnas

alone *adj* solo

along *pre* por, a lo largo de

alongside *pre* al lado de

aloof *adj* distante

aloud *adv* en alta voz

alphabet *n* alfabeto

already *adv* ya

alright *adv* bien

also *adv* también

altar *n* altar

alter *v* alterar

alteration *n* alteración

altercation *n* altercado

alternate *v* alternar

alternate *adj* alterno

alternative *n* alternativa

although *c* aunque

altitude *n* altitud

altogether *adj* en total, juntos

aluminum *n* aluminio
always *adv* siempre
amass *v* amasar
amateur *adj* aficionado
amaze *v* asombrar
amazement *n* asombro
amazing *adj* asombroso
ambassador *n* embajador
ambiguous *adj* ambiguo
ambition *n* ambición
ambitious *adj* ambicioso
ambivalent *adj* ambivalente
ambulance *n* ambulancia
ambush *v* emboscar
amenable *adj* dócil
amend *v* enmendar
amendment *n* enmienda
amenities *n* servicios
American *adj* americano
amiable *adj* amable
amicable *adj* amistoso
amid *pre* en medio de
ammonia *n* amoniaco
ammunition *n* municiones
amnesia *n* amnesia
amnesty *n* amnistía
among *pre* entre
amoral *adj* amoral
amorphous *adj* amorfo
amortize *v* amortizar
amount *n* cantidad
amount to *v* ascender

amphibious *adj* anfibio
amphitheater *n* anfiteatro
ample *adj* amplio
amplifier *n* amplificador
amplify *v* amplificar
amputate *v* amputar
amputation *n* amputación
amuse *v* divertir
amusement *n* diversión
amusing *adj* divertido
an *a* un, una
analogy *n* analogía
analysis *n* análisis
analyze *v* analizar
anarchist *n* anarquista
anarchy *n* anarquía
anatomy *n* anatomía
ancestor *n* antepasado
ancestry *n* ascendencia
anchor *n* ancla
anchovy *n* anchoa
ancient *adj* antiguo
and *c* y
anecdote *n* anécdota
anemia *n* anemia
anemic *adj* anémico
anesthesia *n* anestesia
anew *adv* de nuevo
angel *n* ángel
angelic *adj* angélico
anger *v* enfadar
anger *n* rabia, enojo

angina *n* angina de pecho

angle *n* ángulo

Anglican *adj* anglicano

angry *adj* enfadado

anguish *n* angustia

animal *n* animal

animate *v* animar

animation *n* animación

animosity *n* animosidad

ankle *n* tobillo

annex *n* anexo

annexation *n* anexión

annihilate *v* aniquilar

annihilation *n* aniquilación

anniversary *n* aniversario

annotate *v* anotar

annotation *n* nota; anotación

announce *v* anunciar

announcement *n* anuncio

announcer *n* locutor

annoy *v* molestar, irritar

annoying *adj* fastidioso

annual *adj* anual

annul *v* anular

annulment *n* anulación

anoint *v* ungir

anonymity *n* anonimato

anonymous *adj* anónimo

another *adj* otro

answer *v* responder

answer *n* respuesta

ant *n* hormiga

antagonize *v* antagonizar

antecedent *n* anterior

antecedents *n* antecedentes

antelope *n* antílope

antenna *n* antena

anthem *n* himno

antibiotic *n* antibiótico

anticipate *v* esperar, prever

anticipation *n* expectativa

antidote *n* antídoto

antipathy *n* antipatía

antiquated *adj* anticuado

antiquity *n* antiguedad

anvil *n* yunque

anxiety *n* ansiedad

anxious *adj* ansioso

any *adj* cualquier

anybody *pro* cualquiera

anyhow *pro* de todos modos

anyone *pro* cualquiera

anything *pro* algo, nada

apart *adv* aparte

apartment *n* apartamento

apathy *n* apatía

ape *n* mono

aperitif *n* aperitivo

apex *n* cumbre, ápice

aphrodisiac *adj* afrodisiaco

apiece *adv* cada uno

apocalypse *n* apocalipsis

apologize *v* disculparse

apology *n* disculpa

apostle *n* apóstol
apostolic *adj* apostólico
apostrophe *n* apóstrofe
appall *v* horrorizar
appalling *adj* espantoso
apparel *n* ropa, ropaje
apparent *adj* aparente
apparently *adv* por lo visto
apparition *n* aparición
appeal *n* apelación; atracción
appeal *v* apelar; atraer
appealing *adj* atractivo
appear *v* aparecer; parecer
appearance *n* apariencia
appease *v* apaciguar
appeasement *n* apaciguamiento
appendicitis *n* apendicitis
appendix *n* apéndice
appetite *n* apetito
appetizer *n* aperitivo
applaud *v* aplaudir
applause *n* aplauso
apple *n* manzana
appliance *n* aparato
applicable *adj* aplicable
applicant *n* solicitante
application *n* aplicación; solicitud
apply *v* aplicar; solicitar
apply for *v* solicitar
appoint *v* nombrar
appointment *n* cita;
  nombramiento

appraisal *n* valoración
appraise *v* valorar
appreciate *v* apreciar; revalorizar
appreciation *n* aprecio;
  apreciación
apprehend *v* arrestar; entender
apprehensive *adj* aprensivo
apprentice *n* aprendiz
approach *v* acercarse
approach *n* enfoque
approachable *adj* accesible
approbation *n* aprobación
appropriate *adj* apropiado
approval *n* aprobación
approve *v* aprobar
approximate *adj* aproximado
apricot *n* albaricoque
April *n* abril
apron *n* delantal
aptitude *n* aptitud
aquarium *n* aquario
aquatic *adj* acuático
aqueduct *n* acueducto
Arabic *adj* árabe
arable *adj* arable
arbiter *n* árbitro
arbitrary *adj* arbitrario
arbitrate *v* arbitrar
arbitration *n* arbitraje
arc *n* arco
arch *n* arco
archaeology *n* arqueología

archaic *adj* arcaico
archbishop *n* arzobispo
architect *n* arquitecto
architecture *n* arquitectura
archive *n* archivo
arctic *adj* ártico
ardent *adj* ferviente
ardor *n* ardor
arduous *adj* arduo
area *n* área, región
arena *n* estadio, ruedo
argue *v* discutir
argument *n* argumento
arid *adj* árido
arise *iv* surgir
aristocracy *n* aristocracia
aristocrat *n* aristócrata
arithmetic *n* aritmética
ark *n* arca
arm *n* brazo
arm *v* armar
armaments *n* armamento
armchair *n* sillón
armistice *n* armisticio
armor *n* armadura
armpit *n* sobaco
army *n* ejército
aromatic *adj* aromático
around *pro* alrededor
arouse *v* despertar; excitar
arrange *v* ordenar, organizar
arrangement *n* arreglo

array *n* conjunto
arrest *v* arrestar
arrest *n* arresto
arrival *n* llegada
arrive *v* llegar
arrogance *n* arrogancia
arrogant *adj* arrogante
arrow *n* flecha
arsenal *n* arsenal
arsenic *n* arsénico
arson *n* incendio
arsonist *n* pirómano
art *n* arte
artery *n* arteria
arthritis *n* artritis
artichoke *n* alcachofa
article *n* artículo
articulate *v* articular
articulation *n* articulación
artificial *adj* artificial
artillery *n* artillería
artisan *n* artesano
artist *n* artista
artistic *adj* artístico
artwork *n* ilustraciones
as *c* mientras
as *adv* como
ascend *v* ascender
ascendancy *n* ascendencia
ascertain *v* averiguar
ascetic *adj* ascético
ash *n* ceniza; fresno

ashamed *adj* avergonzado
ashore *adv* en tierra
ashtray *n* cenicero
aside *adv* a un lado
aside from *adv* además de
ask *v* preguntar; pedir
asleep *adj* dormido
asparagus *n* espárrago
aspect *n* aspecto
asphalt *n* asfalto
asphyxiate *v* asfixiar
asphyxiation *n* asfixia
aspiration *n* aspiración
aspire *v* aspirar
aspirin *n* aspirina
assail *v* asaltar
assailant *n* agresor
assassin *n* asesino
assassinate *v* asesinar
assassination *n* asesinato
assault *n* agresión
assault *v* asaltar
assemble *v* juntar; armar
assembly *n* asamblea; montaje
assent *v* aprobar
assert *v* afirmar
assertion *n* afirmación
assess *v* evaluar; valorar
assessment *n* evaluación
asset *n* ventaja
assets *n* fondos
assign *v* asignar

assignment *n* tarea; misión
assimilate *v* asimilar
assimilation *n* asimilación
assist *v* ayudar
assistance *n* ayuda
associate *v* asociar
association *n* asociación
assorted *adj* variado
assortment *n* surtido
assume *v* suponer
assumption *n* suposición
assurance *n* garantía
assure *v* asegurar
asterisk *n* asterisco
asteroid *n* asteroide
asthma *n* asma
asthmatic *adj* asmático
astonish *v* asombrar
astonishing *adj* asombroso
astound *v* pasmar
astounding *adj* pasmoso
astray *v* extraviarse
astrologer *n* astrólogo
astrology *n* astrología
astronaut *n* astronauta
astronomer *n* astrónomo
astronomic *adj* astronómico
astronomy *n* astronomía
astute *adj* astuto, sagaz
asunder *adv* en dos
asylum *n* asilo
at *pre* en

atheism *n* ateísmo
atheist *n* ateo
athlete *n* atleta
athletic *adj* atlético
atmosphere *n* atmósfera
atmospheric *adj* atmosférico
atom *n* átomo
atomic *adj* atómico
atone *v* expiar
atonement *n* expiación
atrocious *adj* atroz
atrocity *n* atrocidad
atrophy *v* atrofiarse
attach *v* unir, atar, pegar
attached *adj* adjunto, junto
attachment *n* apego, archivo
attack *n* ataque
attack *v* atacar
attacker *n* agresor
attain *v* conseguir
attainable *adj* asequible
attainment *n* logro
attempt *v* tratar de
attempt *n* intento
attend *v* acudir, asistir
attendance *n* asistencia
attendant *n* encargado
attention *n* atención
attentive *adj* atento
attenuate *v* atenuar
attenuating *adj* atenuante
attest *v* atestiguar

attic *n* ático, desván
attitude *n* actitud
attorney *n* abogado
attract *v* atraer
attraction *n* atracción, atractivo
attractive *adj* atractivo
attribute *v* atribuir
auction *n* subasta
auction *v* subastar
auctioneer *n* subastador
audacious *adj* audaz
audacity *n* audacidad
audible *adj* audible
audience *n* audiencia
audit *v* revisar
auditorium *n* auditorio
augment *v* agrandar
August *n* agosto
aunt *n* tía
auspicious *adj* favorable
austere *adj* austero
austerity *n* austeridad
authentic *adj* auténtico
authenticate *v* autentificar
authenticity *n* autenticidad
author *n* autor
authoritarian *adj* autoritario
authority *n* autoridad
authorization *n* autorización
authorize *v* autorizar
auto *n* coche, carro
autograph *n* autógrafo

automatic *adj* automático
automobile *n* automóvil
autonomous *adj* autónomo
autonomy *n* autonomía
autopsy *n* autopsia
autumn *n* otoño
auxiliary *adj* auxiliar
avail *v* aprovechar
availability *n* disponibilidad
available *adj* disponible
avalanche *n* avalancha
avarice *n* avaricia
avaricious *adj* avaricioso
avenge *v* vengar
avenue *n* avenida
average *n* promedio, media
averse *adj* reacio
aversion *n* aversión
avert *v* evitar
aviation *n* aviación
aviator *n* aviador
avid *adj* ávido
avoid *v* evitar
avoidable *adj* evitable
avoidance *n* evasión
avowed *adj* declarado
await *v* esperar
awake *iv* despertar
awake *adj* despierto
awakening *n* el despertar
award *v* otorgar
award *n* premio

aware *adj* consciente
awareness *n* conciencia
away *adv* lejos
awe *n* admiración
awesome *adj* formidable
awful *adj* horrible
awkward *adj* torpe; incómodo
awning *n* toldo
ax *n* hacha
axiom *n* axioma
axis *n* eje
axle *n* eje

babble *v* balbucear
baby *n* bebé
babysitter *n* niñera
bachelor *n* soltero, licenciado
back *n* espalda
back *adv* de vuelta
back *v* respaldar
back down *v* echarse a atrás
back up *v* apoyar
backbone *n* espina dorsal
backdoor *n* puerta trasera
backfire *v* fallar
background *n* fondo

backing *n* apoyo, respaldo
backlash *n* reacción fuerte
backlog *n* tarea atrasada
backpack *n* mochila
backup *n* respaldo
backward *adj* atrasado
backwards *adv* hacia atrás
backyard *n* patio trasero
bacon *n* tocino
bacteria *n* bacteria
bad *adj* malo
badge *n* placa, chapa
badly *adv* mal, gravemente
baffle *v* desconcertar
bag *n* bolsa, saco
baggage *n* equipaje
baggy *adj* uango, ancho
baguette *n* barra de pan
bail *n* fianza
bail out *v* pagar la fianza
bailiff *n* alguacil
bait *n* cebo
bake *v* cocer al horno
baker *n* panadero
bakery *n* panadería
balance *v* equilibrar
balance *n* equilibrio; saldo
balcony *n* balcón
bald *adj* calvo
bale *n* fardo
ball *n* pelota
balloon *n* globo

ballot *n* votación
ballroom *n* salón de baile
balm *n* bálsamo
balmy *adj* suave
bamboo *n* bambú
ban *n* prohibición
ban *v* prohibir
banality *n* banalidad
banana *n* plátano
band *n* banda; grupo
bandage *n* venda
bandage *v* vendar
bandit *n* bandido
bang *v* golpear
banish *v* desterrar
banishment *n* destierro
bank *n* banco; ribera
bankrupt *v* arruinar
bankrupt *adj* en quiebra
bankruptcy *n* quiebra
banner *n* estandarte
banquet *n* banquete
baptism *n* bautismo
baptize *v* bautizar
bar *n* barra, tableta
bar *v* prohibir
barbarian *n* bárbaro
barbaric *adj* brutal
barbarism *n* brutalidad
barbecue *n* barbacoa
barber *n* peluquero
bare *adj* desnudo

barefoot *adj* descalzo

barely *adv* apenas

bargain *n* ganga

bargain *v* negociar

bargaining *n* negociación

barge *n* barcaza

bark *v* ladrar

bark *n* corteza; ladrido

barley *n* cebada

barmaid *n* mesera

barman *n* mesero

barn *n* granero

barometer *n* barómetro

barracks *n* cuartel

barrage *n* descarga

barrel *n* barril

barren *adj* estéril; árido

barricade *n* barricada

barrier *n* barrera

barring *pre* excepto

bartender *n* camarero

barter *v* intercambiar

base *n* base

base *v* basarse en

baseball *n* béisbol

baseless *adj* sin pruebas

basement *n* sótano

bashful *adj* tímido

basic *adj* básico, sencillo

basics *n* fundamentos

basin *n* lavabo, cuenca

basis *n* base

bask *v* tomar al sol

basket *n* cesta

basketball *n* baloncesto

bastard *n* bastardo

bat *n* murciélago; bate

batch *n* lote; grupo

bath *n* baño

bathe *v* bañarse

bathrobe *n* bata

bathroom *n* cuarto de baño

bathtub *n* bañera

baton *n* batuta

battalion *n* batallón

batter *v* maltratar

battery *n* batería, pila

battle *n* batalla

battle *v* luchar

battleship *n* acorazado

bay *n* bahía

bayonet *n* bayoneta

bazaar *n* bazar

be *iv* ser; estar

be born *v* nacer

beach *n* playa

beacon *n* faro

beak *n* pico

beam *n* rayo; viga

bean *n* judía, alubia

bear *n* oso

bear *iv* soportar, llevar

bearable *adj* llevadero

beard *n* barba

bearded *adj* barbudo
bearer *n* portador
beast *n* bestia
beat *iv* golpear; vencer
beat *n* latido; ritmo
beaten *adj* golpeado; vencido
beating *n* paliza
beautiful *adj* hermoso
beautify *v* embellecer
beauty *n* hermosura
beaver *n* castor
because *c* porque
because of *pre* por razón de
beckon *v* hacer señas
become *iv* llegar a ser
bed *n* cama, cauce
bedding *n* ropa de cama
bedroom *n* dormitorio
bedspread *n* colcha
bee *n* abeja
beef *n* carne
beef up *v* reforzar
beehive *n* colmena
beer *n* cerveza
beet *n* remolacha
beetle *n* escarabajo
before *adv* antes
before *pre* antes de
beforehand *adv* de antemano
befriend *v* hacerse amigo
beg *v* suplicar
beggar *n* mendigo

begin *iv* empezar
beginner *n* principiante
beginning *n* principio
beguile *v* engañar
behalf (on) *adv* en favor de
behave *v* comportarse
behavior *n* conducta
behead *v* decapitar
behind *pre* detrás de
behold *iv* contemplar
being *n* ser
belated *adj* atrasado
belch *v* eructar
belch *n* eruto
belfry *n* campanario
Belgian *adj* belga
Belgium *n* Bélgica
belief *n* creencia
believable *adj* verosímil
believe *v* creer
believer *n* creyente
belittle *v* menospreciar
bell *n* campana; timbre
bell pepper *n* pimiento
belligerent *adj* agresivo
belly *n* barriga, panza
belly button *n* ombligo
belong *v* pertenecer
belongings *n* pertenencias
beloved *adj* querido
below *adv* abajo
below *pre* debajo de

B

belt *n* correa
bench *n* banco
bend *iv* doblar, torcer
bend down *v* agacharse
beneath *pre* debajo de
benediction *n* bendición
benefactor *n* bienhechor
beneficial *adj* beneficioso
beneficiary *n* beneficiario
benefit *n* beneficio
benefit *v* beneficiar
benevolence *n* benevolencia
benevolent *adj* benévolo
benign *adj* benigno
bequeath *v* legar
bereaved *adj* desconsolado
bereavement *n* duelo
beret *n* boina
berserk *adv* loco
berth *n* litera
beseech *iv* suplicar
beset *iv* acosar
beside *pre* al lado de
besides *pre* además
besiege *iv* asediar
best *adj* el mejor
best man *n* padrino de boda
bestial *adj* bestial
bestiality *n* bestialidad
bestow *v* otorgar
bet *iv* apostar
bet *n* apuesta

betray *v* traicionar; engañar
betrayal *n* traición; engaño
better *adj* mejor
between *pre* entre
beverage *n* bebida
beware *v* tener cuidado
bewilder *v* desconcertar
bewitch *v* hechizar
beyond *adv* más allá
bias *n* prejuicio
bible *n* biblia
biblical *adj* bíblico
bibliography *n* bibliografía
bicycle *n* bicicleta
bid *n* oferta
bid *iv* hacer una oferta
big *adj* grande
bigamy *n* bigamia
bigot *adj* fanático
bigotry *n* fanatismo
bike *n* bicicleta
bile *n* bilis
bilingual *adj* bilingue
bill *n* cuenta, factura
billiards *n* billar
billion *n* billón
billionaire *n* billonario
bimonthly *adj* bimestral
bin *n* bote de basura
bind *iv* obligar; unir
binding *adj* obligatorio
binoculars *n* binoculares

biography *n* biografía
biological *adj* biológico
biology *n* biología
bird *n* pájaro
birth *n* nacimiento
birthday *n* cumpleaños
biscuit *n* galleta
bishop *n* obispo
bison *n* bisonte
bit *n* trozo; un poco
bite *iv* morder; picar
bite *n* mordisco
bitter *adj* amargo
bitterly *adv* amargamente
bitterness *n* amargura
bizarre *adj* extravagante
black *adj* negro
blackberry *n* mora
blackboard *n* pizarra
blackmail *n* chantaje
blackmail *v* chantajear
blackness *n* oscuridad
blackout *n* apagón
blacksmith *n* herrero
bladder *n* vejiga
blade *n* cuchilla
blame *n* culpa
blame *v* culpar
blameless *adj* inocente
bland *adj* soso, insulso
blank *adj* en blanco
blanket *n* manta

blaspheme *v* blasfemar
blasphemy *n* blasfemia
blast *n* explosión
blaze *v* arder
bleach *v* desteñir
bleach *n* lejía
bleak *adj* desolador
bleed *iv* sangrar
bleeding *n* hemorragia
blemish *n* mancha
blemish *v* manchar
blend *n* mezcla
blend *v* mezclar
blender *n* licuadora
bless *v* bendecir
blessed *adj* bendito
blessing *n* bendición
blind *v* cegar
blind *adj* ciego
blindfold *n* venda
blindfold *v* vendar los ojos
blindly *adv* a ciegas
blindness *n* ceguera
blink *v* parpadear
bliss *n* felicidad
blissful *adj* feliz
blister *n* ampolla
blizzard *n* ventisca
bloat *v* hincharse
bloated *adj* hinchado
block *n* bloque; tapón
block *v* atascar; impedir

B

blockade v bloquear

blockade n bloqueo

blockage n obstrucción

blond adj rubio

blood n sangre

bloody adj sangriento

bloom v florecer

blossom v florecer

blot n borrón, mancha

blot v emborronar

blouse n blusa

blow n golpe

blow iv soplar; sonar

blow out iv apagar(se)

blow up iv estallar

blowout n reventón

bludgeon v aporrear

blue adj azul

blueprint n plano, plan

bluff v fanfarronear

blunder n error

blunt adj franco, sin punta

bluntness n franqueza

blur v enturbiar

blurred adj borroso

blush v sonrojarse

blush n rubor, sonrojo

boar n jabalí

board n tablero; tabla

board v embarcarse

boast v alardear

boat n barca

bodily adj corporal

body n cuerpo, grupo

bog n pantano

bog down v atascarse

boil v hervir

boil down to v reducirse a

boil over v rebosar

boiler n caldera

boisterous adj ruidoso

bold adj valiente; letra negra

boldness n valentía

bolster v reforzar, apoyar

bolt n pestillo; rayo

bolt v cerrar con pestillo

bomb n bomba

bomb v bombardear

bombing n bombardeo

bombshell n bomba

bond n fianza; unión

bondage n esclavitud

bone n hueso

bone marrow n médula

bonfire n hoguera

bonus n bonificación

book n libro

bookcase n estantería

bookkeeper n contable

bookkeeping n contabilidad

booklet n folleto

bookseller n librero

bookstore n librería

boom n auge, estruendo

boom *v* crecer

boost *v* estimular

boost *n* estímulo

boot *n* bota

booth *n* cabina

booty *n* botín

booze *n* bebida

border *n* frontera; borde

border on *v* lindar con

borderline *adj* dudoso

bore *v* taladrar

bored *adj* aburrido

boredom *n* aburrimiento

boring *adj* aburrido

born *adj* nacido

borough *n* municipio

borrow *v* tomar prestado

bosom *n* seno, pecho

boss *n* jefe

boss around *v* dar órdenes

bossy *adj* mandón

botany *n* botánica

botch *v* estropear

both *adj* ambos

bother *v* molestar

bothersome *adj* preocupante

bottle *n* botella

bottle *v* embotellar

bottleneck *n* embotellamiento

bottom *n* fondo, pie, final

bottomless *adj* sin fondo

bough *n* rama

boulder *n* roca

boulevard *n* bulevar

bounce *v* rebotar, botar

bounce *n* rebote

bound *adj* obligado

bound for *adj* con destino a

boundary *n* frontera, borde

boundless *adj* sin límites

bounty *n* recompensa

bourgeois *adj* burgués

bow *n* reverencia; proa

bow *v* inclinarse

bow out *v* ceder

bowels *n* entrañas

bowl *n* tazón, plato hondo

box *n* caja

box office *n* taquilla

boxer *n* boxeador

boxing *n* boxeo

boy *n* muchacho

boycott *v* boicotear

boyfriend *n* novio

boyhood *n* mocedad

bra *n* sostén

brace for *v* prepararse para

bracelet *n* pulsera

bracket *n* soporte

brag *v* jactarse

braid *n* trenza

brain *n* cerebro

brainwash *v* lavar el cerebro

brake *n* freno

brake v frenar

branch n rama

branch office n sucursal

branch out v extenderse

brand n marca

brand-new adj reciente

brandy n cognac

brat adj mocoso

brave adj valiente

bravely adv valerosamente

bravery n valentía

brawl n pelea

breach n infracción; brecha

bread n pan

breadth n anchura

break n fractura; descanso

break iv romper

break away v separarse

break down v averiarse, romperse

break free v escaparse

break in v entrar

break off v romperse

break open v forzar

break out v estallar

break up v deshacer(se)

breakable adj frágil

breakdown n avería

breakfast n desayuno

breakthrough n avance

breast n pecho

breath n aliento, respiro

breathe v respirar

breathing n respiración

breathtaking adj imponente

breed iv procrear, generar

breed n raza

breeze n brisa

brethren n hermanos

brevity n brevedad

brew v elaborar

brewery n cervecería

bribe v sobornar

bribe n soborno

bribery n soborno

brick n ladrillo

bricklayer n albañil

bridal adj nupcial

bride n novia

bridegroom n novio

bridesmaid n dama de honor

bridge n puente

bridle n freno

brief adj corto, breve

brief v informar

briefcase n cartera

briefing n informe

briefly adv brevemente

briefs n calzoncillos

brigade n brigada

bright adj brillante

brighten v alumbrar

brightness n brillo

brilliant adj brillante

brim *n* borde
bring *iv* traer
bring back *v* devolver
bring down *v* echar abajo
bring up *v* mencionar
brink *n* borde
brisk *adj* rapido
Britain *n* Gran Bretaña
British *adj* británico
brittle *adj* frágil
broad *adj* ancho
broadcast *v* transmitir
broadcast *n* emisión
broadcaster *n* locutor
broaden *v* ampliar
broadly *adv* en general
broadminded *adj* liberal
brochure *n* folleto
broil *v* asar
broiler *n* asador
broke *adj* quebrado
broken *adj* roto
bronchitis *n* bronquitis
bronze *n* bronce
broom *n* escoba
broth *n* caldo
brothel *n* burdel
brother *n* hermano
brotherhood *n* hermandad
brother-in-law *n* cuñado
brotherly *adj* fraternal
brow *n* ceja, frente

brown *adj* marrón
browse *v* hojear; navegar
browser *n* navegador
bruise *n* moretón
bruise *v* magullar
brunch *n* almuerzo
brunette *adj* morena
brush *n* cepillo
brush *v* cepillar
brush aside *v* ignorar
brush up *v* repasar
brusque *adj* rudo
brutal *adj* brutal
brutality *n* brutalidad
brutalize *v* embrutecer
brute *adj* bruto
bubble *n* burbuja
bubble gum *n* chicle
buck *n* dólar
bucket *n* balde, cubo
buckle *n* hebilla
buckle up *v* abrocharse
bud *n* brote, capullo
buddy *n* compañero
budge *v* moverse; ceder
budget *n* presupuesto
buffalo *n* búfalo
bug *n* bicho, microbio
bug *v* molestar
build *iv* edificar
builder *n* constructor
building *n* edificio

B

buildup *n* acumulación
built-in *adj* empotrado
bulb *n* bombilla
bulge *n* bulto
bulk *n* grueso, mayor parte
bulky *adj* abultado, enorme
bull *n* toro
bull fight *n* corrida de toros
bull fighter *n* torero
bulldoze *v* derribar
bullet *n* bala
bulletin *n* boletín
bully *adj* matón
bulwark *n* baluarte
bum *n* vagabundo
bump *n* chinchón; bache
bump into *v* tropezar con
bumper *n* parachoques
bumpy *adj* lleno de baches
bun *n* bollo
bunch *n* ramo; grupo
bundle *n* fardo, haz
bundle *v* envolver, atar
bunk bed *n* litera
bunker *n* refugio
buoy *n* boya
burden *n* carga
burden *v* cargar
burdensome *adj* pesado
bureau *n* oficina
bureaucracy *n* burocracia
bureaucrat *n* burócrata

burger *n* hamburguesa
burglar *n* ladrón
burglarize *v* robar
burglary *n* robo
burial *n* entierro
burly *adj* fornido
burn *iv* quemar, arder
burn *n* quemadura
burp *v* eructar
burp *n* eructo
burrow *n* madriguera
burst *iv* reventar
burst into *v* irrumpir
bury *v* enterrar
bus *n* autobús
bus *v* llevar en autobús
bush *n* arbusto
busily *adv* afanosamente
business *n* negocio
businessman *n* negociante
bust *n* busto
bustling *adj* ajetreado
busy *adj* ocupado
but *c* pero
butcher *n* carnicero
butchery *n* carnicería
butler *n* mayordomo
butt *n* culata; colilla
butter *n* mantequilla
butterfly *n* mariposa
button *n* botón
buttonhole *n* ojal

buy *iv* comprar
buy off *v* sobornar
buyer *n* comprador
buzz *n* zumbido
buzz *v* zumbar
buzzard *n* buitre
buzzer *n* timbre
by *pre* por, al lado de
bye *e* adiós
bypass *n* desviación
bypass *v* eludir; desviarse
by-product *n* derivado
bystander *n* espectador

C

cab *n* taxi
cabbage *n* berza, repollo
cabin *n* cabina
cabinet *n* armario; gabinete
cable *n* cable
cafeteria *n* cafetería
caffeine *n* cafeína
cage *n* jaula
cake *n* pastel
calamity *n* calamidad
calculate *v* calcular
calculation *n* cálculo

calculator *n* calculadora
calendar *n* calendario
calf *n* ternero
caliber *n* calibre
calibrate *v* calibrar
call *n* llamada; llamamiento
call *v* llamar; convocar
call off *v* cancelar
call on *v* visitar
call out *v* llamar a gritos
calling *n* vocación
callous *adj* cruel
calm *adj* calmado
calm *n* calma
calm down *v* calmar(se)
calorie *n* caloría
calumny *n* calumnia
camel *n* camello
camera *n* cámara
camouflage *v* camuflar
camouflage *n* camuflaje
camp *n* campamento
camp *v* acampar
campaign *v* hacer campaña
campaign *n* campaña
campfire *n* fogata
can *iv* poder
can *v* enlatar
can *n* lata, bote
can opener *n* abrelatas
canal *n* canal
canary *n* canario

cancel v cancelar
cancellation n cancelación
cancer n cáncer
cancerous adj canceroso
candid adj franco
candidacy n candidatura
candidate n candidato
candle n vela, cirio
candlestick n candelero
candor n franqueza
candy n dulces
cane n caña; bastón
canister n bote
canned adj enlatado
cannibal n caníbal
cannon n cañón
canoe n canoa
canonize v canonizar
cantaloupe n melón
canteen n cantina
canvas n lienzo, lona
canvas v solicitar
canyon n cañon
cap n gorra; tapadera
capability n capacidad
capable adj capaz
capacity n capacidad
cape n capa; cabo
capital n capital
capital letter n mayúscula
capitalism n capitalismo
capitalize v aprovecharse

capitulate v capitular
capsize v volcar
capsule n cápsula
captain n capitán
captivate v cautivar
captive n cautivo
captivity n cautiverio
capture v capturar
capture n captura
car n coche, auto
carat n quilate
caravan n caravana
carburetor n carburador
carcass n esqueleto
card n tarjeta; naipe
cardboard n cartón
cardiac adj cardiaco
cardiac arrest n paro cardiaco
cardiology n cardiología
care n cuidado
care v cuidar
care about v preocuparse
care for v importar
career n profesión, carrera
carefree adj despreocupado
careful adj cuidadoso
careless adj descuidado
carelessness n descuido
caress n caricia
caress v acariciar
caretaker n encargado
cargo n cargamento

caricature *n* caricatura
caring *adj* bondadoso
carnage *n* matanza
carnal *adj* carnal
carnation *n* clavel
carol *n* villancico
carpenter *n* carpintero
carpentry *n* carpintería
carpet *n* alfombra
carriage *n* vagón, carruaje
carrot *n* zanahoria
carry *v* llevar
carry on *v* continuar
carry out *v* llevar a cabo
cart *n* carreta
cart *v* acarrear
cartoon *n* caricatura
cartridge *n* cartucho
carve *v* trinchar; tallar
cascade *n* cascada
case *n* caso; caja
cash *n* dinero en efectivo
cashier *n* cajero
casino *n* casino
casket *n* ataúd, cofre
casserole *n* cazuela
cassock *n* sotana
cast *iv* arrojar; fundir
castaway *n* náufrago
caste *n* casta
castle *n* castillo
casual *adj* casual, informal

C

casualty *n* víctima
cat *n* gato
cataclysm *n* cataclismo
catacomb *n* catacumba
catalog *n* catálogo
catalog *v* catalogar
cataract *n* catarata
catastrophe *n* catástrofe
catch *iv* coger, tomar
catch up *v* alcanzar
catching *adj* contagioso
catchword *n* eslogan
catechism *n* catecismo
category *n* categoría
cater to *v* satisfacer
caterpillar *n* oruga
cathedral *n* catedral
catholic *adj* católico
Catholicism *n* catolicismo
cattle *n* ganado
cauliflower *n* coliflor
cause *n* causa, motivo
cause *v* causar
caution *n* cautela, precaución
cautious *adj* precavido
cavalry *n* caballería
cave *n* cueva
cave in *v* derrumbarse; ceder
cavern *n* caverna
cavity *n* cavidad, hoyo
cease *v* cesar
cease-fire *n* tregua

C

ceiling n techo

celebrate v celebrar, festejar

celebration n celebración

celebrity n celebridad

celery n apio

celestial adj celestial

celibacy n celibato

celibate adj célibe

cellar n bodega

cellphone n móvil, celular

cement n cemento

cemetery n cementerio

censorship n censura

censure v censurar

census n censo

cent n céntimo

centenary n centenario

center n centro

center v centrar

centimeter n centímetro

central adj central

centralize v centralizar

century n siglo

ceramic n cerámica

cereal n cereal

cerebral adj cerebral

ceremony n ceremonia

certain adj cierto

certainty n certeza

certificate n certificado

certify v certificar

chagrin n disgusto

chain n cadena

chain v encadenar

chainsaw n sierra eléctrica

chair n silla

chair v presidir

chairman n presidente

chalet n chalet, villa

chalice n cáliz

chalk n tiza

chalkboard n pizarra

challenge v desafiar

challenge n desafío

challenging adj estimulante

chamber n cámara, sala

champ n campeón

champion n campeón

champion v promover

chance n oportunidad; riesgo

chancellor n canciller

chandelier n araña (lámpara)

change v cambiar

change n cambio

channel n canal

chant n canto

chaos n caos

chaotic adj caótico

chapel n capilla

chaplain n capellán

chapter n capítulo

char v carbonizar

character n carácter

characteristic adj característico

charade *n* farsa

charbroil *adj* asar a la brasa

charcoal *n* carbón

charge *v* acusar; cobrar

charge *n* cargo; precio

charisma *n* carisma

charismatic *adj* carismático

charitable *adj* caritativo

charity *n* caridad

charm *v* encantar

charm *n* encanto

charming *adj* encantador

chart *n* gráfico; mapa

charter *n* estatutos; alquiler

charter *v* alquilar

chase *n* persecución

chase *v* perseguir

chase away *v* ahuyentar

chasm *n* sima, abismo

chaste *adj* casto

chastise *v* castigar

chastisement *n* castigo

chastity *n* castidad

chat *v* charlar

chauffeur *n* chófer

cheap *adj* barato

cheat *v* estafar, engañar

cheater *n* estafador

check *n* cheque; cuenta

check *v* comprobar

check in *v* registrar(se)

check up *n* examen

checkbook *n* chequera

cheek *n* mejilla

cheekbone *n* pómulo

cheeky *adj* descarado

cheer *v* vitorear

cheer up *v* animar

cheerful *adj* alegre

cheers *n* aclamaciones

cheese *n* queso

chef *n* jefe de cocina

chemical *adj* químico

chemist *n* farmacéutico

chemistry *n* química

cherish *v* apreciar

cherry *n* cereza

chess *n* ajedrez

chest *n* pecho; cofre

chestnut *n* castaña

chew *v* mascar

chick *n* pollito, jovencita

chicken *n* pollo

chicken out *v* acobardarse

chicken pox *n* viruela

chide *v* regañar

chief *n* jefe

chiefly *adv* principalmente

child *n* niño

childhood *n* niñez

childish *adj* pueril

childless *adj* sin hijos

children *n* niños

chill *n* resfriado**

C

C

chill *v* enfriar
chill out *v* calmarse
chilly *adj* fresco, frío
chimney *n* chimenea
chimpanzee *n* chimpancé
chin *n* barbilla
chip *n* ficha; papa frita
chisel *n* cincel
chocolate *n* chocolate
choice *n* elección
choir *n* coro
choke *v* ahogar(se)
cholera *n* cólera
cholesterol *n* colesterol
choose *iv* escoger, elegir
choosy *adj* exigente
chop *v* cortar
chop *n* chuleta
chopper *n* helicóptero
chore *n* faena, tarea
chorus *n* coro
christen *v* bautizar
christening *n* bautizo
christian *adj* cristiano
Christianity *n* Cristiandad
Christmas *n* Navidad
chronic *adj* crónico
chronicle *n* crónica
chronology *n* cronología
chubby *adj* regordete
chuckle *v* reirse entre dientes
chunk *n* trozo, pedazo

church *n* iglesia
chute *n* rampa
cider *n* sidra
cigar *n* cigarro
cigarette *n* cigarrillo
cinder *n* ceniza
cinema *n* cine
cinnamon *n* canela
circle *n* círculo
circle *v* rodear; volar
circuit *n* circuito
circular *adj* circular
circulate *v* circular
circulation *n* circulación
circumcise *v* circuncidar
circumcision *n* circuncisión
circumstance *n* circunstancia
circumstancial *adj* circunstancial
circus *n* circo
cistern *n* cisterna
citizen *n* ciudadano
citizenship *n* ciudadanía
city *n* ciudad
city hall *n* ayuntamiento
civic *adj* cívico
civil *adj* civil, cortés
civilization *n* civilización
civilize *v* civilizar
claim *v* reclamar, afirmar
claim *n* reclamación
clam *n* almeja
clamor *v* clamar

clamp *n* abrazadera
clamp down *v* suprimir
clan *n* clan, grupo
clandestine *adj* clandestino
clap *v* aplaudir
clarification *n* clarificación
clarify *v* clarificar, aclarar
clarinet *n* clarinete
clarity *n* claridad
clash *v* chocar
clash *n* choque
class *n* clase; categoría
classic *adj* clásico
classify *v* clasificar
classmate *n* compañero
classroom *n* aula
classy *adj* elegante
clause *n* cláusula
claw *n* garra, zarpa
claw *v* arañar
clay *n* arcilla
clean *adj* limpio
clean *v* limpiar
cleaner *n* quitamanchas
cleanliness *n* limpieza
cleanse *v* limpiar
cleanser *n* crema de limpiar
clear *adj* claro, despejado
clear *v* despejar; absolver
clearance *n* rebaja; espacio
clear-cut *adj* definido
clearly *adv* claramente

clearness *n* claridad
cleft *n* grieta
clemency *n* clemencia
clench *v* apretar
clergy *n* clero
clergyman *n* cura, ministro
clerical *adj* clerical
clerk *n* dependiente
clever *adj* listo
click *v* chasquear
client *n* cliente
clientele *n* clientela
cliff *n* acantilado
climate *n* clima
climatic *adj* climático
climax *n* apogeo
climb *v* escalar, subir
climbing *n* ascenso
clinch *v* afianzar, rematar
cling *iv* agarrarse
clinic *n* clínica
clip *v* recortar; cortar
clipping *n* recorte; fragmento
cloak *n* capa, manto
clock *n* reloj
clog *v* atascar
cloister *n* claustro
clone *v* clonar
cloning *n* clonación
close *v* cerrar
close *adj* cercano
close to *pre* cerca de

C

C

closed *adj* cerrado
closely *adv* de cerca
closet *n* armario
closure *n* cierre, fin
clot *n* coágulo
cloth *n* tela, trapo
clothe *v* vestir
clothes *n* ropa
clothing *n* ropa
cloud *n* nube
cloudless *adj* sin nubes
cloudy *adj* nubloso
clown *n* payaso
club *n* club, porra
club *v* apporrear
clue *n* pista
clumsiness *n* torpeza
clumsy *adj* torpe
cluster *n* agrupación
cluster *v* agruparse
clutch *n* embrague
coach *v* entrenar, preparar
coach *n* entrenador
coaching *n* entrenamiento
coagulate *v* coagular
coagulation *n* coagulación
coal *n* carbón
coalition *n* coalición
coarse *adj* áspero; grosero
coast *n* costa, litoral
coastal *adj* costero
coastline *n* litoral

coat *n* chaqueta; mano
coax *v* persuadir
cob *n* mazorca
cobblestone *n* adoquín
cobweb *n* telaraña
cocaine *n* cocaína
cock *n* gallo
cockpit *n* cabina
cockroach *n* cucaracha
cocktail *n* cóctel
cocky *adj* arrogante
cocoa *n* cacao
coconut *n* coco
cod *n* bacalao
code *n* código; clave
codify *v* codificar
coefficient *n* coeficiente
coerce *v* coaccionar
coercion *n* coacción
coexist *v* coexistir
coffee *n* café
coffin *n* ataúd
cohabit *v* cohabitar
coherent *adj* coherente
cohesion *n* cohesión
coin *n* moneda
coincide *v* coincidir
coincidence *n* coincidencia
coincidental *adj* casual
cold *adj* frío
coldness *n* frialdad
colic *n* cólico

collaborate _v_ colaborar
collaboration _n_ colaboración
collaborator _n_ colaborador
collapse _v_ hundirse
collapse _n_ desplome
collar _n_ collar, cuello
collarbone _n_ clavícula
collateral _adj_ colateral
colleague _n_ colega
collect _v_ colectar
collection _n_ colección
collector _n_ coleccionista
college _n_ colegio
collide _v_ chocar
collision _n_ choque
cologne _n_ colonia
colon _n_ colon; dos puntos
colonel _n_ coronel
colonial _adj_ colonial
colonization _n_ colonización
colonize _v_ colonizar
colony _n_ colonia
color _n_ color
color _v_ teñir; colorear
colorful _adj_ colorido
colossal _adj_ colosal
colt _n_ potro
column _n_ columna
coma _n_ coma
comb _n_ peine
comb _v_ peinar
combat _n_ combate

combat _v_ combatir
combatant _n_ combatiente
combination _n_ combinación
combine _v_ combinar
combustible _n_ combustible
combustion _n_ combustión
come _iv_ venir
come about _v_ acontecer
come across _v_ topar con
come apart _v_ deshacerse
come back _v_ volver
come down _v_ bajar; caer
come forward _v_ presentarse
come from _v_ ser de, venir de
come in _v_ entrar
come out _v_ salir; descubrirse
come over _v_ venir
come up _v_ surgir; subir
comeback _n_ vuelta
comedian _n_ comediante
comedy _n_ comedia
comet _n_ cometa
comfort _n_ bienestar
comfortable _adj_ cómodo
comforter _n_ colcha
comical _adj_ cómico
coming _n_ llegada
coming _adj_ próximo
comma _n_ coma
command _v_ mandar
commander _n_ comandante
commandment _n_ mandamiento**

C

C

commemorate *v* conmemorar
commence *v* comenzar
commend *v* elogiar
commendation *n* elogio
comment *v* comentar
comment *n* comentario
commerce *n* comercio
commercial *adj* comercial
commission *n* comisión, tarea
commit *v* cometer; comprometer
commitment *n* compromiso
committed *adj* dedicado
committee *n* comité
common *adj* común
commotion *n* alboroto
communicate *v* comunicar
communication *n* comunicación
communion *n* comunión
communism *n* comunismo
communist *adj* comunista
community *n* comunidad
commute *v* conmutar; viajar
compact *adj* compacto
compact *v* comprimir
companion *n* compañero
companionship *n* compañía
company *n* compañía
comparable *adj* comparable
comparative *adj* comparativo
compare *v* comparar(se)
comparison *n* comparación
compartment *n* compartimento

compass *n* brújula
compassion *n* compasión
compassionate *adj* compasivo
compatibility *n* compatibilidad
compatible *adj* compatible
compatriot *n* paisano
compel *v* forzar, obligar
compelling *adj* contundente
compendium *n* compendio
compensate *v* compensar
compensation *n* compensación
compete *v* competir
competence *n* competencia
competent *adj* competente
competition *n* concurso
competitive *adj* competitivo
competitor *n* competidor
compile *v* compilar
complain *v* quejarse
complaint *n* queja
complement *n* complemento
complete *adj* completo
complete *v* completar
completely *adv* completamente
completion *n* terminación
complex *adj* complejo
complexion *n* tez
complexity *n* complejidad
compliance *n* cumplimiento
compliant *adj* obediente
complicate *v* complicar
complication *n* complicación

complicity *n* complicidad
compliment *n* elogio, piropo
complimentary *adj* gratis, elogioso
comply *v* cumplir con
component *n* componente
compose *v* componer, calmarse
composed *adj* compuesto, calmado
composer *n* compositor
composition *n* composición
compost *n* abono
composure *n* compostura
compound *n* recinto; compuesto
compound *v* agravar
comprehend *v* comprender
comprehensive *adj* completo
compress *v* comprimir
compression *n* compresión
comprise *v* consistir en
compromise *n* arreglo
compromise *v* transigir
compulsion *n* compulsión
compulsive *adj* compulsivo
compulsory *adj* obligatorio
compute *v* calcular
computer *n* computadora
comrade *n* camarada
con man *n* estafador
conceal *v* ocultar
concede *v* conceder
conceited *adj* presumido

conceive *v* concebir
concentrate *v* concentrar
concentration *n* concentración
concentric *adj* concéntrico
concept *n* concepto
conception *n* concepción
concern *v* concernir, preocupar
concern *n* preocupación
concerning *pre* acerca de, sobre
concert *n* concierto
concession *n* concesión
conciliate *v* conciliar
conciliatory *adj* conciliatorio
conciousness *n* conciencia
concise *adj* conciso
conclude *v* concluir, terminar
conclusion *n* conclusión, final
conclusive *adj* concluyente
concoct *v* mezclar; urdir
concoction *n* brebaje
concrete *n* hormigón, cemento
concrete *adj* concreto, sucinto
concur *v* coincidir
concurrent *adj* simultáneo
concussion *n* golpe cerebral
condemn *v* condenar
condemnation *n* condenación
condensation *n* condensación
condense *v* condensar
condescend *v* condescender
condiment *n* condimento
condition *n* condición

conditional *adj* condicional
conditioner *n* suavizante
condo *n* condominio
condolences *n* pésame
condone *v* justificar
conducive *adj* conducente
conduct *n* conducta
conduct *v* comportarse, dirigir
conductor *n* chófer, director
cone *n* cono
confer *v* otorgar; deliberar
conference *n* conferencia
confess *v* confesar(se)
confession *n* confesión
confessional *n* confesionario
confessor *n* confesor
confidant *n* confidente
confide *v* confiar
confidence *n* confianza
confident *adj* confiado
confidential *adj* confidencial
confine *v* limitarse; recluir
confinement *n* prisión
confirm *v* confirmar
confirmation *n* confirmación
confiscate *v* confiscar
confiscation *n* confiscación
conflict *n* conflicto
conflict *v* chocar
conflicting *adj* opuesto
conform *v* conformarse
conformist *adj* conformista

conformity *n* conformidad
confound *v* confundir
confront *v* enfrentarse
confrontation *n* confrontación
confuse *v* confundir
confusing *adj* confuso
confusion *n* confusión
congenial *adj* agradable
congested *adj* congestionado
congestion *n* congestión
congratulate *v* felicitar
congratulations *n* felicitaciones
congregate *v* congregar
congregation *n* congregación
congress *n* congreso
conjecture *n* conjetura
conjugal *adj* conyugal
conjugate *v* conjugar
conjunction *n* conjunción
conjure up *v* evocar
connect *v* conectar
connection *n* conexión
connive *v* ser cómplice
connote *v* connotar
conquer *v* conquistar
conqueror *n* conquistador
conquest *n* conquista
conscience *n* conciencia
conscious *adj* consciente
conscript *n* recluta
consecrate *v* consagrar
consecration *n* consagración**

consecutive *adj* consecutivo

consensus *n* consenso

consent *v* consentir

consent *n* consentimiento

consequence *n* consecuencia

consequent *adj* consistente

conservation *n* conservación

conservative *adj* conservador

conserve *v* conservar

conserve *n* mermelada

consider *v* considerar

considerable *adj* considerable

considerate *adj* considerado

consideration *n* consideración

consignment *n* envío

consist *v* consistir

consistency *n* consistencia

consistent *adj* coherente;
  constante

consolation *n* consuelo

console *v* consolar

consolidate *v* consolidar

consonant *n* consonante

conspicuous *adj* visible

conspiracy *n* conspiración

conspirator *n* conspirador

conspire *v* conspirar

constancy *n* constancia

constant *adj* constante

constellation *n* constelación

consternation *n* consternación

constipate *v* estreñir

constipated *adj* estreñido

constipation *n* estreñimiento

constitute *v* constituir

constitution *n* constitución

constrain *v* restringir, limitar

constraint *n* restricción, límite

construct *v* construir

construction *n* construcción

constructive *adj* constructivo

consul *n* cónsul

consulate *n* consulado

consult *v* consultar

consultation *n* consulta

consume *v* consumir

consumer *n* consumidor

consumption *n* consumo

contact *v* contactar

contact *n* contacto

contagious *adj* contagioso

contain *v* contener

container *n* recipiente

contaminate *v* contaminar

contamination *n* contaminación

contemplate *v* contemplar

contemporary *adj*
  contemporáneo

contempt *n* desprecio

contend *v* competir

contender *n* contendiente

content *adj* contento

content *v* contentar

contentious *adj* polémico

C

contents *n* contenido
contest *n* concurso; lucha
contestant *n* concursante
context *n* contexto
continent *n* continente
continental *adj* continental
contingency *n* contingencia
contingent *adj* contingente
continuation *n* continuación
continue *v* continuar
continuity *n* continuidad
continuous *adj* continuo
contour *n* contorno
contraband *n* contrabando
contract *v* contraer(se)
contract *n* contrato
contraction *n* contracción
contradict *v* contradecir
contradiction *n* contradicción
contrary *adj* contrario
contrast *v* contrastar
contrast *n* contraste
contribute *v* contribuir, aportar
contribution *n* aportación
contributor *n* colaborador; donante
contrition *n* contrición
control *n* control
control *v* controlar
controversial *adj* polémico
controversy *n* controversia
convalescent *adj* convaleciente

convene *v* convocar
convenience *n* conveniencia
convenient *adj* conveniente
convent *n* convento
convention *n* convención
conventional *adj* convencional
converge *v* convergir
conversation *n* conversación
converse *v* conversar
conversely *adv* por el contrario
conversion *n* conversión
convert *v* convertir
convert *n* converso
convey *v* transmitir; transportar
convict *v* declarar culpable
conviction *n* convicción; condena
convince *v* convencer
convincing *adj* convincente
convoluted *adj* enrevesado
convoy *n* convoy
convulse *v* retorcerse
convulsion *n* convulsión
cook *v* cocinar
cook *n* cocinero
cookie *n* galleta
cooking *n* cocina
cool *adj* fresco; sereno
cool *v* enfriar
cool down *v* calmar; enfriar
cooling *adj* refrescante
coolness *n* frialdad; frío
cooperate *v* cooperar

cooperation *n* cooperación
cooperative *adj* servicial
coordinate *v* coordinar
coordination *n* coordinación
coordinator *n* coordinador
cop *n* policía
cope *v* arreglárselas
copier *n* copiadora
copper *n* cobre
copy *v* copiar
copy *n* copia
copyright *n* derechos de autor
cord *n* cuerda; cable
cordial *adj* cordial
cordless *adj* inalámbrico
cordon *n* cordón
cordon off *v* acordonar
core *n* núcleo; meollo
cork *n* corcho
corn *n* maíz
corner *n* esquina; rincón
cornerstone *n* piedra angular
cornet *n* corneta
corollary *n* consecuencia
coronary *adj* coronario
coronation *n* coronación
corporal *adj* corporal
corporal *n* cabo
corporation *n* corporación
corpse *n* cadáver
corpulent *adj* corpulento
corpuscle *n* corpúsculo

correct *v* corregir
correct *adj* correcto
correction *n* corrección
correlate *v* correlacionar
correspond *v* corresponder
correspondent *n* corresponsal
corresponding *adj* correspondiente
corridor *n* pasillo
corroborate *v* corroborar
corrode *v* corroer
corrupt *v* corromper
corrupt *adj* corrupto; corrompido
corruption *n* corrupción
cosmetic *n* cosmético
cosmic *adj* cósmico
cosmonaut *n* cosmonauta
cost *iv* costar
cost *n* costo, coste
costly *adj* costoso, caro
costume *n* traje
cottage *n* casita
cotton *n* algodón
couch *n* sofá
cough *n* tos
cough *v* toser
council *n* consejo
counsel *v* aconsejar
counsel *n* abogado; consejo
counselor *n* consejero
count *v* contar
count *n* cuenta, conde
countdown *n* cuenta atrás

C

countenance *n* semblante
counter *n* mostrador
counter *v* responder
counteract *v* contrarrestar
counterfeit *v* falsificar
counterfeit *adj* falso
counterpart *n* homólogo
countess *n* condesa
countless *adj* innumerables
country *n* país; campo
countryman *n* compatriota
countryside *n* campo
county *n* condado
coup *n* golpe
couple *n* pareja; par
coupon *n* cupón
courage *n* valentía
courageous *adj* valiente
courier *n* mensajero
course *n* curso; plato
court *n* tribunal; cancha
court *v* cortejar
courteous *adj* cortés
courtesy *n* cortesía
courthouse *n* juzgado
courtship *n* noviazgo
courtyard *n* patio
cousin *n* primo
cove *n* cala
covenant *n* pacto
cover *n* cubierta; funda
cover *v* cubrir(se); cobijar

cover up *v* encubrir
coverage *n* cobertura
covert *adj* secreto
coverup *n* encubrimiento
covet *v* desear
cow *n* vaca
coward *n* cobarde
cowardice *n* cobardía
cowardly *adv* cobardemente
cowboy *n* vaquero
cozy *adj* cómodo
crab *n* cangrejo
crack *n* grieta, raja
crack *v* rajarse; descifrar
cradle *n* cuna
craft *n* oficio; arte
craftsman *n* artesano
cram *v* meter a la fuerza
cramp *n* calambre, retorcijón
cramped *adj* apretado
crane *n* grúa
crank *n* manivela
cranky *adj* malhumorado
crap *n* porquería
crappy *adj* de mala calidad
crash *n* choque; desplome
crash *v* estrellarse; hundirse
crass *adj* grosero
crater *n* cráter
crave *v* ansiar
craving *n* ansia
crawl *v* arrastrarse

crayon *n* tiza
craziness *n* locura
crazy *adj* loco
creak *v* rechinar, crujir
creak *n* chirrido
cream *n* crema
creamy *adj* cremoso
crease *n* pliegue, arruga
crease *v* arrugar
create *v* crear
creation *n* creación
creative *adj* creativo
creativity *n* creatividad
creator *n* creador
creature *n* criatura
credibility *n* credibilidad
credible *adj* creíble
credit *n* crédito
creditor *n* acreedor
creed *n* credo
creek *n* arroyo
creep *v* moverse lento
creepy *adj* horroroso
cremate *v* incinerar
crematorium *n* crematorio
crest *n* cresta, cima
crevice *n* grieta
crew *n* tripulación
crib *n* cuna
cricket *n* grillo; cricket
crime *n* crimen
criminal *adj* criminal

cripple *adj* inválido, lisiado
cripple *v* paralizar
crisis *n* crisis
crisp *adj* fresco
crispy *adj* crujiente
criss-cross *v* atravesar
criterion *n* criterio
critical *adj* crítico; crucial
criticism *n* crítica
criticize *v* criticar
critique *n* critica
crockery *n* loza, platos
crocodile *n* cocodrilo
crony *n* amigo
crook *n* ladrón
crooked *adj* torcido, malo
crop *n* cosecha
cross *n* cruz
cross *adj* enfadado
cross *v* cruzar, atravesar
cross out *v* tachar
crossfire *n* fuego cruzado
crossing *n* travesía
crossroads *n* cruce
crosswalk *n* paso de peatones
crossword *n* crucigrama
crouch *v* agacharse
crow *n* cuervo
crow *v* cacarear
crowbar *n* palanca
crowd *n* muchedumbre
crowd *v* aglomerarse

C

C

crowded *adj* abarrotado
crown *n* corona
crown *v* coronar
crowning *n* coronación
crucial *adj* crucial, decisivo
crucifix *n* crucifijo
crucifixion *n* crucifixión
crucify *v* crucificar
crude *adj* grosero; crudo
cruel *adj* cruel
cruelty *n* crueldad
cruise *v* viajar en crucero
crumb *n* miga
crumble *v* desmoronarse
crunchy *adj* crujiente
crusade *n* cruzada
crusader *n* cruzado
crush *v* aplastar
crushing *adj* aplastante
crust *n* corteza; costra
crusty *adj* crujiente
crutch *n* muleta
cry *n* grito, llanto
cry *v* llorar
cry out *v* gritar
crying *n* lloro
crystal *n* cristal
cub *n* cachorro
cube *n* cubo
cubic *adj* cúbico
cubicle *n* cubículo
cucumber *n* pepino

cuddle *v* abrazar
cuff *n* puño; dobladillo
cuisine *n* cocina
culminate *v* culminar
culpability *n* culpabilidad
culprit *n* culpable
cult *n* secta
cultivate *v* cultivar
cultivation *n* cultivo
cultural *adj* cultural
culture *n* cultura
cumbersome *adj* enrevesado
cunning *adj* astuto
cup *n* taza
cupboard *n* alacena
curable *adj* curable
curator *n* director
curb *v* frenar; limitar
curb *n* borde
curdle *v* cuajarse, cortarse
cure *v* curar
cure *n* cura
curfew *n* toque de queda
curiosity *n* curiosidad
curious *adj* curioso
curl *v* rizar
curl *n* rizo
curly *adj* rizado
currency *n* moneda
current *adj* corriente, actual
currently *adv* actualmente
curse *v* maldecir

curtail *v* restringir, acortar
curtain *n* cortina, telón
curve *n* curva
curve *v* curvarse
cushion *n* cojín
cushion *v* amortiguar
cuss *v* maldecir
custard *n* natillas
custodian *n* guardián
custody *n* custodia
custom *n* costumbre
customary *adj* habitual
customer *n* cliente
custom-made *adj* a medida
customs *n* aduana
cut *n* cortada
cut *iv* cortar
cut back *v* reducir
cut down *v* cortar, talar
cut off *v* aislar
cut out *v* recortar
cute *adj* gracioso, lindo
cutlery *n* cubiertos
cutter *n* alicates
cyanide *n* cianuro
cycle *n* ciclo
cyclist *n* ciclista
cyclone *n* ciclón
cylinder *n* cilindro
cynic *adj* cínico
cynicism *n* cinismo
cypress *n* ciprés

cyst *n* quiste
czar *n* zar

C
D

dad *n* papá, padre
dagger *n* puñal, daga
daily *adv* diariamente
dairy farm *n* lechería
daisy *n* margarita
dam *n* presa
damage *n* daño
damage *v* dañar
damaging *adj* perjudicial
damn *v* condenar
damnation *n* condenación
damp *adj* húmedo
dampen *v* mojar; desanimar
dance *n* baile
dance *v* bailar
dancing *n* baile
dandruff *n* caspa
danger *n* peligro
dangerous *adj* peligroso
dangle *v* colgar
dare *v* atreverse
dare *n* atrevimiento
daring *adj* atrevido

dark *adj* oscuro

darken *v* oscurecer

darkness *n* oscuridad

darling *adj* querido

darn *v* zurcir

dart *n* dardo

dash *v* correr; frustrar

dashing *adj* deslumbrante

data *n* datos

database *n* base de datos

date *n* fecha; dátil

date *v* fechar; salir con

daughter *n* hija

daughter-in-law *n* nuera

daunt *v* desalentar

daunting *adj* desalentador

dawn *n* amanecer, alba

day *n* día

daydream *v* soñar despierto

daze *v* aturdir

dazed *adj* aturdido

dazzle *v* deslumbrar

dazzling *adj* deslumbrante

de luxe *adj* lujoso

deacon *n* diácono

dead *adj* muerto

dead end *n* sin salida

deaden *v* amortiguar

deadline *n* fecha tope

deadlock *adj* estancado

deadly *adj* mortal

deaf *adj* sordo

deafen *v* ensordecer

deafening *adj* ensordecedor

deafness *n* sordera

deal *iv* tratar (de, con)

deal *n* pacto, acuerdo

dealer *n* comerciante

dealings *n* tratos

dean *n* decano

dear *adj* querido

dearly *adv* caramente

death *n* muerte

death toll *n* número de víctimas

death trap *n* trampa mortal

deathbed *n* lecho de muerte

debase *v* rebajar(se)

debatable *adj* discutible

debate *v* debatir

debate *n* debate

debit *n* débito

debrief *v* interrogar

debris *n* escombros

debt *n* deuda

debtor *n* deudor

debunk *v* refutar

debut *n* estreno

decade *n* década

decadence *n* decadencia

decaff *adj* descafeinado

decapitate *v* decapitar

decay *v* pudrirse

decay *n* descomposición

deceased *adj* difunto

deceit *n* engaño, mentira
deceitful *adj* engañoso
deceive *v* engañar
December *n* diciembre
decency *n* decencia
decent *adj* decente
deception *n* engaño
deceptive *adj* engañoso
decide *v* decidir
deciding *adj* decisivo
decimal *adj* decimal
decimate *v* diezmar
decipher *v* descifrar
decision *n* decisión
decisive *adj* decisivo
deck *n* cubierta
declaration *n* declaración
declare *v* declarar
declension *n* declinación
decline *v* rehusar
decline *n* descenso
decompose *v* descomponerse
décor *n* decoración
decorate *v* decorar
decorative *adj* decorativo
decorum *n* decoro
decrease *v* disminuir
decrease *n* disminución
decree *n* decreto
decree *v* decretar
decrepit *adj* decrépito
dedicate *v* dedicar

dedication *n* dedicación
deduce *v* deducir
deduct *v* descontar
deductible *adj* deducible
deduction *n* deducción
deed *n* acción, hecho
deem *v* juzgar, estimar
deep *adj* profundo
deepen *v* profundizar
deer *n* ciervo
deface *v* desfigurar
defame *v* difamar
defeat *v* derrotar
defeat *n* derrota
defect *n* defecto
defect *v* desertar
defection *n* defección
defective *adj* defectuoso
defend *v* defender
defendant *n* acusado
defender *n* defensor
defense *n* defensa
defenseless *adj* indefenso
defer *v* aplazar, diferir
defiance *n* desafío
defiant *adj* desafiante
deficiency *n* falta, carencia
deficient *adj* deficiente
deficit *n* déficit
defile *v* manchar
define *v* definir
definite *adj* definitivo

definition n definición
definitive adj definitivo
deflate v desinflar
deform v deformar
deformity n deformidad
defraud v defraudar
defray v sufragar
defrost v descongelar
deft adj diestro
defuse v desactivar
defy v desafiar
degenerate v degenerar
degenerate adj degenerado
degeneration n degeneracion
degradation n degradacion
degrade v degradar
degrading adj degradante
degree n grado, título
dehydrate v deshidratar
deign v dignarse
deity n deidad
dejected adj desanimado
delay v aplazar
delay n retraso, demora
delegate v delegar
delegate n delegado
delegation n delegación
delete v borrar, tachar
deliberate v deliberar
deliberate adj intencionado
delicacy n delicadeza
delicate adj delicado

delicious adj delicioso
delight n placer
delight v agradar
delightful adj agradable
delinquency n delincuencia
delinquent adj delincuente
deliver v entregar, dar
delivery n entrega; parto
delude v engañar
deluge n diluvio
delusion n engaño
demand v exigir
demand n reclamación
demanding adj exigente
demean v rebajarse
demeaning adj degradante
demeanor n conducta
demented adj demente
demise n fin, final
democracy n democracia
democratic adj democrático
demolish v derribar
demolition n demolición
demon n demonio
demonstrate v demostrar
demonstrative adj demonstrativo
demoralize v desmoralizar
demote v degradar
den n guarida; estudio
denial n negación
denigrate v denigrar
Denmak n Dinamarca

denominator *n* denominador
denote *v* denotar
denounce *v* denunciar
dense *adj* denso; espeso
density *n* densidad
dent *v* abollar
dent *n* abolladura
dental *adj* dental
dentist *n* dentista
dentures *n* dentadura postiza
deny *v* negar
deodorant *n* desodorante
depart *v* salir, marchar
department *n* departamento
departure *n* salida
depend *v* depender
dependable *adj* confiable
dependence *n* dependencia
dependent *adj* dependiente
depict *v* describir
deplete *v* agotar
deplorable *adj* deplorable
deplore *v* deplorar
deploy *v* desplegar
deployment *n* despliegue
deport *v* deportar
deportation *n* deportatión
depose *v* deponer
deposit *n* depósito
depot *n* almacén, cochera
deprave *adj* depravado
depravity *n* depravación

depreciate *v* depreciarse
depreciation *n* depreciación
depress *v* deprimir
depressing *adj* deprimente
depression *n* depresión
deprivation *n* privación
deprive *v* privar·
deprived *adj* necesitado
depth *n* profundidad
derail *v* descarrilar
derailment *n* descarrilamiento
deranged *adj* transtornado
derelict *adj* abandonado
deride *v* mofarse de
derivative *adj* derivado
derive *v* derivar(se); obtener
derogatory *adj* despectivo
descend *v* descender
descendant *n* descendiente
descent *n* descendencia, bajada
describe *v* describir
description *n* descripción
descriptive *adj* descriptivo
desecrate *v* desecrar
desegregate *v* desegregar
desert *n* desierto
desert *v* desertar; dejar
deserted *adj* abandonado
deserter *n* desertor
deserve *v* merecer
deserving *adj* merecedor
design *n* diseño, designio

designate *v* designar
desirable *adj* deseable
desire *n* deseo
desire *v* desear
desist *v* desistir
desk *n* escritorio, recepción
desolate *adj* desolado
desolation *n* desolación
despair *n* desesperación
desperate *adj* desesperado
despicable *adj* despreciable
despise *v* despreciar
despite *c* a pesar de
despondent *adj* desanimado
despot *n* déspota
despotic *adj* despótico
dessert *n* postre
destination *n* destino
destiny *n* destino
destitute *adj* desamparado
destroy *v* destruir
destroyer *n* destructor
destruction *n* destrucción
destructive *adj* destructivo
detach *v* separar
detachable *adj* separable
detail *n* detalle
detail *v* enumerar
detain *v* detener
detect *v* detectar
detective *n* detective
detector *n* detector

detention *n* detención
deter *v* disuadir
detergent *n* detergente
deteriorate *v* deteriorar
deterioration *n* deterioro
determination *n* determinación
determine *v* determinar
deterrence *n* disuasión
detest *v* odiar
detestable *adj* detestable
detonate *v* detonar
detonation *n* detonación
detonator *n* detonador
detour *n* desviación
detriment *n* detrimento
detrimental *adj* perjudicial
devaluation *n* devaluación
devalue *v* devaluar
devastate *v* desvastar
devastating *adj* desvastador
devastation *n* devastación
develop *v* desarrollar
development *n* desarrollo
deviation *n* desviación
device *n* aparato
devil *n* demonio
devious *adj* engañoso
devise *v* idear
devoid *adj* vacío
devote *v* dedicarse
devotion *n* devoción
devour *v* devorar

devout *adj* devoto
dew *n* rocío
diabetes *n* diabetes
diabetic *adj* diabético
diabolical *adj* diabólico
diagnose *v* diagnosticar
diagnosis *n* diagnóstico
diagonal *adj* diagonal
diagram *n* diagrama
dial *n* esfera
dial *v* marcar
dial tone *n* tono de marcar
dialect *n* dialecto
dialogue *n* diálogo
diameter *n* diámetro
diamond *n* diamante
diaper *n* pañal
diarrhea *n* diarrea
diary *n* diario
dice *n* dados
dictate *v* dictar
dictator *n* dictador
dictatorial *adj* dictatorial
dictatorship *n* dictadura
dictionary *n* diccionario
die *v* morir
die out *v* desaparecer
diet *n* dieta
differ *v* discrepar
difference *n* diferencia
different *adj* diferente
difficult *adj* difícil

difficulty *n* dificultad
diffuse *v* difundir(se)
dig *iv* cavar
digest *v* digerir
digestion *n* digestión
digestive *adj* digestivo
digit *n* dígito
dignify *v* dignarse
dignitary *n* dignatario
dignity *n* dignidad
digress *v* divagar
dilapidated *adj* desmoronado
dilemma *n* dilema
diligence *n* diligencia
diligent *adj* diligente
dilute *v* diluir
dim *adj* oscuro, tenue
dim *v* atenuar
dime *n* diez centavos
dimension *n* dimensión
diminish *v* disminuir
dine *v* cenar, comer
diner *n* restaurante
dining room *n* comedor
dinner *n* comida, cena
dinosaur *n* dinosaurio
diocese *n* diócesis
diphthong *n* diptongo
diploma *n* diploma
diplomacy *n* diplomacia
diplomat *n* diplomático
diplomatic *adj* diplomático

D

dire _adj_ desesperado

direct _adj_ directo

direct _v_ dirigir

direction _n_ dirección

director _n_ director

directory _n_ directorio

dirt _n_ suciedad

dirty _adj_ sucio

disability _n_ incapacidad

disabled _adj_ incapacitado

disadvantage _n_ desventaja

disagree _v_ discrepar

disagreeable _adj_ desagradable

disagreement _n_ desacuerdo

disappear _v_ desaparecer

disappearance _n_ desaparición

disappoint _v_ decepcionar

disappointing _adj_ decepcionante

disappointment _n_ decepción

disapproval _n_ desaprobación

disapprove _v_ desaprobar

disarm _v_ desarmar

disarmament _n_ desarme

disaster _n_ desastre

disastrous _adj_ desastroso

disband _v_ disolver

disbelief _n_ incredulidad

disburse _v_ desembolsar

discard _v_ descartar, tirar

discern _v_ discernir

discharge _v_ dar de alta; supurar

discharge _n_ descarga; emisión

disciple _n_ discípulo

discipline _n_ disciplina

disclaim _v_ negar

disclose _v_ revelar

discomfort _n_ incomodidad

disconnect _v_ desconectar

discontent _adj_ descontento

discontinue _v_ descontinuar

discord _n_ discordia

discordant _adj_ discordante

discount _n_ descuento

discount _v_ descontar

discourage _v_ desanimar

discouragement _n_ desaliento

discouraging _adj_ desalentador

discourtesy _n_ descortesía

discover _v_ descubrir

discovery _n_ descubrimiento

discredit _v_ desacreditar

discreet _adj_ discreto

discrepancy _n_ discrepancia

discretion _n_ discreción

discriminate _v_ discriminar

discrimination _n_ discriminación

discuss _v_ discutir

discussion _n_ discusión

disdain _n_ menosprecio

disease _n_ enfermedad

disembark _v_ desembarcar

disenchanted _adj_ desencantado

disentangle _v_ desenredar

disfigure _v_ desfigurar

disgrace *n* deshonor
disgrace *v* deshonrar
disgraceful *adj* vergonzoso
disgruntled *adj* descontento
disguise *v* disfrazar(se)
disguise *n* disfraz
disgust *n* asco, repugnancia
disgusting *adj* repugnante
dish *n* plato
dishearten *v* desalentar
dishonest *adj* deshonesto
dishonesty *n* deshonestidad
dishonor *n* deshonra
dishonorable *adj* deshonroso
dishwasher *n* lavaplatos
disillusion *n* desilusión
disinfect *v* desinfectar
disinfectant *v* desinfectante
disinherit *v* desheredar
disintegrate *v* desintegrar
disintegration *n* desintegración
disinterested *adj* desinteresado
disk *n* disco
dislike *v* tener antipatía
dislike *n* antipatía
dislocate *v* dislocar
dislodge *v* desplazar
disloyal *adj* desleal
disloyalty *n* deslealtad
dismal *adj* espantoso
dismantle *v* desarmar
dismay *n* consternación

dismay *v* consternar
dismiss *v* despedir; rechazar
dismissal *n* despido
dismount *v* desmontar
disobedience *n* desobediencia
disobedient *adj* desobediente
disobey *v* desobedecer
disorder *n* desorden
disorganized *adj* desorganizado
disoriented *adj* desorientado
disown *v* repudiar
disparity *n* disparidad
dispatch *v* enviar
dispel *v* disipar
dispensation *n* dispensa
dispense *v* dispensar, dar
dispersal *n* dispersión
disperse *v* dispersar(se)
displace *v* desplazar
display *n* muestra
display *v* exponer, mostrar
displease *v* desagradar
displeasing *adj* desagradable
displeasure *n* desagrado
disposable *adj* desechable
disposal *n* eliminación
dispose *v* deshacerse
disprove *v* refutar
dispute *n* disputa
dispute *v* discutir
disqualify *v* descalificar
disregard *v* ignorar

disrepair *n* deterioro
disrespect *n* falta de respeto
disrespectful *adj* irrespetuoso
disrupt *v* trastornar
disruption *n* trastorno
dissatisfied *adj* insatisfecho
disseminate *v* propagar
dissent *v* discrepar
dissident *adj* disidente
dissimilar *adj* distinto
dissipate *v* esfumarse
dissolute *adj* disoluto
dissolution *n* disolución
dissolve *v* disolver(se)
dissonant *adj* disonante
dissuade *v* disuadir
distance *n* distancia
distant *adj* distante
distaste *n* desagrado
distasteful *adj* desagradable
distill *v* destilar
distinct *adj* distinto, claro
distinction *n* distinción
distinctive *adj* distintivo
distinguish *v* distinguir
distort *v* distorsionar
distortion *n* distorsión
distract *v* distraer
distraction *n* distracción
distraught *adj* angustiado
distress *n* angustia
distress *v* afligir, angustiar

distressing *adj* angustioso
distribute *v* distribuir
distribution *n* distribución
district *n* distrito
distrust *n* desconfianza
distrust *v* desconfiar
distrustful *adj* desconfiado
disturb *v* perturbar
disturbance *n* disturbio
disturbing *adj* perturbador
disunity *n* desunión
disuse *n* desuso
ditch *n* zanja
ditch *v* dejar
dive *v* zambullirse
diver *n* buzo
diverse *adj* diverso
diversify *v* diversificar
diversion *n* desvío
diversity *n* diversidad
divert *v* desviar
divide *v* dividir
dividend *n* dividendo
divine *adj* divino
diving *n* buceo
divinity *n* divinidad
divisible *adj* divisible
division *n* división
divorce *n* divorcio
divorce *v* divorciar
divorcee *n* divorciado
divulge *v* divulgar**

D

dizziness *n* mareo
dizzy *adj* mareado
do *iv* hacer
docile *adj* dócil
docility *n* docilidad
dock *n* muelle
dock *v* atracar, amarrar
doctor *n* doctor, médico
doctrine *n* doctrina
document *n* documento
documentary *n* documental
documentation *n* documentación
dodge *v* esquivar
dog *n* perro
dogmatic *adj* dogmático
dole out *v* repartir
doll *n* muñeca
dollar *n* dólar
dolphin *n* delfín
dome *n* cúpula
domestic *adj* doméstico, nacional
domesticate *v* domesticar
dominate *v* dominar
domination *n* dominación
domineering *adj* dominante
dominion *n* dominio, poder
donate *v* donar
donation *n* donativo
donkey *n* asno
donor *n* donante
doom *n* destino, suerte
doomed *adj* condenado

door *n* puerta
doorbell *n* timbre
doorstep *n* peldaño
doorway *n* entrada
dope *n* droga
dope *v* drogarse
dormitory *n* dormitorio
dosage *n* dosis
dossier *n* expediente
dot *n* punto
double *adj* doble
double *v* doblar
double-check *v* asegurarse
double-cross *v* traicionar
doubt *n* duda
doubt *v* dudar
doubtful *adl* dudoso
dough *n* masa
dove *n* paloma
down *adv* abajo
down payment *n* entrada
downcast *adj* deprimido
downfall *n* caída
downhill *adv* cuesta abajo
downpour *n* aguacero
downsize *v* reducir
downstairs *adv* abajo
down-to-earth *adj* práctico
downtown *n* centro
downtrodden *adj* pordiosero
downturn *n* bajón
dowry *n* dote

doze *n* cabezada

doze *v* dormitar

dozen *n* docena

draft *n* corriente; borrador

draft *v* reclutar

draftsman *n* dibujante

drag *v* arrastrar

dragon *n* dragón

drain *v* escurrir, drenar

drainage *n* drenaje, desague

dramatic *adj* dramático

dramatize *v* dramatizar

drape *n* cortina

drastic *adj* drástico

draw *n* empate

draw *iv* dibujar; atraer

drawback *n* inconveniente

drawer *n* cajón

drawing *n* dibujo

dread *v* tener horror

dreaded *adj* temible

dreadful *adj* horroroso

dream *iv* soñar

dream *n* sueño

dress *n* vestido

dress *v* vestirse

dresser *n* tocador

dressing *n* vendaje

dried *adj* seco

drift *v* ir a la deriva

drift apart *v* distanciarse

drifter *n* vagamundo

drill *v* taladrar; practicar

drill *n* broca; instrucción

drink *iv* beber

drink *n* bebida

drinkable *adj* potable

drinker *n* bebedor

drip *v* gotear

drip *n* gota

drive *n* vuelta; energía

drive *iv* conducir, manejar

drive at *v* insinuar

drive away *v* marcharse

driver *n* conductor

driveway *n* entrada

drizzle *v* lloviznar

drizzle *n* llovizna

drop *n* gota; descenso

drop *v* dejar caer, caer

drop in *v* visitar

drop off *v* dejar, entregar

drop out *v* abandonar

drought *n* sequía

drown *v* ahogar(se)

drowsy *adj* soñoliento

drug *n* droga

drug *v* drogar(se)

drugstore *n* farmacia

drum *n* tambor; barril

drunk *adj* borracho

drunkenness *n* borrachera

dry *v* secar

dry *adj* seco

dryclean *v* limpiar en seco
dryer *n* secadora
dual *adj* doble
dubious *adj* dudoso
duchess *n* duquesa
duck *n* pato
duck *v* agacharse, evitar
duct *n* conducto
due *adj* debido
duel *n* duelo
dues *n* cuota
duke *n* duque
dull *adj* aburrido; sordo
duly *adv* debídamente
dumb *adj* mudo; estúpido
dummy *n* copia
dummy *adj* falso, idiota
dump *v* tirar, arrojar
dump *n* basurero
dung *n* estiércol
dungeon *n* calabozo
dupe *v* engañar
duplicate *v* duplicar
duplication *n* duplicado
durable *adj* duradero
duration *n* duración
during *pre* durante
dusk *n* anochecer
dust *n* polvo
dusty *adj* polvoriento
Dutch *adj* holandés
duty *n* deber

dwarf *n* enano
dwell *iv* habitar
dwelling *n* alojamiento
dwindle *v* disminuir
dye *v* teñir
dye *n* tinte
dying *adj* moribundo
dynamic *adj* dinámico
dynamite *n* dinamita
dynasty *n* dinastía

D
E

each *adj* cada
each other *adj* cada uno
eager *adj* deseoso
eagerness *n* entusiasmo
eagle *n* águila
ear *n* oreja; espiga
earache *n* dolor de oídos
eardrum *n* tímpano
early *adv* temprano
earmark *v* destinar
earn *v* ganar
earnestly *adv* en serio
earnings *n* salario
earphones *n* auriculares
earring *n* pendiente

earth *n* tierra
earthquake *n* terremoto
earwax *n* cera del oído
ease *v* aliviar; facilitar
ease *n* facilidad
easily *adv* fácilmente
east *n* este
eastbound *adj* hacia el este
Easter *n* Pascua
eastern *adj* oriental
easterner *n* del oriente
eastward *adv* hacia el este
easy *adj* fácil
eat *iv* comer
eat away *v* corroer
eavesdrop *v* escuchar
ebb *v* bajar, disminuir
eccentric *adj* escéntrico
echo *n* eco
eclipse *n* eclipse
ecology *n* ecología
economical *adj* económico
economize *v* ahorrar
economy *n* economía
ecstasy *n* éxtasis
ecstatic *adj* extático
edge *n* borde
edgy *adj* nervioso, tenso
edible *adj* comestible
edifice *n* edificio
edit *v* editar; cambiar
edition *n* edición

educate *v* educar
educational *adj* educativo
eerie *adj* misterioso
effect *n* efecto
effective *adj* vigente
effectiveness *n* eficacia
efficiency *n* eficiencia
efficient *adj* eficaz, eficiente
effigy *n* efigie
effort *n* esfuerzo
effusive *adj* efusivo
egg *n* huevo
egg white *n* clara
egoism *n* egoísmo
egoist *n* egoísta
eight *adj* ocho
eighteen *adj* dieciocho
eighth *adj* octavo
eighty *adj* ochenta
either *adj* cada uno (de dos)
either *adv* tampoco
eject *v* expulsar
elapse *v* transcurrir
elastic *adj* elástico
elated *adj* eufórico
elbow *n* codo
elder *n* mayor
elderly *adj* de edad
elect *v* elegir
election *n* elección
electric *adj* eléctrico
electrician *n* electricista

electricity *n* electricidad
electrify *v* electrificar
electrocute *v* electrocutar
electronic *adj* electrónico
elegance *n* elegancia
elegant *adj* elegante
element *n* elemento
elementary *adj* elemental
elephant *n* elefante
elevate *v* elevar
elevation *n* altura
elevator *n* ascensor
eleven *adj* once
eleventh *adj* undécimo
eligible *adj* elegible
eliminate *v* eliminar
elm *n* olmo
eloquence *n* elocuencia
else *adv* otro
elsewhere *adv* en otra parte
elude *v* eludir
elusive *adj* evasivo
emaciated *adj* demacrado
emanate *v* emanar
emancipate *v* emancipar
embalm *v* embalsamar
embark *v* embarcar
embarrass *v* avergonzar
embassy *n* embajada
embellish *v* embellecer
embers *n* ascua
embezzle *v* malversar

embitter *v* amargar
emblem *n* emblema
embody *v* personificar
emboss *v* grabar
embrace *v* abrazar; abarcar
embrace *n* abrazo
embroider *v* bordar
embroidery *n* bordado
embroil *v* meterse en líos
embryo *n* embrio
emerald *n* esmeralda
emerge *v* emergir, brotar
emergency *n* emergencia
emigrant *n* emigrante
emigrate *v* emigrar
emission *n* emisión
emit *v* emitir
emotion *n* emoción
emotional *adj* emocional
emperor *n* emperador
emphasis *n* énfasis
emphasize *v* hacer énfasis
empire *n* imperio
employ *v* emplear
employee *n* empleado
employer *n* patrón
employment *n* empleo
empress *n* emperatriz
emptiness *n* vacío
empty *adj* vacío
empty *v* vacíar
enable *v* permitir

enchant *v* encantar

enchanting *adj* encantador

encircle *v* cercar, rodear

enclave *n* enclave

enclose *v* adjuntar; rodear

enclosure *n* recinto

encompass *v* abarcar; rodear

encounter *v* encontrarse

encounter *n* encuentro

encourage *v* animar

encroach *v* usurpar

encyclopedia *n* enciclopedia

end *n* fin

end *v* terminar

end up *v* acabar en

endanger *v* poner en peligro

endeavor *v* esforzarse

endeavor *n* esfuerzo

ending *n* final

endless *adj* sin fin

endorse *v* endorsar; apoyar

endorsement *n* apoyo, respaldo

endure *v* aguantar

enemy *n* enemigo

energetic *adj* enérgetico

energy *n* energía

enforce *v* hacer cumplir

engage *v* dedicarse a

engaged *adj* comprometido

engagement *n* compromiso; batalla

engine *n* motor

engineer *n* ingeniero

England *n* Inglaterra

English *adj* inglés

engrave *v* grabar

engraving *n* grabado

engrossed *adj* absorto

engulf *v* envolver, devorar

enhance *v* realzar

enjoy *v* gozar

enjoyable *adj* agradable

enjoyment *n* gozo

enlarge *v* ampliar

enlargement *n* aumento

enlighten *v* iluminar

enlist *v* alistarse

enormous *adj* enorme

enough *adv* bastante

enrage *v* enfurecer

enrich *v* enriquecer

enroll *v* inscribir(se)

enrollment *n* inscripción

ensure *v* asegurar

entail *v* llevar consigo

entangle *v* enredarse

enter *v* entrar

enterprise *n* empresa

entertain *v* entretener

entertaining *adj* divertido

entertainment *n* diversión

enthrall *v* cautivar

enthralling *adj* cautivador

enthuse *v* entusiasmar

enthusiasm *n* entusiasmo

entice *v* atraer

enticement *n* incentivo

enticing *adj* tentador

entire *adj* entero

entirely *adv* totalmente

entrance *n* entrada

entreat *v* suplicar

entree *n* plato

entrenched *adj* arraigado

entrepreneur *n* empresario

entrust *v* confiar

entry *n* entrada

enumerate *v* enumerar

envelop *v* envolver, cubrir

envelope *n* sobre

envious *adj* envidioso

environment *n* ambiente

envisage *v* imaginar

envoy *n* enviado

envy *n* envidia

envy *v* envidiar

epidemic *n* epidemia

epilepsy *n* epilepsia

episode *n* episodio

epistle *n* carta

epitaph *n* epitafio

epitomize *v* resumir

epoch *n* época

equal *adj* igual

equality *n* igualdad

equate *v* equiparar

equation *n* ecuación

equator *n* ecuador

equilibrium *n* equilibrio

equip *v* equipar

equipment *n* equipo

equivalent *adj* equivalente

era *n* época

eradicate *v* erradicar

erase *v* borrar

eraser *n* goma de borrar

erect *v* erigir, levantar

erect *adj* erguido, derecho

err *v* equivocarse

errand *n* mandado

erroneous *adj* erróneo

error *n* error

erupt *v* estallar, brotar

eruption *n* erupción, brote

escalate *v* intensificar

escalator *n* escalera eléctrica

escapade *n* aventura

escape *v* escaparse

escort *n* acompañar

esophagus *n* esófago

especially *adv* especialmente

espionage *n* espionaje

essay *n* ensayo; artículo

essence *n* esencia

essential *adj* esencial

establish *v* establecer

estate *n* finca, hacienda

esteem *v* estimar, apreciar

E

estimate *v* calcular
estimation *n* estima
estranged *adj* separado
estuary *n* estuario
eternity *n* eternidad
ethical *adj* ético
ethics *n* ética
etiquette *n* etiqueta
euphoria *n* euforia
Europe *n* Europa
European *adj* europeo
evacuate *v* evacuar
evade *v* evadir
evaluate *v* evaluar
evaporate *v* evaporar
evasion *n* evasión
evasive *adj* evasivo
eve *n* víspera
even *adj* llano, igualado
even if *c* aún si
even more *c* aún más
evening *n* tarde
event *n* acontecimiento
eventuality *n* eventualidad
eventually *adv* tarde o temprano
ever *adv* alguna vez
everlasting *adj* perenne
every *adj* cada
everybody *pro* cada uno
everyday *adj* cotidiano
everyone *pro* cada uno
everything *pro* cualquier cosa

evict *v* desahuciar
evidence *n* evidencia
evil *n* mal
evil *adj* malo
evoke *v* evocar
evolution *n* evolución
evolve *v* evolucionar
exact *adj* exacto
exaggerate *v* exagerar
exalt *v* exaltar
examination *n* exámen
examine *v* examinar
example *n* ejemplo
exasperate *v* irritar
excavate *v* excavar
exceed *v* exceder
exceedingly *adv* sumamente
excel *v* sobresalir
excellence *n* excelencia
excellent *adj* excelente
except *pre* excepto
exception *n* excepción
exceptional *adj* excepcional
excerpt *n* extracto
excess *n* exceso
excessive *adj* excesivo
exchange *v* cambiar
excite *v* entusiasmar
excitement *n* emoción
exciting *adj* emocionante
exclaim *v* exclamar
exclude *v* excluir

excruciating *adj* doloroso
excursion *n* excursión
excuse *v* excusar
excuse *n* excusa
execute *v* ejecutar
executive *n* ejecutivo
exemplary *adj* ejemplar
exemplify *v* ejemplificar
exempt *adj* exento
exemption *n* exención
exercise *n* ejercicio
exercise *v* hacer ejercicios
exert *v* esforzarse; ejercer
exertion *n* esfuerzo; ejercicio
exhaust *v* agotar, cansar
exhausting *adj* agotador
exhaustion *n* agotamiento
exhibit *v* exponer
exhibition *n* exposición
exhilarating *adj* estimulante
exhort *v* exhortar
exile *v* desterrar
exile *n* destierro
exist *v* existir
existence *n* existencia
exit *n* salida
exodus *n* éxodo
exonerate *v* exculpar
exorbitant *adj* exorbitante
exorcist *n* exorcista
exotic *adj* exótico
expand *v* ampliar, extender

expansion *n* ampliación
expect *v* esperar; suponer
expectancy *n* esperanza
expectation *n* expectativa
expediency *n* conveniencia
expedient *adj* conveniente
expedition *n* expedición
expel *v* expulsar
expenditure *n* gastos
expense *n* gasto
expensive *adj* caro
experience *n* experiencia
experiment *n* experimento
expert *adj* experto
expiate *v* expiar
expiation *n* expiación
expiration *n* caducidad
expire *v* caducar
explain *v* explicar
explicit *adj* explícito
explode *v* estallar
exploit *v* explotar
exploit *n* hazaña
explore *v* explorar
explorer *n* explorador
explosion *n* explosión
explosive *adj* explosivo
explotation *n* explotación
export *v* exportar
expose *v* exponer
exposed *adj* expuesto
express *adj* expreso, rápido

expression *n* expresión
expressly *adv* expresamente
expropriate *v* expropiar
expulsion *n* expulsión
exquisite *adj* exquisito
extend *v* extender(se)
extension *n* prórroga, extensión
extent *n* medida, alcance
extenuating *adj* atenuante
exterior *adj* exterior
exterminate *v* exterminar
external *adj* externo
extinct *adj* extinguido
extinguish *v* extinguir(se), apagar
extort *v* extorsionar
extortion *n* extorsión
extra *adv* de más
extract *v* sacar, extraer
extradite *v* extraditar
extradition *n* extradición
extraneous *adj* ajeno
extravagance *n* derroche
extravagant *adj* extravagante
extreme *adj* extremo
extremist *adj* extremista
extremities *n* extremidades
extricate *v* liberar
extroverted *adj* extrovertido
exude *v* rebosar
exult *v* alegrarse
eye *n* ojo
eyebrow *n* cejas

eye-catching *adj* llamativo
eyeglasses *n* gafas
eyelash *n* pestaña
eyelid *n* párpado
eyesight *n* vista
eyewitness *n* testigo ocular

fable *n* fábula
fabric *n* tela, tejido
fabricate *v* fabricar
fabulous *adj* fabuloso
face *n* cara
face up to *v* afrontar
facet *n* faceta; lado
facilitate *v* facilitar
facing *pre* frente a
fact *n* hecho
factor *n* factor
factory *n* fábrica
factual *adj* real
faculty *n* facultad
fad *n* novedad, moda
fade *v* desteñirse
faded *adj* descolorido
fail *v* fracasar
failure *n* fracaso

faint *v* desmayarse

faint *n* desmayo

faint *adj* vago, débil

fair *n* feria

fair *adj* justo; rubio, blanco

fairness *n* imparcialidad

fairy *n* hada

faith *n* fe; confianza

faithful *adj* fiel

fake *v* falsificar

fake *adj* falso

fall *n* caída; bajón

fall *iv* caer, descender

fall back *v* recurrir a

fall behind *v* retrasarse

fall down *v* caerse

fall through *v* fracasar

fallacy *n* error

fallout *n* consecuencia

falsehood *n* falsedad

falsify *v* falsificar

falter *v* fallar

fame *n* fama

familiar *adj* familiar

family *n* familia

famine *n* hambre

famous *adj* famoso

fan *n* ventilador; hincha

fanatic *adj* fanático

fancy *adj* lujoso

fang *n* colmillo

fantastic *adj* fantástico

fantasy *n* fantasía

far *adv* lejos

faraway *adj* lejano

farce *n* farsa

fare *n* precio del billete

farewell *n* despedida

farm *n* granja

farmer *n* agricultor

farming *n* cultivo

farmyard *n* corral

farther *adv* más lejos

fascinate *v* fascinar

fashion *n* moda

fashionable *adj* de moda

fast *adj* rápido

fasten *v* sujetar

fat *n* grasa

fat *adj* gordo

fatal *adj* fatal

fate *n* destino

fateful *adj* fatídico

father *n* padre

fatherhood *n* paternidad

father-in-law *n* suegro

fatherly *adj* paternal

fathom out *v* comprender

fatigue *n* fatiga

fatten *v* engordar

fatty *adj* grasoso

faucet *n* grifo, llave

fault *n* culpa, defecto

faulty *adj* defectuoso

F

F

favor *n* favor
favorable *adj* favorable
favorite *adj* favorito
fear *v* temer
fear *n* miedo
fearful *adj* miedoso, temeroso
feasible *adj* factible, viable
feast *n* fiesta
feat *n* proeza
feather *n* pluma
feature *n* característica, rasgo
February *n* febrero
fed up *adj* harto
federal *adj* federal
fee *n* pago, cuota
feeble *adj* débil
feed *iv* alimentar
feedback *n* reacción
feel *iv* sentir; pensar
feeling *n* sensación
feelings *n* sentimientos
feet *n* pies
feign *v* fingir
fellow *n* compañero
fellowship *n* compañerismo
felon *n* criminal
felony *n* crimen
female *n* hembra, mujer
feminine *adj* femenino
fence *n* valla, cerca
fencing *n* esgrima
fend *v* defenderse

fend off *v* evitar, esquivar
fender *n* parachoque
ferment *v* fermentar
ferment *n* fermento
ferocious *adj* feroz
ferocity *n* ferocidad
ferry *n* barco
fertile *adj* fértil
fertility *n* fertilidad
fertilize *v* fertilizar
fervent *adj* ferviente
fester *v* enconarse
festive *adj* festivo
festivity *n* festividad
fetid *adj* fétido
fetus *n* feto
feud *n* enemistad
fever *n* fiebre
feverish *adj* con fiebre
few *adj* pocos
fewer *adj* menos
fiancé *n* novio
fiber *n* fibra
fickle *adj* voluble
fiction *n* ficción
fictitious *adj* ficticio
fiddle *n* violín
fidelity *n* fidelidad
field *n* campo
fierce *adj* feroz
fiery *adj* ardiente
fifteen *adj* quince

fifth *adj* quinto
fifty *adj* cincuenta
fifty-fifty *adv* a medias
fig *n* higo
fight *iv* luchar
fight *n* lucha
fighter *n* combatiente
figure *n* figura
figure out *v* resolver
file *v* archivar; limar
file *n* archivo; lima
fill *v* llenar
filling *n* relleno
film *n* película
filter *n* filtro
filter *v* filtrar
filth *n* suciedad
filthy *adj* sucio
fin *n* aleta
final *adj* final
finalize *v* finalizar
finance *v* financiar
financial *adj* financiero
find *iv* encontrar
find out *v* descubrir
fine *n* multa
fine *v* multar
fine *adv* bien
fine *adj* elegante; bueno
fine print *n* letra pequeña
finger *n* dedo
fingernail *n* uña

fingerprint *n* huella dactilar
fingertip *n* punta del dedo
finish *v* terminar
Finland *n* Finlandia
Finnish *adj* finlandés
fire *v* disparar; despedir
fire *n* fuego
firearm *n* arma de fuego
firecracker *n* cohete
firefighter *n* bombero
fireman *n* bombero
fireplace *n* chimenea
firewood *n* leña
fireworks *n* fuegos artificiales
firm *adj* firme
firm *n* empresa
firmness *n* firmeza
first *adj* primero
fish *n* pescado, pez
fisherman *n* pescador
fishy *adj* sospechoso
fist *n* puño
fit *n* ataque
fit *v* ajustar(se)
fitness *n* salud
fitting *adj* apropiado
five *adj* cinco
fix *v* arreglar
fjord *n* fiordo
flag *n* bandera
flagpole *n* asta de bandera
flamboyant *adj* extravagante

F

flame *n* llama

flammable *adj* inflamable

flank *n* flanquear

flare *n* llamarada

flare-up *v* encenderse

flash *n* destello

flashlight *n* linterna

flashy *adj* ostentoso

flat *n* apartamento

flat *adj* llano

flatten *v* allanar

flatter *v* halagar

flattery *n* piropo

flaunt *v* alardear

flavor *n* gusto, sabor

flaw *n* defecto, fallo

flawless *adj* impecable

flea *n* pulga

flee *iv* huir

fleece *n* desplumar

fleet *n* flota

fleeting *adj* fugaz

flesh *n* carne

flex *v* tensar

flexible *adj* flexible

flicker *v* parpadear

flier *n* folleto; aviador

flight *n* vuelo, huida

flimsy *adj* débil

flip *v* dar la vuelta a

flirt *v* coquetear, flirtear

float *v* flotar

flock *n* rebaño

flog *v* azotar

flood *v* inundar

floodgate *n* compuerta

flooding *n* inundación

floodlight *n* foco

floor *n* suelo

flop *n* fracaso

floss *n* hilo dental

flour *n* harina

flourish *v* florecer

flow *v* circular

flow *n* flujo

flower *n* flor

flowerpot *n* tiesto

flu *n* gripe

fluctuate *v* fluctuar

fluently *adv* con fluidez

fluid *n* líquido, fluído

flunk *v* suspender

flush *v* tirar de

flute *n* flauta

flutter *v* aletear

fly *iv* volar

fly *n* mosca

foam *n* espuma

focus *n* foco

focus on *v* concentrarse

foe *n* enemigo

fog *n* niebla

foggy *adj* brumoso, nubloso

foil *v* frustrar

fold v doblar
folder n carpeta
folks n familiares
folksy adj popular
follow v seguir
follower n seguidor
folly n locura
fond adj aficionado; cariñoso
fondle v tocar, acariciar
fondness n cariño
food n comida
foodstuff n comestibles
fool v engañar
fool adj tonto
foolproof adj infalible
foot n pie
football n fútbol
footnote n nota
footprint n huella
footstep n paso
footwear n calzado
for pre para
forbid iv prohibir
force n fuerza
force v forzar
forceful adj enérgico
forcibly adv a la fuerza
forecast iv pronosticar
forefront n vanguardia
foreground n primer plano
forehead n frente
foreign adj extranjero; ajeno

foreigner n extranjero
foreman n capataz
foremost adj principal
foresee iv prever
foreshadow v presagiar
foresight n previsión
forest n bosque
foretaste n anticipo
foretell v pronosticar
forever adv para siempre
forewarn v avisar
foreword n prólogo
forfeit v renunciar
forge v falsificar
forgery n falsificación
forget v olvidar
forgivable adj perdonable
forgive v perdonar
forgiveness n perdón
fork n tenedor
form n forma
formal adj formal
formality n trámite
formalize v formalizar
formally adv oficialmente
format n formato
formation n formación
former adj anterior, primero
formerly adv antes
formidable adj formidable
formula n fórmula
forsake iv abandonar

F

fort *n* fuerte

forthcoming *adj* próximo

forthright *adj* franco, directo

fortify *v* fortificar

fortitude *n* fortaleza

fortress *n* fortaleza

fortunate *adj* afortunado

fortune *n* fortuna

forty *adj* cuarenta

forward *adv* adelante

fossil *n* fósil

foster *v* fomentar; acoger

foul *adj* asqueroso

foundation *n* cimiento; fundación

founder *n* fundador

foundry *n* fundición

fountain *n* fuente

four *adj* cuatro

fourteen *adj* catorce

fourth *adj* cuarto

fox *n* zorro

foxy *adj* atractiva

fraction *n* fracción

fracture *n* fractura

fragile *adj* frágil

fragment *n* fragmento, trozo

fragrance *n* fragancia

fragrant *adj* oloroso

frail *adj* frágil, débil

frailty *n* fragilidad

frame *n* marco; montura

frame *v* enmarcar

framework *n* estructura; marco

France *n* Francia

franchise *n* franquicia

frank *adj* franco

frankly *adv* francamente

frankness *n* franqueza

frantic *adj* fuera de sí

fraternal *adj* fraternal

fraternity *n* fraternidad

fraud *n* fraude

fraudulent *adj* fraudulento

freckle *n* peca

freckled *adj* pecoso

free *v* liberar

free *adj* libre; gratis

freedom *n* libertad

freeway *n* autopista

freeze *iv* helar

freezer *n* congelador

freezing *adj* helado

freight *n* carga

French *adj* francés

frenetic *adj* frenético

frenzied *adj* frenético

frenzy *n* frenesí

frequency *n* frecuencia

frequent *adj* frecuente

frequent *v* frecuentar

fresh *adj* fresco, nuevo

freshen *v* refrescar

freshness *n* frescura

friar *n* fraile
friction *n* fricción, roce
Friday *n* viernes
fried *adj* frito, freído
friend *n* amigo
friendship *n* amistad
fries *n* papas fritas
frigate *n* fragata
fright *n* susto
frighten *v* asustar
frightening *adj* aterrador
frigid *adj* frígido
fringe *n* margen, flequillo
frivolous *adj* frívolo
frog *n* rana
from *pre* de, desde
front *n* portada; fachada
front *adj* delantero
frontage *n* fachada
frontier *n* frontera
frost *n* helada, escarcha
frostbite *n* congelación
frostbitten *adj* congelado
frosty *adj* glacial
frown *v* fruncir el ceño
frozen *adj* helado
frugal *adj* frugal
frugality *n* frugalidad
fruit *n* fruta, fruto
fruitful *adj* provechoso
fruity *adj* afrutado
frustrate *v* frustrar

frustration *n* frustración
fry *v* freír
frying pan *n* sartén
fuel *n* combustible
fuel *v* mantener
fugitive *n* fugitivo
fulfill *v* realizar
fulfillment *n* satisfacción
full *adj* lleno
fully *adv* completamente
fumes *n* gases
fumigate *v* fumigar
fun *n* diversión
function *n* función
fund *n* fondo, reserva
fund *v* financiar
fundamental *adj* fundamental
funds *n* fondos
funeral *n* funeral
fungus *n* hongos
funny *adj* gracioso
fur *n* piel
furious *adj* furioso
furiously *adv* furiosamente
furnace *n* horno
furnish *v* amueblar; proveer
furnishings *n* muebles
furniture *n* muebles
furor *n* furor
furrow *n* surco
furry *adj* peludo
further *adv* más lejos

F

F
G

furthermore *adv* además
fury *n* furia
fuse *n* fusible
fusion *n* fusión
fuss *n* conmoción
fussy *adj* exigente
futile *adj* inútil
futility *n* inutilidad
future *n* futuro
fuzzy *adj* borroso

G

gadget *n* aparato
gag *n* mordaza
gag *v* amordazar
gage *v* medir
gain *v* ganar
gain *n* ganancia
gal *n* moza
galaxy *n* galacia
gale *n* vendaval
gall bladder *n* vesícula biliar
gallant *adj* galante
gallery *n* galería
gallon *n* galón
gallop *v* galopar
gallows *n* horca

galvanize *v* galvanizar
gamble *v* arriesgar
game *n* juego
gang *n* pandilla
gangrene *n* gangrena
gangster *n* gangster
gap *n* hueco; intervalo
garage *n* garaje
garbage *n* basura
garden *n* jardín
gardener *n* jardinero
gargle *v* hacer gárgaras
garland *n* guirnalda
garlic *n* ajo
garment *n* vestido
garnish *v* adornar
garnish *n* adorno, aderezo
garrison *n* guarnición
garrulous *adj* charlatán
garter *n* liga
gas *n* gas
gash *n* corte profundo
gasoline *n* gasolina
gasp *v* jadear
gastric *adj* gástrico
gate *n* puerta
gather *v* recoger
gathering *n* reunión
gauge *v* medir, calibrar
gauze *n* gasa, venda
gaze *v* mirar fijamente
gear *n* marcha; equipo

geese _n_ gansos

gem _n_ piedra preciosa

gender _n_ género

gene _n_ gen

general _n_ general

generalize _v_ generalizar

generate _v_ generar

generation _n_ generación

generator _n_ generador

generic _adj_ genérico

generosity _n_ generosidad

genetic _adj_ genético

genial _adj_ simpático

genius _n_ genio

genocide _n_ genocidio

genteel _adj_ elegante

gentle _adj_ suave, tierno

gentleman _n_ caballero

gentleness _n_ suavidad

genuflect _v_ arrodillarse

genuine _adj_ auténtico

geography _n_ geografía

geology _n_ geología

geometry _n_ geometría

germ _n_ microbio, germen

German _adj_ alemán

Germany _n_ Alemania

germinate _v_ brotar

gerund _n_ gerundio

gestation _n_ gestación

gesticulate _v_ hacer gestos

gesture _n_ gesto, muestra

get _iv_ obtener

get along _v_ llevarse bien

get away _v_ escaparse

get back _v_ volver

get by _v_ manejarse

get down _v_ bajarse

get down to _v_ ponerse a

get in _v_ entrar

get off _v_ apearse

get out _v_ salir

get over _v_ recobrarse

get together _v_ reunirse

get up _v_ levantarse

getaway _n_ fuga

geyser _n_ géiser

ghastly _adj_ espantoso

ghost _n_ fantasma

giant _n_ gigante

gift _n_ regalo

gifted _adj_ dotado

gigantic _adj_ enorme

giggle _v_ reírse tontamente

gimmick _n_ truco

ginger _n_ jenjibre

gingerly _adv_ con cuidado

giraffe _n_ girafa

girl _n_ chica

girlfriend _n_ amiga

give _iv_ dar

give away _v_ regalar

give back _v_ devolver

give in _v_ ceder

G

give out *v* distribuir

give up *v* rendirse

glacier *n* glaciar

glad *adj* contento

gladiator *n* gladiador

glamorous *adj* atractivo

glance *v* ojear

glance *n* ojeada

gland *n* glándula

glare *n* brillo

glass *n* cristal; vaso

glasses *n* gafas

glassware *n* cristalería

gleam *n* resplandor

gleam *v* brillar

glide *v* planear

glimmer *n* luz tenue; rayo

glimpse *n* vistazo

glimpse *v* vislumbrar

glitter *v* relucir

globe *n* globo

globule *n* glóbulo

gloom *n* obscuridad

gloomy *adj* obscuro; triste

glorify *v* glorificar

glorious *adj* glorioso

glory *n* gloria

gloss *n* brillo

glossary *n* glosario

glossy *adj* brilloso

glove *n* guante

glow *v* brillar

glucose *n* glucosa

glue *n* goma de pegar

glue *v* pegar

glut *n* abundancia

glutton *n* glotón

gnaw *v* roer

go *iv* ir

go ahead *v* seguir adelante

go away *v* marcharse

go back *v* volver

go down *v* bajar

go in *v* entrar

go on *v* continuar

go out *v* salir

go over *v* examinar

go through *v* atravesar

go under *v* hundirse

go up *v* subir

goad *v* aguijonear

goal *n* meta; gol

goalkeeper *n* portero

goat *n* cabra

gobble *v* engullir, devorar

go-between *n* mediador

God *n* Dios

goddess *n* diosa

godless *adj* ateo

godsend *n* bendición

goggles *n* gafas

gold *n* oro

golden *adj* dorado

good *adj* bueno

good-looking *adj* guapo
goodness *n* bondad
goods *n* mercancía
goodwill *n* buena voluntad
goof *v* meter la pata
goof *n* metedura de pata
goose *n* ganso
gore *v* cornear
gorge *n* barranco
gorgeous *adj* muy bueno
gorilla *n* gorila
gory *adj* sangriento
gosh *e* caramba
gospel *n* evangelio
gossip *v* cotillear
gossip *n* chisme
gout *n* gota
govern *v* gobernar
government *n* gobierno
governor *n* gobernador
gown *n* bata; toga
grab *v* coger, agarrar
grace *n* gracia
graceful *adj* elegante
gracious *adj* amable
grade *n* nota
gradual *adj* gradual
graduate *v* graduarse
graduation *n* graduación
graft *v* injertar
graft *n* injerto; soborno
grain *n* grano

gram *n* gramo
grammar *n* gramática
grand *adj* grandioso
grandchild *n* nieto
granddad *n* abuelito
grandfather *n* abuelo
grandmother *n* abuela
grandparents *n* abuelos
grandson *n* nieto
grandstand *n* tribuna
granite *n* granito
granny *n* abuelita
grant *v* conceder, otorgar
grant *n* beca; subvención
grape *n* uva
grapefruit *n* toronja
grapevine *n* vid
graphic *adj* gráfico
grasp *n* comprensión
grasp *v* agarrar; entender
grass *n* hierba, césped
grassroots *adj* popular
grate *v* rallar
grateful *adj* agradecido
gratify *v* gratificar
gratifying *adj* grato
gratitude *n* gratitud
gratuity *n* propina
grave *adj* grave, serio
grave *n* sepultura
gravel *n* grava
gravely *adv* gravemente

G

gravestone *n* lápida
graveyard *n* cementerio
gravitate *v* gravitar
gravity *n* gravedad
gravy *n* salsa
gray *adj* gris
grayish *adj* canoso
graze *v* pacer; rozar
graze *n* rasguño; roce
grease *v* engrasar
grease *n* grasa
greasy *adj* grasoso
great *adj* magnífico
greatness *n* grandeza
Greece *n* Grecia
greed *n* avaricia
greedy *adj* avaro
Greek *adj* griego
green *adj* verde
green bean *n* vaina, ejote
greenhouse *n* invernadero
Greenland *n* Groenlandia
greet *v* saludar
greetings *n* saludos
gregarious *adj* social
grenade *n* granada
greyhound *n* galgo
gridlock *n* atasco
grief *n* pena
grievance *n* queja
grieve *v* sufrir por
grill *v* asar; interrogar

grill *n* parrilla
grim *adj* sombrío
grimace *n* mueca
grime *n* mugre, suciedad
grind *iv* moler; rechinar
grip *v* agarrar
grip *n* asa
gripe *n* queja
grisly *adj* horrible
groan *v* gemir, gruñir
groan *n* quejido
groceries *n* comestibles
groin *n* ingle
groom *n* novio
groom *v* arreglarse
groove *n* ranura
gross *adj* grosero; bruto
grossly *adv* sumamente
grotesque *adj* grotesco
grotto *n* gruta
grouch *v* refunfuñar
grouchy *adj* quejón, gruñón
ground *n* tierra; motivo
ground floor *n* planta baja
groundless *adj* sin fundamento
groundwork *n* preparación
group *n* grupo
grow *iv* crecer
grow up *v* criarse
growl *v* gruñir; rugir
grown-up *n* adulto
growth *n* crecimiento**

grudge *n* rencor
grudgingly *adv* de mala gana
gruelling *adj* duro, agotador
gruesome *adj* horrible
grumble *v* refunfuñar
grumpy *adj* gruñón
guarantee *v* garantizar
guarantee *n* garantía
guarantor *n* garante
guard *n* guarda
guard *v* vigilar
guardian *n* guardián
guerrilla *n* guerrillero
guess *v* adivinar
guess *n* conjetura
guest *n* invitado
guidance *n* orientación
guide *v* guiar
guide *n* guía
guidebook *n* manual
guidelines *n* normas
guild *n* gremio
guile *n* astucia, fraude
guillotine *n* guillotina
guilt *n* culpa
guilty *adj* culpable
guise *n* apariencia
guitar *n* guitarra
gulf *n* golfo
gull *n* gaviota
gullible *adj* crédulo
gulp *v* tragar

gulp *n* trago
gulp down *v* engullir
gum *n* encía; goma
gun *n* pistola
gun down *v* matar a tiros
gunfire *n* disparos
gunman *n* pistolero
gunpowder *n* pólvora
gunshot *n* tiro
gust *n* ráfaga de viento
gusto *n* ilusión, gusto
gusty *adj* ventoso
gut *n* intestino, tripa
guts *n* agallas, valor
gutter *n* canalón, cuneta
guy *n* tipo, gente
guzzle *v* tragar
gymnasium *n* gimnasio
gynecology *n* ginecología
gypsy *n* gitano
gyrate *v* girar

G
H

habit *n* costumbre
habitable *adj* habitable
habitual *adj* habitual
hack *v* dar tajos; piratear

haggle v regatear
hail n granizo
hail v granizar; aclamar
hair n pelo
hairbrush n cepillo de pelo
haircut n corte de pelo
hairdo n peinado
hairdresser n peluquera
hairpiece n peluca
hairy adj peludo
half n mitad
half adj medio
hall n pasillo, sala
hallucinate v halucinar
hallway n pasillo
halt v parar, detenerse
halve v partir por la mitad
ham n jamón
hamburger n hamburguesa
hamlet n aldea
hammer n martillo
hammer v martillar
hammock n hamaca
hamper n cesta
hamper v poner trabas
hand n mano
hand down v transmitir
hand in v entregar
hand out v repartir
hand over v entregar
handbag n bolso
handbook n manual

handcuff v esposar
handcuffs n esposas
handful n puñado
handgun n pistola
handicap n desventaja
handkerchief n pañuelo
handle v manejar
handle n asa
handmade adj hecho a mano
handout n limosna
handrail n barandilla
handshake n apretón de manos
handsome adj guapo
handwritting n escritura
handy adj práctico
hang iv ahorcar
hang around v quedarse
hang on v esperar
hang up v colgar
hanger n percha
hangup n complejo
happen v suceder
happening n suceso
happiness n felicidad
happy adj feliz
harass v acosar
harassment n acoso
harbor n puerto
harbor v proteger, albergar
hard adj duro
harden v endurecer
hardly adv apenas

hardness *n* dureza
hardship *n* privación
hardware *n* ferretería
hardwood *n* leña
hardy *adj* fuerte
hare *n* liebre
harm *v* dañar
harm *n* daño
harmful *adj* dañino
harmless *adj* inofensivo
harmonize *v* armonizar
harmony *n* armonía
harp *n* arpa
harpoon *n* arpón
harrowing *adj* horrendo
harsh *adj* severo
harshly *adv* con dureza
harshness *n* dureza
harvest *n* cosecha
harvest *v* cosechar
hashish *n* hachís
hassle *v* molestar
hassle *n* lata
haste *n* prisa
hasten *v* apresurar(se)
hastily *adv* apresudaramente
hasty *adj* apresurado
hat *n* sombrero
hatch *v* tramar
hatchet *n* hacha
hate *v* odiar
hateful *adj* odioso

hatred *n* odio
haughty *adj* altanero
haul *v* transportar
haunt *v* perseguir
have *iv* tener
have to *v* tener que
haven *n* refugio
havoc *n* estragos
hawk *n* halcón
hay *n* heno
haystack *n* pajar
hazard *n* peligro
hazardous *adj* peligroso
haze *n* neblina
hazelnut *n* avellana
hazy *adj* brumoso
he *pro* él
head *n* cabeza
head for *v* dirigirse a
headache *n* dolor de cabeza
heading *n* encabezamiento
head-on *adv* de frente
headphones *n* auriculares
headquarters *n* sede central
headway *n* progreso
heal *v* curar
healer *n* curandero
health *n* salud
healthy *adj* sano
heap *n* montón
heap *v* amontonar
hear *iv* oir

H

hearing *n* oído
hearsay *n* rumor
hearse *n* coche fúnebre
heart *n* corazón
heartbeat *n* latido
heartburn *n* acidez
hearten *v* animar
heartfelt *adj* sincero
hearth *n* chimenea
heartless *adj* despiadado
hearty *adj* sano, bueno
heat *v* calentar
heat *n* calor
heater *n* calentador
heathen *n* pagano
heating *n* calefacción
heatstroke *n* insolación
heatwave *n* ola de calor
heaven *n* cielo
heavenly *adj* celestial
heaviness *n* pesadez
heavy *adj* pesado
heckle *v* abuchear
hectic *adj* agitado
heed *v* hacer caso
heel *n* talón, tacón
hefty *adj* sustancial
height *n* altura
heighten *v* elevar
heinous *adj* horrible
heir *n* heredero
heiress *n* heredera

heist *n* robo violento
helicopter *n* helicóptero
hell *n* infierno
hello *e* hola
helm *n* timón
helmet *n* casco
help *v* ayudar
help *n* ayuda
helper *n* ayudante
helpful *adj* útil
helpless *adj* impotente
hem *n* dobladillo
hemisphere *n* hemisferio
hemorrhage *n* hemorragia
hen *n* gallina
hence *adv* por lo tanto
henchman *n* sicario
her *adj* su, de ella
herald *v* anunciar
herald *n* heraldo, anuncio
herb *n* hierba
here *adv* aquí
hereafter *adv* en el futuro
hereby *adv* por la presente
hereditary *adj* hereditario
heresy *n* herejía
heretic *adj* herético
heritage *n* patrimonio
hermetic *adj* hermético
hermit *n* ermitaño
hernia *n* hernia
hero *n* héroe

heroic *adj* heróico
heroin *n* heroína
heroism *n* heroísmo
hers *pro* suya, de ella
herself *pro* ella misma
hesitant *adj* vacilante
hesitate *v* vacilar
hesitation *n* vacilación
heyday *n* apogeo
hiccup *n* hipo
hidden *adj* oculto
hide *iv* esconder
hideaway *n* escondite
hideous *adj* horrendo
hierarchy *n* jerarquía
high *adj* alto
highlight *n* punto culminante
highlight *v* resaltar
highly *adv* altamente
Highness *n* Alteza
highway *n* carretera
hijack *v* secuestrar
hijacking *n* secuestro
hijacker *n* secuestrador
hike *v* caminar; aumentar
hike *n* caminata; subida
hilarious *adj* divertido
hill *n* colina
hillside *n* ladera
hilltop *n* cima
hilly *adj* montañoso
hilt *n* puño

himself *pro* el mismo
hinder *v* obstaculizar
hindrance *n* impedimento
hindsight *n* retrospectiva
hinge *v* depender
hinge *n* bisagra
hint *n* pista
hint *v* dar a entender
hip *n* cadera
hire *v* alquilar
his *adj* su
his *pro* suyo, de él
Hispanic *adj* hispano
hiss *v* silbar
historian *n* historiador
historic *adj* histórico
history *n* historia
hit *n* golpe, éxito
hit *iv* golpear
hit back *v* responder
hitch *n* problema
hitch up *v* enganchar
hitchhike *n* autostop
hitherto *adv* hasta ahora
hive *n* colmena
hoard *v* acumular
hoarse *adj* ronco
hoax *n* engaño
hobby *n* pasatiempo
hoe *n* azada
hog *n* cerdo
hoist *v* levantar, alzar

hoist *n* montacargas
hold *iv* sostener, tener
hold back *v* guardar
hold on to *v* afferrarse
hold out *v* aguantar
hold up *v* atracar
holdup *n* atraco
hole *n* agujero
holiday *n* día de fiesta
holiness *n* santidad
Holland *n* Holanda
hollow *adj* hueco
holocaust *n* holocausto
holy *adj* santo
homage *n* homenaje
home *n* casa
homeland *n* patria
homeless *adj* sin hogar
homely *adj* acogedor
homemade *adj* casero
homesick *adj* nostálgico
hometown *n* ciudad natal
homework *n* tareas
homicide *n* homicidio
homily *n* sermón
honest *adj* honesto
honesty *n* honestidad
honey *n* miel
honeymoon *n* luna de miel
honk *v* pitar, tocar
honor *n* honor
hood *n* capucha

hoodlum *n* malvado
hoof *n* pezuña
hook *n* gancho; anzuelo
hook *v* enganchar
hooligan *n* gamberro
hoop *n* aro
hop *v* saltar, brincar
hope *n* esperanza
hope *v* esperar
hopeful *adj* optimista
hopefully *adv* con tiempo
hopeless *adj* sin remedio, inútil
horizon *n* horizonte
horizontal *adj* horizontal
hormone *n* hormona
horn *n* cuerno
horrendous *adj* horrendo
horrible *adj* horrible
horrific *adj* horroroso
horrify *v* horrorizar
horror *n* horror
horror *adj* de miedo
horse *n* caballo
horseshoe *n* herradura
hose *n* manguera
hospital *n* hospital
hospitality *n* hospitalidad
hospitalize *v* hospitalizar
host *n* anfitrión
hostage *n* rehén
hostess *n* anfitriona
hostile *adj* hostil, enemigo

hostility *n* hostilidad
hot *adj* caliente
hotel *n* hotel
hound *n* perro de caza
hound *v* acosar
hour *n* hora
hourly *adv* cada hora
house *n* casa
household *n* hogar, familia
household *adj* familiar
housekeeper *n* sirvienta
housewife *n* ama de casa
housework *n* faenas de casa
hover *v* flotar en el aire
how *adv* cómo
however *c* sin embargo
howl *v* aullar
howl *n* aullido
hub *n* centro
huddle *v* acurrucarse
hug *v* abrazar
hug *n* abrazo
huge *adj* grande, enorme
hull *n* casco
hum *v* tararear
human *adj* humano
human being *n* ser humano
humane *adj* humano
humanitarian *adj* humanitario
humanities *n* humanidades
humankind *n* humanidad
humble *adj* humilde

humbly *adv* humíldemente
humid *adj* húmedo
humidity *n* humedad
humiliate *v* humillar
humility *n* humildad
humor *n* humor
humorous *adj* gracioso
hump *n* joroba
hunch *n* presentimiento
hunchback *n* joroba
hunched *adj* jorobado
hundred *adj* cien
hundredth *adj* centésimo
hunger *n* hambre
hungry *adj* hambriento
hunt *v* cazar
hunter *n* cazador
hunting *n* caza
hurdle *n* obstáculo
hurl *v* arrojar, lanzar
hurricane *n* huracán
hurriedly *adv* apresuradamente
hurry *v* apresurarse
hurry up *v* dase prisa
hurt *iv* herir, doler
hurt *adj* herido
hurtful *adj* hiriente
husband *n* marido
hush *n* silencio
hush up *v* encubrir
husky *adj* ronco
hustle *n* ajetreo, bullicio**

H

hut *n* cabaña
hydraulic *adj* hidráulico
hydrogen *n* hidrógeno
hyena *n* hiena
hygiene *n* higiene
hymn *n* himno
hyphen *n* guión
hypnosis *n* hipnosis
hypnotize *v* hipnotizar
hypocrisy *n* hipocresía
hypocrite *adj* hipócrita
hypothesis *n* hipótesis
hysteria *n* histeria
hysterical *adj* histérico

I *pro* yo
ice *n* hielo
ice cream *n* helado
ice cube *n* cubo de hielo
ice skate *v* patinar
iceberg *n* iceberg
icebox *n* congelador
ice-cold *adj* helado
icon *n* icono
icy *adj* helado
idea *n* idea

ideal *adj* ideal
identical *adj* idéntico
identify *v* identificar
identity *n* identidad
ideology *n* ideología
idiom *n* modismo
idiot *n* idiota
idiotic *adj* idiota
idle *adj* ocioso
idol *n* ídolo
idolatry *n* idolatría
if *c* si
ignite *v* encender
ignorance *n* ignorancia
ignorant *adj* ignorante
ignore *v* ignorar
ill *adj* enfermo
illegal *adj* ilegal
illegible *adj* ilegible
illegitimate *adj* ilegítimo
illicit *adj* ilícito
illiterate *adj* analfabeto
illness *n* enfermedad
illogical *adj* ilógico
illuminate *v* iluminar
illusion *n* ilusión
illustrate *v* ilustrar
illustration *n* ilustración
illustrious *adj* ilustre
image *n* imagen
imagination *n* imaginación
imagine *v* imaginarse

imbalance *n* desequilibrio
imitate *v* imitar
imitation *n* imitación
immaculate *adj* inmaculado
immature *adj* inmaduro
immaturity *n* inmadurez
immediately *adv* inmediatamente
immense *adj* inmenso
immensity *n* inmensidad
immerse *v* sumergir
immersion *n* inmersión
immigrant *n* inmigrante
immigrate *v* inmigrar
immigration *n* inmigración
imminent *adj* inminente
immobile *adj* inmóvil
immobilize *v* inmobilizar
immoral *adj* inmoral
immorality *n* inmoralidad
immortal *adj* inmortal
immortality *n* inmortalidad
immune *adj* inmune
immunity *n* inmunidad
immunize *v* inmunizar
immutable *adj* inmutable
impact *n* impacto
impact *v* impactar
impair *v* perdudicar
impartial *adj* imparcial
impatience *n* impaciencia
impatient *adj* impaciente
impeccable *adj* impecable

impediment *n* obstáculo
impending *adj* inminente
imperfection *n* imperfección
imperial *adj* imperial
imperialism *n* imperialismo
impersonal *adj* impersonal
impertinence *n* impertinencia
impertinent *adj* impertinente
impetuous *adj* impetuoso
implacable *adj* implacable
implant *v* implantar
implement *v* implementar
implicate *v* implicar
implication *n* implicación
implicit *adj* implícito
implore *v* implorar
imply *v* implicar
impolite *adj* mal educado
import *v* importar
importance *n* importancia
importation *n* importación
impose *v* imponer
imposing *adj* imponente
imposition *n* imposición
impossibility *n* imposibilidad
impossible *adj* imposible
impotent *adj* impotente
impound *v* embargar
impoverished *adj* empobrecido
impractical *adj* impráctico
imprecise *adj* impreciso
impress *v* impresionar

I

impressive *adj* impresionante
imprison *v* encarcelar
improbable *adj* improbable
impromptu *adv* improvisado
improper *adj* incorrecto
improve *v* mejorar
improvement *n* mejora
improvise *v* improvisar
impulse *n* impulso
impulsive *adj* impulsivo
impunity *n* impunidad
impure *adj* impuro
in *pre* en
in depth *adv* a fondo
inability *n* incapacidad
inaccessible *adj* inacesible
inaccurate *adj* incorrecto
inadequate *adj* insuficiente
inadmissible *adj* inadmisible
inappropriate *adj* inapropiado
inasmuch as *c* ya que
inaugurate *v* inaugurar
inauguration *n* inaguración
incalculable *adj* incalculable
incapable *adj* incapaz
incapacitate *v* incapacitar
incarcerate *v* encarcelar
incense *n* incienso
incentive *n* incentivo
inception *n* principio
incessant *adj* incesante
inch *n* pulgada

incident *n* incidente
incidentally *adv* a propósito
incision *n* incisión
incite *v* provocar
incitement *n* provocación
inclination *n* inclinación
incline *v* inclinar
include *v* incluir
inclusive *adv* incluído
incoherent *adj* incoherente
income *n* ingresos
incoming *adj* entrante
incompatible *adj* incompatible
incompetence *n* incompetencia
incompetent *adj* incompetente
incomplete *adj* incompleto
inconsistent *adj* incongruente
incontinence *n* incontinencia
inconvenient *adj* inconveniente
incorporate *v* incorporar
incorrect *adj* incorrecto
incorrigible *adj* incorregible
increase *v* aumentar
increase *n* aumento
increasing *adj* creciente
incredible *adj* increíble
increment *n* incremento
incriminate *v* incriminar
incur *v* incurrir
incurable *adj* incurable
indecency *n* indecencia
indecision *n* indecisión

indecisive *adj* indeciso
indeed *adv* ciertamente
indefinite *adj* indefinido
indemnify *v* indemnizar
indemnity *n* indemnización
independence *n* independencia
independent *adj* independiente
index *n* índice
indicate *v* indicar
indication *n* indicio
indict *v* acusar
indifference *n* indiferencia
indifferent *adj* indiferente
indigent *adj* indigente
indigestion *n* indigestión
indirect *adj* indirecto
indiscreet *adj* indiscreto
indiscretion *n* indiscreción
indispensable *adj* indispensable
indisposed *adj* indispuesto
indisputable *adj* indiscutible
indivisible *adj* indivisible
indoctrinate *v* adoctrinar
indoor *adv* dentro
induce *v* provocar
indulge *v* satisfacer
indulgent *adj* indulgente
industrious *adj* trabajador
industry *n* industria
ineffective *adj* ineficaz
inefficient *adj* ineficiente
inept *adj* inepto

inequality *n* desigualdad
inevitable *adj* inevitable
inexcusable *adj* inexcusable
inexpensive *adj* económico
inexperienced *adj* inexperto
inexplicable *adj* inexplicable
infallible *adj* infalible
infamous *adj* infame
infancy *n* infancia
infant *n* bebé
infantry *n* infantería
infect *v* infectar
infection *n* infección
infectious *adj* contagioso
infer *v* inferir
inferior *adj* inferior
infertile *adj* estéril
infested *adj* plagado
infidelity *n* infidelidad
infiltrate *v* infiltrar
infiltration *n* infiltración
infinite *adj* infinito
infirmary *n* enfermería
inflammation *n* inflamación
inflate *v* inflar, hinchar
inflation *n* inflación
inflexible *adj* inflexible
inflict *v* infligir
influence *n* influencia
influential *adj* influyente
influenza *n* gripe
influx *n* afluencia

inform *v* informar
informal *adj* informal
informality *n* informalidad
informant *n* confidente
information *n* información
informer *n* chivato
infraction *n* infracción
infrequent *adj* infrecuente
infringe *v* infringir, vulnerar
infringement *n* vulneración
infuriate *v* enloquecer
infusion *n* infusión
ingenuity *n* ingeniosidad
ingest *v* ingerir
ingot *n* lingote
ingrained *adj* arraigado
ingratiate *v* engraciarse
ingratitude *n* ingratitud
ingredient *n* ingrediente
inhabit *v* habitar
inhabitable *adj* inhabitable
inhabitant *n* habitante
inhale *v* inhalar
inherit *v* heredar
inheritance *n* herencia
inhibit *v* impedir
inhuman *adj* inhumano
initial *adj* inicial
initially *adv* al principio
initials *n* iniciales
initiate *v* empezar
initiative *n* iniciativa

inject *v* inyectar
injection *n* inyección
injure *v* herir
injurious *adj* dañoso
injury *n* herida
injustice *n* injusticia
ink *n* tinta
inkling *n* sospecha
inlaid *adj* incrustado
inland *adv* adentro
inland *adj* interior
in-laws *n* suegros
inmate *n* recluso
inn *n* posada, mesón
innate *adj* innato
inner *adj* interior
innocence *n* inocencia
innocent *adj* inocente
innovation *n* novedad
innuendo *n* indirecta
innumerable *adj* innumerable
input *n* aportación
inquest *n* investigación
inquire *v* preguntar
inquiry *n* consulta
inquisition *n* inquisición
insane *adj* loco
insanity *n* locura
insatiable *adj* insaciable
inscription *n* inscripción
insect *n* insecto
insecurity *n* inseguridad

insensitive *adj* insensible
inseparable *adj* inseparable
insert *v* introducir
insertion *n* inserción
inside *adj* interior
inside *pre* dentro de
inside out *adv* al revés
insignificant *adj* insignificante
insincere *adj* falso
insincerity *n* insinceridad
insinuate *v* insinuar
insinuation *n* insinuación
insipid *adj* insípido
insist *v* insistir
insistence *n* insistencia
insolent *adj* descarado
insoluble *adj* insoluble
insomnia *n* insomnio
inspect *v* inspeccionar
inspection *n* inspeción
inspector *n* inspector
inspiration *n* inspiración
inspire *v* inspirar
instability *n* inestabilidad
install *v* instalar
installation *n* instalación
installment *n* plazo
instance *n* ejemplo
instant *n* instante
instantly *adv* al momento
instead *adv* en lugar de
instigate *v* instigar

instil *v* inculcar
instinct *n* instinto
institute *v* establecer
institution *n* institución
instruct *v* instruír
instructor *n* instructor
insufficient *adj* insuficiente
insulate *v* aislar
insulation *n* aislamiento
insult *v* insultar
insult *n* insulto
insurance *n* seguro
insure *v* asegurar
insurgency *n* insurgencia
insurrection *n* insurrección
intact *adj* intacto
intake *n* ingestión
integrate *v* integrar
integration *n* integración
integrity *n* integridad
intelligent *adj* inteligente
intend *v* tener intención
intense *adj* intenso
intensify *v* intensificar
intensity *n* intensidad
intensive *adj* intensivo
intention *n* intención
intercede *v* interceder
intercept *v* interceptar
intercession *n* intercesión
interchange *v* intercambiar
interchange *n* intersección

interest *n* interés
interested *adj* interesado
interesting *adj* interesante
interfere *v* interferir
interference *n* interferencia
interior *adj* interior
interlude *n* intervalo
intermediary *n* intermediario
intern *v* internar
interpret *v* interpretar
interpretation *n* interpretación
interpreter *n* intérprete
interrogate *v* interrogar
interrupt *v* interrumpir
interruption *n* interrupción
intersect *v* cruzarse
intertwine *v* entrelazar
interval *n* intervalo
intervene *v* intervenir
intervention *n* intervención
interview *n* entrevista
intestine *n* intestino
intimacy *n* intimidad
intimate *adj* íntimo
intimidate *v* meter miedo
intolerable *adj* intolerable
intolerance *n* intolerancia
intoxicated *adj* embriagado
intravenous *adj* intravenoso
intrepid *adj* intrépido
intricate *adj* intrincado
intrigue *n* intriga

intriguing *adj* intrigante
intrinsic *adj* intrínsico
introduce *v* introducir
introduction *n* introducción
introvert *adj* introvertido
intrude *v* entrometerse
intruder *n* intruso
intrusion *n* intromisión
intuition *n* intuición
inundate *v* inundar
invade *v* invadir
invader *n* invasor
invalid *n* inválido
invalidate *v* invalidar
invaluable *adj* inestimable
invasion *n* invasión
invent *v* inventar
invention *n* invención
inventory *n* inventario
invest *v* invertir
investigate *v* investigar
investigation *n* investigación
investment *n* inversión
investor *n* inversor
invincible *adj* invencible
invisible *adj* invisible
invitation *n* invitación
invite *v* invitar
invoice *n* factura
invoke *v* invocar
involve *v* implicar, participar
involved *adj* complicado, implicado

involvement _n_ participación
inward _adj_ interior
inwards _adv_ hacia dentro
iodine _n_ yodo
irate _adj_ enojado
Ireland _n_ Irlanda
Irish _adj_ irlandés
iron _n_ hierro
iron _v_ planchar
ironic _adj_ irónico
irony _n_ ironía
irrational _adj_ irracional
irrefutable _adj_ irrefutable
irregular _adj_ irregular
irrelevant _adj_ irrelevante
irreparable _adj_ irreparable
irresistible _adj_ irresistible
irrespective _adj_ independiente de
irreversible _adj_ irreversible
irrevocable _adj_ irrevocable
irrigate _v_ regar
irrigation _n_ regadío
irritate _v_ irritar
irritating _adj_ fastidioso
Islamic _adj_ islámico
island _n_ isla
isle _n_ isla
isolate _v_ aislar
isolation _n_ aislamiento
issue _n_ cuestión, tema
issue _v_ emiti, publicar
Italian _adj_ italiano

italics _adj_ cursiva
Italy _n_ Italia
itch _v_ picar
itchiness _n_ picazón
item _n_ artículo
itemize _v_ detallar
itinerary _n_ intinerario
ivory _n_ marfil

I
J

J

jackal _n_ chacal
jacket _n_ chaqueta
jackpot _n_ premio gordo
jaguar _n_ jaguar
jail _n_ cárcel
jail _v_ encarcelar
jailer _n_ carcelero
jam _n_ mermelada; atasco
janitor _n_ conserje
January _n_ enero
Japan _n_ Japón
Japanese _adj_ japonés
jar _n_ tarro, jarro, jarra
jasmine _n_ jazmín
jaw _n_ mandíbula
jealous _adj_ celoso
jealousy _n_ celos, envidia

jeans *n* vaqueros
jeopardize *v* poner en peligro
jerk *v* tirar
jerk *n* sacudida; tirón
jersey *n* suéter
Jew *n* judío
jewel *n* joya
jeweler *n* joyero
jewelry store *n* joyería
Jewish *adj* judío
jigsaw *n* rompecabezas
job *n* trabajo
jobless *adj* desempleado
join *v* juntar, unirse
joint *n* articulación, unión
jointly *adv* juntos
joke *n* chiste
joke *v* bromear
jokingly *adv* en broma
jolly *adj* alegre
jolt *v* sacudir
jolt *n* sacudida
journal *n* revista; diario
journalist *n* corresponsal
journey *n* camino
jovial *adj* jovial
joy *n* alegría
joyful *adj* alegre
joyfully *adv* alegremente
jubilant *adj* jubiloso
Judaism *n* Judaísmo
judge *n* juez

judgment *n* juicio
judicious *adj* juicioso
jug *n* jarra
juggler *n* malabarista
juice *n* jugo
juicy *adj* jugoso
July *n* julio
jump *v* saltar
jump *n* salto
jumpy *adj* nervioso
junction *n* cruce, unión
June *n* junio
jungle *n* selva, jungla
junior *adj* más joven
junk *n* trastos
jury *n* jurado
just *adj* justo
justice *n* justicia
justify *v* justificar
justly *adv* con razón
juvenile *n* menor
juvenile *adj* juvenil

kangaroo *n* canguro
karate *n* karate
keep *iv* guardar.

keep on *v* continuar
keep up *v* seguir
keg *n* barril
kennel *n* perrera
kettle *n* tetera, hervidor
key *n* llave; clave
key ring *n* llavero
keyboard *n* teclado
kick *v* dar una patada
kickback *n* soborno
kickoff *n* saque
kid *n* chiquillo; cabrito
kidnap *v* secuestrar
kidnapper *n* secuestrador
kidnapping *n* secuestro
kidney *n* riñón
kidney bean *n* frijol rojo
kill *v* matar
killer *n* asesino
killing *n* asesinato
kilogram *n* kilogramo
kilometer *n* kilómetro
kilowatt *n* kilovatio
kind *adj* amable
kindle *v* avivar
kindly *adv* amablemente
kindness *n* amabilidad
king *n* rey
kingdom *n* reino
kinship *n* parentesco
kiosk *n* quiosco
kiss *v* besar

kiss *n* beso
kitchen *n* cocina
kite *n* cometa
kitten *n* gatito
knee *n* rodilla
kneecap *n* rótula
kneel *iv* arrodillarse
knife *n* cuchillo
knight *n* caballero
knit *v* tejer
knob *n* tirador
knock *n* golpe
knock *v* golpear, llamar
knot *n* nudo
know *iv* conocer
know-how *n* conocimientos
knowingly *adv* a sabiendas
knowledge *n* conocimiento

lab *n* laboratorio
label *n* etiqueta
labor *n* trabajo
laborer *n* trabajador
labyrinth *n* laberinto
lace *n* encaje
lack *v* carecer

lack *n* falta, carencia
lad *n* muchacho
ladder *n* escalera
laden *adj* cargado
lady *n* señora
ladylike *adj* femenino
lag *v* rezagarse
lagoon *n* laguna
lake *n* lago
lamb *n* cordero
lame *adj* cojo; pobre
lament *v* lamentarse
lament *n* lamento
laminate *v* laminar
lamp *n* lámpara
lamppost *n* farol
lampshade *n* pantalla
lance *n* lanza
land *n* tierra
land *v* aterrizar
landfill *n* vertedero
landing *n* aterrizaje
landlady *n* dueña
landlocked *adj* encerrado
landlord *n* dueño
landscape *n* paisaje
lane *n* carril; callejón
language *n* lengua
languid *adj* lánguido
languish *v* languidecer
lantern *n* linterna, farol
lap *n* regazo; vuelta

lapse *n* desliz; intervalo
lapse *v* transcurrir
larceny *n* latrocinio
lard *n* manteca
large *adj* grande
largely *adv* en gran parte
larynx *n* laringe
laser *n* láser
lash *n* pestaña; azote
lash *v* azotar
lash out *v* arremeter
last *v* durar
last *adj* último
last name *n* apellido
last night *adv* anoche
lasting *adj* duradero
lastly *adv* por último
latch *n* pestillo
late *adv* tarde
late *adj* difunto; tardío
lately *adv* últimamente
latent *adj* latente
later *adv* más tarde
later *adj* posterior
lateral *adj* lateral
latest *adj* el último
lather *n* espuma
latitude *n* latitud
latter *adj* último
laudable *adj* loable
laugh *v* reírse
laugh *n* risa**

laughable *adj* ridículo, risible
laughing stock *n* hazmerreir
laughter *n* risa
launch *n* lanzamiento
launch *v* lanzar; botar
launder *v* lavar, blanquear
laundry *n* lavandería
lavatory *n* baño
lavish *adj* espléndido
lavish *v* prodigar, derrochar
law *n* ley
law-abiding *adj* respetuoso
lawful *adj* legítimo, lícito
lawmaker *n* legislador
lawn *n* céspez
lawsuit *n* pleito
lawyer *n* abogado
lax *adj* negligente
laxative *adj* laxante
lay *adj* laico, lego
lay *iv* poner; dejar
lay off *v* despedir
layer *n* capa, estrato
layman *n* laico, lego
layout *n* plano, diseño
laziness *n* pereza
lazy *adj* perezoso
lead *iv* guiar, conducir
lead *n* pista; plomo
leaded *adj* con plomo
leader *n* jefe, líder
leadership *n* liderazgo

leading *adj* principal
leaf *n* hoja
leaflet *n* folleto
league *n* liga
leak *v* gotear, salirse
leak *n* gotera, escape
leakage *n* escape, fuga
lean *adj* flaco, magro
lean *iv* inclinarse
lean back *v* reclinarse
lean on *v* apoyarse
leaning *n* inclinación
leap *iv* saltar
leap *n* salto
leap year *n* año bisiesto
learn *iv* aprender
learned *adj* culto
learner *n* estudiante
learning *n* aprendizaje
lease *v* arrendar
lease *n* arriendo
leash *n* correa
least *adj* el menor, el menos
leather *n* cuero, piel
leave *iv* dejar; salir
leave out *v* omitir
leaven *n* levadura
lectern *n* atril
lecture *n* conferencia
ledger *n* libro de cuentas
leech *n* sanguijuela
leeway *n* libertad

L

leftover _adj_ sobrante
leftovers _n_ sobras
leg _n_ pierna
legacy _n_ legado
legal _adj_ legal
legality _n_ legalidad
legalize _v_ legalizar
legend _n_ leyenda
legendary _adj_ legendario
legible _adj_ legible
legion _n_ legión
legislate _v_ legislar
legislation _n_ legislación
legislature _n_ legislatura
legitimate _adj_ legítimo
legitimate _v_ legitimar
leisure _n_ ocio
lemon _n_ limón
lemonade _n_ limonada
lend _iv_ prestar
lender _n_ prestamista
length _n_ longitud
lengthen _v_ alargar
lengthy _adj_ largo
leniency _n_ compasión
lenient _adj_ indulgente
lens _n_ lente
Lent _n_ cuaresma
lentil _n_ lenteja
leopard _n_ leopardo
leper _n_ leproso
leprosy _n_ lepra

less _adj_ menos
lessee _n_ inquilino
lessen _v_ disminuir
lesser _adj_ menor
lesson _n_ lección
lessor _n_ arrendador
lest _c_ para que no
let _iv_ permitir
let down _v_ decepcionar
let go _v_ soltar
let in _v_ dejar entrar
let out _v_ dejar salir
letdown _n_ decepción
lethal _adj_ mortal
lethargy _n_ letargo
letter _n_ carta; letra
lettuce _n_ lechuga
leukemia _n_ leucemia
level _v_ nivelar, allanar
level _n_ nivel, altura
level with _v_ sincerarse
level-headed _adj_ sensato
lever _n_ palanca, resorte
leverage _n_ influencia
levy _v_ recaudar
lewd _adj_ obsceno
liability _n_ obligación
liable _adj_ responsable
liaison _n_ enlace, contacto
liar _n_ mentiroso
libel _n_ calumnia
liberate _v_ liberar

liberation *n* liberación
liberty *n* libertad
librarian *n* bibliotecario
library *n* biblioteca
lice *n* piojos
licence *n* licencia
license *v* autorizar
lick *v* lamer
lid *n* tapa, tapadera
lie *iv* acostarse
lie *v* mentir
lie *n* mentira
lieu *n* lugar
lieutenant *n* teniente
life *n* vida
lifeguard *n* socorrista
lifeless *adj* sin vida
lifespan *n* vida
lifestyle *n* estilo de vida
lifetime *adj* de por vida
lift *v* levantar, alzar
lift off *v* despegar
lift-off *n* despegue
ligament *n* ligamento
light *iv* encender
light *adj* ligero
light *n* luz
lighten *v* aclarar, brillar
lighter *n* mechero
lighthouse *n* faro
lighting *n* iluminación
lightly *adv* ligeramente

lightning *n* rayo
lightweight *n* peso ligero
likable *adj* simpático
like *pre* como
like *v* gustar
likelihood *n* probabilidad
likely *adv* probablemente
liken *v* comparar
likeness *n* parecido
likewise *adv* del mismo modo
liking *n* gusto, simpatía
limb *n* miembro; rama
lime *n* cal; lima
limestone *n* piedra caliza
limit *n* límite; colmo
limit *v* límitar
limitation *n* limitación
limp *v* cojear
limp *n* cojera
linchpin *n* cimiento, base
line *n* línea
line up *v* hacer cola
lined *adj* reglado
linen *n* ropa blanca, lino
linger *v* perdurar
lingerie *n* lencería
lingering *adj* persistente
lining *n* forro
link *v* unir, conectar
link *n* eslabón, enlace
lion *n* león
lioness *n* leona

L

lip *n* labio

lipstick *n* barra de labios

liqueur *n* licor

liquid *n* líquido

liquidate *v* liquidar

liquidation *n* liquidación

liquor *n* licor

list *v* enumerar

list *n* lista

listen *v* escuchar

listener *n* oyente

litany *n* letanía

liter *n* litro

literal *adj* literal

literally *adv* literalmente

literate *adj* culto

literature *n* literatura

litigate *v* litigar

litigation *n* litigio

litre *n* litro

litter *n* basura

litter *v* ensuciar

little *adj* poco

little bit *n* poquito

little by little *adv* poco a poco

liturgy *n* liturgia

live *adj* vivo; en directo

live *v* vivir

live off *v* vivir de gorra

live up *v* gozar

livelihood *n* sustento

lively *adj* animado

liver *n* hígado

livestock *n* ganado

livid *adj* furioso

living room *n* sala de estar

lizard *n* lagarto

load *v* cargar

load *n* carga, peso

loaded *adj* cargado, borracho

loaf *n* barra de pan

loan *v* prestar

loan *n* préstamo

loathe *v* odiar

loathing *n* odio

loathsome *adj* odioso

lobby *n* vestíbulo

lobby *v* presionar

lobster *n* langosta

local *adj* local, de aquí

localize *v* localizar

locate *v* situar; localizar

located *adj* situado

location *n* lugar

lock *v* cerrar con llave

lock *n* cerradura, candado

lock up *v* encarcelar

locker room *n* vestuario

locksmith *n* cerrajero

locust *n* langosta

lodge *v* alojarse

lodging *n* alojamiento

lofty *adj* elevado, noble

log *n* tronco; diario

log *v* anotar

log in *v* entrar

log off *v* salir

logic *n* lógica

logical *adj* lógico

loin *n* lomo

loiter *v* vagar

loneliness *n* soledad

lonely *adv* solo

loner *n* solitario

lonesome *adj* triste, solo

long *adj* largo

long for *v* anhelar

longing *n* anhelo

longitude *n* longitud

long-standing *adj* antiguo

long-term *adj* duradero

look *n* mirada, aspecto

look *v* mirar; parecer

look after *v* cuidar

look at *v* mirar

look down *v* despreciar

look for *v* buscar

look forward *v* desear

look into *v* investigar

look out *v* tener cuidado

look over *v* repasar

look through *v* hojear

looking glass *n* espejo

looks *n* aspecto

loom *n* telar

loom *v* surgir; amenazar

loop *n* lazo

loophole *n* resquicio

loose *v* soltar

loose *adj* suelto, ancho

loosen *v* aflojar

loot *v* saquear

loot *n* botín

lopsided *adj* ladeado

lord *n* señor

lordship *n* señoría

lose *iv* perder

loser *n* fracasado

loss *n* pérdida

lost *adj* perdido

lot *adv* mucho

lotion *n* loción

lots *adj* muchos

lottery *n* lotería

loud *adj* alto, fuerte

loudly *adv* fuertemente

loudspeaker *n* altavoz

lounge *n* salón, sala de estar

louse *n* piojo

lousy *adj* asqueroso

lovable *adj* adorable

love *v* amar, encantar

love *n* amor

lovely *adj* encantador

lover *n* amante

loving *adj* cariñoso

low *adj* bajo, corto

lower *adj* más bajo

L

lowkey *adj* callado
lowly *adj* humilde
loyal *adj* leal
loyalty *n* lealtad
lubricate *v* engrasar
lubrication *n* engrase
lucid *adj* lúcido
luck *n* suerte
lucky *adj* afortunado
lucrative *adj* lucrativo
ludicrous *adj* ridículo
luggage *n* equipaje
lukewarm *adj* tibio
lull *n* tregua
lumber *n* madera
luminous *adj* luminoso
lump *n* bulto, hinchazón
lump sum *n* pago único
lump together *v* poner juntos
lumpy *adj* lleno de bultos
lunacy *n* locura
lunatic *adj* loco
lunch *n* almuerzo
lung *n* pulmón
lure *v* atraer
lure *n* cebo, atractivo
lurid *adj* llamativo, sensacional
lurk *v* acechar
luscious *adj* sensual
lush *adj* exhuberante
lust *v* codiciar
lust *n* lujuria

lustful *adj* lujurioso
luxurious *adj* lujoso
luxury *n* lujo
lynch *v* linchar
lynx *n* lince
lyrics *n* letra de canción

machinary *n* maquinaria
machine *n* máquina
machine gun *n* ametralladora
mad *adj* enfadado
madam *n* señora
madden *v* volver loco
maddening *adj* exasperante
made-up *adj* inventado, falso
madhouse *n* manicomio
madly *adv* locamente
madman *n* loco
madness *n* locura
magazine *n* revista
magic *n* magia
magical *adj* mágico
magician *n* mago
magistrate *n* magistrado
magnet *n* imán
magnetic *adj* magnético

magnetism *n* magnetismo
magnificent *adj* magnífico
magnify *v* aumentar
magnitude *n* inmensidad
maid *n* criada
maiden *n* doncella
mail *v* echar a correos
mail *n* correo
mailbox *n* buzón
mailman *n* cartero
maim *v* mutilar
main *adj* principal
mainland *n* tierra firme
mainly *adv* principalmente
mainstream *adj* corriente
maintain *v* mantener
maintenance *n* mantenimiento
majestic *adj* majestuoso
majesty *n* majestad
major *n* comandante
major *adj* principal; grande
major in *v* especializarse
majority *n* mayoría
make *n* marca
make *iv* hacer, obligar
make up *v* maquillarse
make up for *v* compensar por
maker *n* fabricante
makeshift *adj* improvisado
makeup *n* maquillaje
malaria *n* malaria
male *n* macho, varón

male *adj* masculino
malevolent *adj* malévolo
malfunction *v* funcionar mal
malfunction *n* fallo
malice *n* malicia
malicious *adj* malicioso
malign *v* calumniar
malignancy *n* maldad
malignant *adj* maligno
mall *n* centro comercial
malnourished *adj* malnutrido
malnutrition *n* desnutrición
malpractice *n* negligencia
maltreatment *n* maltrato
mammal *n* mamífero
mammoth *n* mamut
man *n* hombre
man *v* tripular; manejar
manage *v* apañarse; dirigir
manageable *adj* manejable
management *n* dirección
manager *n* director
mandate *n* misión; mandato
mandatory *adj* obligatorio
maneuver *n* maniobra
maneuver *v* maniobrar
manger *n* pesebre
mangle *v* destrozar
manhandle *v* maltratar
manhood *n* edad adulta
manhunt *n* búsqueda
maniac *adj* maniático

M

manifest *v* manifestar
manifold *adj* múltiple
manipulate *v* manipular
mankind *n* humanidad
manliness *n* virilidad
manly *adj* varonil
manner *n* manera, forma
mannerism *n* peculariedad
manners *n* modales
manor *n* finca
manpower *n* mano de obra
mansion *n* mansión
manslaughter *n* homicidio
manual *n* handbook
manual *adj* manual
manufacture *v* fabricar
manure *n* estiércol
manuscript *n* manuscrito
many *adj* muchos
map *n* mapa, plano
map *v* delinear, dibujar
marathon *n* maratón
marble *n* mármol
march *v* marchar, desfilar
march *n* marcha, desfile
March *n* marzo
mare *n* yegua
margin *n* márgen
marginal *adj* marginal
marinate *v* marinar
marine *adj* marino
marital *adj* conyugal, marital

mark *n* marca, huella
mark *v* marcar
mark down *v* rebajar
mark up *v* aumentar
marker *n* marcador
market *n* mercado
marksman *n* tirador
marmalade *n* mermelada
maroon *adj* rojo oscuro
marriage *n* matrimonio
married *adj* casado
marrow *n* médula, meollo
marry *v* casar(se)
Mars *n* Marte
marshal *n* mariscal; jefe
martial *adj* marcial, militar
martyr *n* mártir
martyr *v* martirizar
martyrdom *n* martirio
marvel *n* maravilla
marvel *v* maravillarse
marvelous *adj* maravilloso
marxist *adj* marxista
masculine *adj* masculino
mash *v* machacar, moler
mask *n* máscara
mask *v* encubrir
masochism *n* masoquismo
mason *n* albañi; masón
masquarade *n* farsa
masquerade *v* disfrazarse
mass *n* masa; cantidad

mass *v* juntarse
massacre *n* masacre
massage *n* masaje
massage *v* dar masajes
masseur *n* masajista
masseuse *n* masajista
massive *adj* masivo
mast *n* mástil
master *n* amo, dueño
master *v* dominar
masterful *adj* magistral
mastermind *n* cerebro
mastermind *v* dirigir
masterpiece *n* obra maestra
mastery *n* maestría
mat *n* estera
match *n* cerilla; partido
match *v* igualar; hacer juego
mate *n* pareja; colega
mate *adj* sin brillo
material *n* material; tejido
materialism *n* materialismo
maternal *adj* maternal
maternity *n* maternidad
math *n* matemáticas
matriculate *v* matricular
matrimony *n* matrimonio
matter *n* asunto; problema
matter *v* importar
mattress *n* colchón
mature *adj* maduro
mature *v* madurar

maturity *n* madurez
maul *v* magullar
maxim *n* máxima
maximize *v* maximizar
maximum *adj* máximo
May *n* mayo
may *iv* poder
may-be *adv* quizá, tal vez
mayhem *n* caos
mayor *n* alcalde
maze *n* laberinto
meadow *n* pradera, prado
meager *adj* escaso; flaco
meal *n* comida
mean *iv* significar, pretender
mean *adj* tacaño, cruel
mean *n* promedio
meander *v* serpentear, vagar
meaning *n* significado
meaningful *adj* significativo
meaningless *adj* sin sentido
meanness *n* tacañería
means *n* medios
meantime *adv* mientras tanto
meanwhile *adv* mientras tanto
measles *n* sarampión
measure *v* medir
measure *n* medida
measure up *v* estar a la altura
measurement *n* medida
meat *n* carne; meollo
meatball *n* albóndiga**

M

mechanic _n_ mecánico
mechanism _n_ mecanismo
mechanize _v_ mecanizar
medal _n_ medalla
medallion _n_ medallón
meddle _v_ entrometerse
mediate _v_ mediar
mediation _n_ mediación
mediator _n_ intermediario
medication _n_ medicación
medicinal _adj_ medicinal
medicine _n_ medicina
medieval _adj_ medieval
mediocre _adj_ mediocre
mediocrity _n_ mediocridad
meditate _v_ meditar
meditation _n_ meditación
medium _adj_ mediano, medio
meek _adj_ manso, dócil
meekness _n_ mansedumbre
meet _iv_ reunir(se)
meeting _n_ reunión
melancholic _adj_ melancólico
melancholy _n_ melancolía
melee _n_ pelea, barullo
mellow _adj_ suave, blando
mellow _v_ sosegar, madurar
melodic _adj_ melódico
melody _n_ melodía
melon _n_ melón
melt _v_ derritir(se)
member _n_ miembro

membership _n_ membrecía
membrane _n_ membrana
memento _n_ recuerdo
memo _n_ nota
memoirs _n_ memorias
memorable _adj_ memorable
memorize _v_ memorizar
memory _n_ memoria; recuerdo
men _n_ hombres
menace _n_ amenaza
menacing _adj_ amenazador
mend _v_ reparar
meningitis _n_ meningitis
menopause _n_ menopausia
menstruation _n_ menstruación
mental _adj_ mental
mentality _n_ mentalidad
mentally _adv_ mentalmente
mention _v_ mencionar
mention _n_ mención
menu _n_ menú
mercenary _n_ mercenario
merchandise _n_ mercancía
merchant _n_ comerciante
merciful _adj_ compasivo
merciless _adj_ despiadado
mercury _n_ mercurio
mercy _n_ compasión
mere _adj_ mero, simple
merely _adv_ simplemente
merge _v_ unir, fundirse
merger _n_ unión; fusión

M

merit *n* mérito
merit *v* merecer
mermaid *n* sirena
merry *adj* alegre
mesh *n* malla, trama
mesh *v* enredarse
mesmerize *v* hechizar
mess *n* desorden
mess around *v* perder el tiempo
mess up *v* desordenar
message *n* mensaje
messenger *n* mensajero
Messiah *n* Mesías
messy *adj* sucio; revuelto
metal *n* metal
metallic *adj* metálico
metaphor *n* metáfora
meteor *n* meteoro
meteoric *adj* meteórico
meter *n* metro; contador
method *n* método
methodical *adj* metódico
meticulous *adj* cuidadoso
metric *adj* métrico
metropolis *n* metrópolis
Mexican *adj* mexicano
mice *n* ratones
microbe *n* microbio
microphone *n* micrófono
microscope *n* microscopio
microscopic *adj* microscópico
microwave *n* microondas

midair *n* en el aire
midday *n* mediodía
middle *n* centro; medio
middleman *n* intermediario
midget *n* enano
midget *adj* diminutivo
midnight *n* medianoche
midst *pre* en medio de
midsummer *n* pleno verano
midwife *n* comadrona
mighty *adj* poderoso
migraine *n* jaqueca migraña
migrant *n* emigrante
migrate *v* emigrar
mild *adj* suave, apacible
mildew *n* moho
mile *n* milla
mileage *n* millaje
milestone *n* hito
milieu *n* entorno
militant *adj* militante
milk *n* leche
milky *adj* lechoso
mill *n* molino
millennium *n* milenio
milligram *n* miligramo
millimeter *n* milímetro
million *n* millón
millionaire *adj* millonario
mime *v* mímica
mimic *v* imitar
mince *v* picar; ser franco

M

mincemeat *n* carne picada
mind *v* importar; cuidar
mind *n* mente, intención
mind-boggling *adj* increíble
mindful *adj* consciente
mindless *adj* inconsciente
mine *n* mina
mine *v* minar
mine *pro* mío
minefield *n* campo minado
miner *n* minero
mineral *n* mineral
mingle *v* mezclar(se)
miniature *n* miniatura
minimal *adj* mínimo
minimize *v* minimizar
minimum *n* mínimo
miniskirt *n* minifalda
minister *n* ministro, sacerdote
minister *v* atender
ministry *n* ministerio
minor *adj* menor
minority *n* minoría
mint *n* menta
mint *v* acuñar
minus *adj* menos
minute *n* minuto
miracle *n* milagro
miraculous *adj* milagroso
mirage *n* espejismo
mirror *n* espejo
mirror *v* reflejar

misbehave *v* portarse mal
miscalculate *v* calcular mal
miscarriage *v* fracaso, aborto
mischief *n* travesura
mischievous *adj* travieso
misconduct *n* mala conducta
misconstrue *v* interpretar mal
misdemeanor *n* delito
miser *n* avaro
miserable *adj* miserable
misery *n* miseria
misfit *n* inadaptado
misfortune *n* desgracia
misgivings *n* dudas
misguided *adj* equivocado
mishap *n* percance
misinterpret *v* interpretar mal
misjudge *v* juzgar mal
mislead *v* engañar
misleading *adj* engañoso
mismanage *v* administrar mal
misplace *v* extraviar
misprint *n* errata
miss *v* extrañar
miss *n* señorita
missile *n* projectil
missing *adj* perdido
mission *n* misión
missionary *n* misionero
mist *n* neblina
mistake *iv* equivocarse
mistake *n* error

mistaken *adj* equivocado
mister *n* señor
mistreat *v* maltratar
mistreatment *n* maltrato
mistress *n* amante
mistrust *n* desconfianza
mistrust *v* desconfiar
misty *adj* brumoso
misunderstand *v* entender mal
misuse *n* mal uso
misuse *v* usar mal
mitigate *v* mitigar
mix *v* mezclar
mixed-up *adj* confuso
mixer *n* mezcladora
mixture *n* mezcla
mix-up *n* confusión
moan *v* gemir
moan *n* gemido
mob *v* acosar, asediar
mob *n* gentío, turba
mobile *adj* móvil
mobilize *v* mobilizar
mobster *n* gángster
mock *v* burlarse, imitar
mock *adj* simulado
mockery *n* burla
mode *n* modo
model *n* modelo
model *v* modelar
moderate *adj* moderado
moderate *v* moderar(se)

moderation *n* moderación
modern *adj* moderno
modernize *v* modernizar
modest *adj* modesto, ligero
modesty *n* modestia, pudor
modify *v* modificar
module *n* módulo
moisten *v* humedecer, mojar
moisture *n* humedad
molar *n* muela
mold *v* moldear
mold *n* molde
moldy *adj* mohoso
mole *n* lunar; topo; espía
molecule *n* molécula
molest *v* molestar, acosar
mollify *v* calmar
molten *adj* derritido
mom *n* mamá
moment *n* momento
momentarily *adv* en un rato
momentary *adj* momentáneo
momentous *adj* importante
monarch *n* monarca
monarchy *n* monarquía
monastery *n* monasterio
monastic *adj* monástico
Monday *n* lunes
money *n* dinero
money order *n* giro
monitor *v* controlar
monk *n* monje

M

monkey *n* mono
monogamy *n* monogamia
monologue *n* monólogo
monopolize *v* monopolizar
monopoly *n* monopolio
monotonous *adj* monótono
monotony *n* monotonía
monster *n* monstruo
monstrous *adj* monstruoso
month *n* mes
monthly *adv* mensualmente
monthly *adj* mensual
monument *n* monumento
monumental *adj* monumental
mood *n* humor
moody *adj* triste
moon *n* luna
moor *v* amarrar
mop *v* limpiar, fregar
moral *adj* moral
moral *n* moraleja
morality *n* moralidad
moralize *v* moralizar
morbid *adj* morboso
more *adj* más
moreover *adv* además
morning *n* mañana
moron *adj* imbécil
morphine *n* morfina
morsel *n* bocado, porción
mortal *adj* mortal
mortality *n* mortalidad

mortar *n* cemento
mortgage *n* hipoteca
mortification *n* mortificación
mortify *v* mortificar
mortuary *n* funeraria
mosaic *n* mosaico
mosque *n* mezquita
mosquito *n* mosquito
moss *n* musgo
most *adj* mayor parte
mostly *adv* principalmente
motel *n* motel
moth *n* polilla
mother *n* madre
motherhood *n* maternidad
mother-in-law *n* suegra
motion *n* movimiento
motionless *adj* inmóvil
motivate *v* motivar
motive *n* motivo
motor *n* motor
motorcycle *n* motocicleta
motto *n* lema
mouldy *adj* mohoso
mount *n* monte
mount *v* montar
mountain *n* montaña
mountainous *adj* montañoso
mourn *v* llorar la muerte
mourning *n* luto, duelo
mouse *n* ratón
mouth *n* boca

mouthpiece *n* boquilla
movable *adj* movible
move *n* jugada
move *v* mover
move back *v* retroceder
move forward *v* avanzar
move out *v* mudarse
move over *v* dejar sitio
move up *v* ascender
movement *n* movimiento
movie *n* película
moving *adj* conmovedor
mow *v* cortar, segar
much *adv* mucho
mucus *n* mucosidad
mud *n* barro
muddle *n* enturbiar
muddy *adj* embarrado
muffle *v* amortiguar
muffler *n* silenciador
mug *v* atracar, asaltar
mugger *n* atracador
mugging *n* atraco
mule *n* mula
multiple *adj* múltiple
multiplication *n* multiplicación
multiply *v* multiplicar
multitude , multitud
mumble *v* refunfuñar
mummy *n* momia
mumps *n* paperas
munch *v* mascar

munitions *n* armamento
murder *n* asesinato
murder *v* asesinar
murderer *n* asesino
murky *adj* turbio
murmur *v* murmurar
murmur *n* murmullo
muscle *n* músculo
museum *n* museo
mushroom *n* hongo, seta
mushy *adj* pastoso
music *n* música
musician *n* músico
Muslim *adj* musulmán
must *iv* tener que
mustache *n* bigote
mustard *n* mostaza
muster *v* reunir, juntar
mutate *v* transformarse
mute *adj* mudo
mute *v* atenuar
mutilate *v* mutilar
mutiny *n* motín
mutter *v* murmullar
mutually *adv* mutuamente
muzzle *v* amordazar
muzzle *n* hocico; bozal
my *adj* mi
myopia *n* miopía
myopic *adj* miope
myself *pro* yo mismo
mysterious *adj* misterioso

M

mystery _n_ misterio
mystic _adj_ místico
mystify _v_ dejar perplejo
myth _n_ mito

N

nag _v_ dar la lata
nagging _adj_ continuo
nail _n_ uña; clavo
nail down _v_ clavar
naive _adj_ ingenuo
naked _adj_ desnudo
name _n_ nombre
namely _adv_ a saber
nanny _n_ niñera
nap _n_ siesta
napkin _n_ servilleta
narcotic _n_ narcótico
narrate _v_ narrar
narration _n_ narración
narrow _adj_ estrecho
narrowly _adv_ por poco
nasty _adj_ asqueroso
nation _n_ nación
national _adj_ nacional
nationality _n_ nacionalidad
nationalize _v_ nacionalizar

native _adj_ nativo
natural _adj_ natural
naturally _adv_ naturalmente
nature _n_ naturaleza
naughty _adj_ travieso
nausea _n_ náusea
nave _n_ nave
navel _n_ ombligo
navigate _v_ navegar
navigation _n_ navegación
navy _n_ armada
navy blue _adj_ azul marino
near _pre_ cerca de
nearby _adj_ cercano
nearly _adv_ casi
nearsighted _adj_ miope
neat _adj_ ordenado, limpio
neatly _adv_ esmeradamente
necessary _adj_ necesario
necessitate _v_ necesitar
necessity _n_ necesidad
neck _n_ cuello
necklace _n_ collar
necktie _n_ corbata
need _v_ necesitar
need _n_ necesidad
needle _n_ aguja
needle _v_ pinchar
needless _adj_ innecesario
needy _adj_ necesitado
negative _adj_ negativo
neglect _v_ descuidar

neglect *n* descuido
negligence *n* negligencia
negligent *adj* negligente
negotiate *v* negociar
negotiation *n* negociación
neighbor *n* vecino
neighborhood *n* barrio
neighboring *adj* vecino
neither *adj* ninguno
neither *adv* tampoco
nephew *n* sobrino
nerve *n* nervio
nervous *adj* nervioso
nervousness *n* nerviosismo
nest *n* nido
net *n* red
net *v* atrapar
Netherlands *n* Países Bajos
network *n* red, cadena
neurotic *adj* neurótico
neuter *v* capar
neuter *adj* neutro
neutral *adj* neutral
neutralize *v* neutralizar
never *adv* nunca
nevertheless *adv* sin embargo
new *adj* nuevo
newborn *n* recién nacido
newcomer recién llegado
newly *adv* recientemente
newlywed *adj* recién casados
news *n* noticias

newscast *n* noticiero
newsletter *n* boletín
newspaper *n* periódico
newsstand *n* quiosco
next *adj* próximo
next door *adj* de al lado
nibble *v* picar, morder
nibble *n* mordisco
nice *adj* simpático
nicely *adv* amablemente
nickel *n* níquel
nickname *n* apodo, mote
nicotine *n* nicotina
niece *n* sobrina
night *n* noche
nightfall *n* anochecer
nightgown *n* bata de dormir
nightingale *n* ruiseñor
nightly *adj* cada noche
nightmare *n* pesadilla
nil *n* nada
nine *adj* nueve
nineteen *adj* diecinueve
ninety *adj* noventa
ninth *adj* noveno
nip *n* pellizco
nip *v* pellizcar
nipple *n* pezón
nitpicking *adj* quisquilloso
nitrogen *n* nitrógeno
no one *pro* ninguno
nobility *n* nobleza

N

noble *adj* noble
nobleman *n* hidalgo
nobody *pro* nadie
nocturnal *adj* nocturno
nod *v* saludar; asentir
noise *n* ruido
noisily *adv* ruidosamente
noisy *adj* ruidoso
nomad *adj* nómada
nominate *v* nombrar
nomination *n* nombramiento
nominee *n* candidato
none *pre* ninguno
nonetheless *c* no obstante
nonsense *n* disparate
nonsmoker *n* no fumador
nonstop *adv* sin parar
noodles *n* fideos
noon *n* mediodía
noose *n* lazo, soga
nor *c* ni
norm *n* norma
normal *adj* normal
normalize *v* normalizar
normally *adv* normalmente
north *n* norte
northeast *n* noroeste
northern *adj* del norte
northerner *adj* norteño
Norway *n* Noruega
Norwegian *adj* noruego
nose *n* nariz; hocico

nosedive *v* caer en picado
nostalgia *n* nostalgia
nostril *n* orificio nasal
nosy *adj* curioso
not *adv* no
notable *adj* notable
notably *adv* notablemente
notary *n* notario
note *n* nota, anotación
note *v* notar
note down *v* anotar
notebook *n* cuaderno
noteworthy *adj* notable, digno
nothing *n* nada
notice *v* observar; notar
notice *n* aviso; letrero
noticeable *adj* obvio
notification *n* notificación
notify *v* notificar
notion *n* noción, idea
notorious *adj* notorio
notwithstanding *pre* a pesar de
noun *n* nombre
nourish *v* nutrir
nourishing *adj* nutritivo
nourishment *n* alimento
novel *n* novela
novelist *n* novelista
novelty *n* novedad
November *n* noviembre
novice *n* novicio, novato
now *adv* ahora

N

nowadays *adv* hoy en día
nowhere *adv* en ningún lugar
noxious *adj* nocivo
nozzle *n* boquilla
nuance *n* matiz
nuclear *adj* nuclear
nude *adj* desnudo
nudism *n* nudismo
nudist *n* nudista
nudity *n* desnudez
nuisance *n* molestia
null *adj* nulo
nullify *v* anular
numb *adj* entumecido
number *n* número
numbness *n* entumecimiento
numerous *adj* numeroso
nun *n* monja
nurse *n* enfermera
nurse *v* cuidar
nursery *n* guardería; vivero
nurture *v* criar, nutrir
nut *n* nuez; tuerca
nutrient *adj* nutriente
nutrition *n* nutrición
nutritious *adj* nutritivo
nutshell *n* cáscara de nuez
nutty *adj* tocado, chalado
nylon *n* nilón

oak *n* roble
oar *n* remo
oasis *n* oasis
oath *n* juramento
oatmeal *n* avena
obedience *n* obediencia
obedient *adj* obediente
obese *adj* obeso, gordo
obey *v* obedecer
object *v* oponerse
object *n* objeto
objection *n* objeción
objective *n* objetivo
obligate *v* obligar
obligation *n* obligación
obligatory *adj* obligatorio
oblige *v* obligar
obliged *adj* agradecido
oblique *adj* oblicuo
obliterate *v* borrar, destruir
oblivion *n* olvido
oblivious *adj* inconsciente
oblong *adj* rectangular
obnoxious *adj* detestable
obscene *adj* obsceno
obscenity *n* obscenidad
obscure *adj* obscuro
obscurity *n* obscuridad
observation *n* observación

N
O

observatory *n* observatorio
observe *v* observar, notar
observer *n* observador
obsess *v* obsesionar
obsession *n* obsesión
obsolete *adj* en desuso
obstacle *n* obstáculo
obstinacy *n* terquedad
obstinate *adj* terco
obstruct *v* obstruir
obstruction *n* obstrucción
obtain *v* obtener
obvious *adj* evidente
obviously *adv* evidentemente
occasion *n* ocasión
occasionally *adv* a veces
occult *adj* oculto
occupant *n* ocupante
occupation *n* ocupación
occupy *v* ocupar
occur *v* ocurrir
ocean *n* océano
October *n* octubre
octopus *n* pulpo
ocurrence *n* suceso
odd *adj* raro, extraño
oddity *n* rareza
odds *n* probabilidades
odious *adj* odioso
odometer *n* odómetro
odor *n* olor
odyssey *n* odisea

of *pre* de
off *adv* lejos
offend *v* ofender
offense *n* ofensa
offensive *adj* ofensivo
offer *v* ofrecer
offer *n* oferta
offering *n* ofrenda
office *n* oficina
officer *n* agente
official *adj* oficial
officiate *v* oficiar
offset *v* compensar
offspring *n* descendencia
off-the-record *adj* confidencial
often *adv* a menudo
oil *n* aceite, petróleo
oily *adj* grasiento
ointment *n* unguento
okay *adv* bien
okay *v* aprobar
old *adj* viejo, antiguo
old age *n* vejez
old-fashioned *adj* anticuado
olive *n* aceituna
olympics *n* olimpiada
omelette *n* tortilla
omen *n* presagio
ominous *adj* amenazador
omission *n* omisión
omit *v* omitir
on *pre* en, encima

once *adv* una vez
once *c* una vez que
oncoming *adj* venidero
one *adj* uno
oneself *pre* uno mismo
ongoing *adj* continuo
onion *n* cebolla
onlooker *n* espectador
only *adv* solamente
onset *n* comienzo
onslaught *n* embestida
onwards *adv* hacia adelante
opaque *adj* opaco, obscuro
open *v* abrir
open *adj* abierto
open up *v* abrirse
opener *n* abridor
opening *n* vacante
open-minded *adj* imparcial
openness *n* franqueza
opera *n* ópera
operate *v* operar, actuar
operation *n* operación
opinion *n* opinión
opinionated *adj* testarudo
opium *n* opio
opponent *n* adversario
opportune *adj* oportuno
opportunity *n* oportunidad
oppose *v* oponerse
opposite *adj* opuesto
opposite *adv* en frente

opposite *n* contrario
opposition *n* oposición
oppress *v* oprimir
oppression *n* opresión
oppressive *adj* agobiante
opt for *v* optar por
optical *adj* óptico
optician *n* optometrista
optimism *n* optimismo
optimistic *adj* optimista
option *n* opción
optional *adj* opcional
opulence *n* opulencia
or *c* o
oracle *n* oráculo
orally *adv* oralmente
orange *n* naranja
orbit *n* órbita
orchard *n* huerto
orchestra *n* orquesta
ordain *v* ordenar
ordeal *n* tormento
order *n* orden
ordinarily *adv* ordinariamente
ordinary *adj* corriente
ordination *n* ordenación
ore *n* mineral
organ *n* órgano
organism *n* organismo
organist *n* organista
organization *n* organización
organize *v* organizar

O

orient n oriente
oriental adj oriental
orientation n orientación
oriented adj orientado
origin n origen
original adj original
originally adv al principio
originate v originar(se)
ornament n adorno
ornamental adj decorativo
orphan n huérfano
orphanage n orfanatorio
orthodox adj ortodoxo
ostentatious adj ostentoso
ostrich n avestruz
other adj otro
otherwise adv de lo contrario
otter n nutria
ought to iv deber
ounce n onza
our adj nuestro
ours pro nuestro
ourselves pro nosotros mismos
oust v desalojar
out adv afuera, fuera
outbreak n estallido; comienzo
outburst n arrebato
outcast adj abandonado
outcome n resultado
outcry n protesta
outdated adj anticuado
outdo v superar

outdoor adj al aire libre, exterior
outdoors adv fuera
outer adj exterior
outfit n conjunto
outgoing adj extrovertido
outgrow v dejar atrás
outing n excursión
outlast v durar más que
outlaw v prohibir
outlet n salida; enchufe
outline n perfil; esquema
outline v resumir, esbozar
outlive v sobrevivir
outlook n perspectiva
outmoded adj anticuado
outnumber v superar a
outpatient n paciente
outperform v superar
outpouring n manifestación
output n producción
outrage n indignación
outraged adj indignado
outrageous adj atroz
outright adj rotundo, claro
outrun v adelantar
outset n principio
outshine v eclipsar
outside adv afuera
outside adj exterior
outsider n forastero
outskirts n alrededores
outspoken adj muy franco

outstanding *adj* destacado
outstretched *adj* extendido
outward *adj* externo
outweigh *v* sobrepesar
oval *adj* ovalado
ovary *n* ovario
ovation *n* ovación
oven *n* horno
over *pre* sobre
overall *adv* en general
overall *adj* general
overbearing *adj* abrumador
overboard *adv* por la borda
overcast *adj* nublado
overcharge *v* cobrar de más
overcoat *n* abrigo
overcome *v* superar
overcrowded *adj* superpoblado
overdo *v* exagerar
overdone *adj* demasiado hecho
overdose *n* sobredosis
overdue *adj* retrasado
overestimate *v* sobreestimar
overflow *v* desbordarse
overhaul *v* revisar
overlap *v* coincidir, duplicar
overload *v* sobrecargar
overlook *v* pasar por alto
overnight *adv* por la noche
overpower *v* dominar
overrate *v* sobreestimar
override *v* invalidar

overrule *v* anular
overrun *v* invadir
overseas *adv* en el extranjero
oversee *v* supervisar
overshadow *v* eclipsar
oversight *n* descuido
overstate *v* exagerar
overstep *v* pasarse de la raya
overtake *v* adelantar
overthrow *v* derrocar
overthrow *n* derrocamiento
overtime *adv* horas extras
overturn *v* volcar
overview *n* vista general
overweight *adj* obeso
overwhelm *v* abrumar
owe *v* deber
owing to *adv* debido a
owl *n* buho
own *v* poseer
own *adj* propio
owner *n* dueño
ownership *n* posesión
ox *n* buey
oxen *n* bueyes
oxygen *n* oxígeno
oyster *n* ostra

O

P

pace *v* dar pasos
pace *n* paso
pacify *v* pacificar
pack *v* empaquetar
package *n* paquete
package *v* empaquetar
packed *adj* abarrotado
pact *n* pacto
pad *v* rellenar
padding *n* relleno
paddle *v* chapotear
padlock *n* candado
pagan *adj* pagano
page *n* página; paje
pail *n* balde, cubo
pain *n* dolor
painful *adj* doloroso
painkiller *n* calmante
painless *adj* sin dolor
painstaking *adj* esmerado
paint *v* pintar
paint *n* pintura
paintbrush *n* brocha
painter *n* pintor
painting *n* pintura; cuadro
pair *n* par
pajamas *n* pijamas
pal *n* compañero
palace *n* palacio

palatable *adj* aceptable
palate *n* paladar
pale *adj* pálido
paleness *n* palidez
palm *n* palma; palmera
palpable *adj* palpable
paltry *adj* miserable
pamper *v* mimar
pamphlet *n* folleto
pan *n* cazuela
pancreas *n* pancreas
pander *v* complacer
pang *n* punzada
panic *n* pánico
panorama *n* panorama
pant *v* jadear
panther *n* pantera
pantry *n* despensa
pants *n* pantalones
pantyhose *n* media
papacy *n* papado
paper *n* papel
paper *v* empapelar
paperclip *n* sujetapapeles
paperwork *n* papeleo
parable *n* parábola
parachute *n* paracaídas
parade *n* desfile
parade *v* desfilar
paradise *n* paraíso
paradox *n* paradoja
paragraph *n* párrafo

parakeet *n* periquito, loro
parallel *n* paralelo
paralysis *n* parálisis
paralyze *v* paralizar
parameters *n* límites
paramount *adj* primordial
paranoid *adj* paranoico
parasite *n* parásito
paratrooper *n* paracaidista
parcel *n* paquete
parcel post *n* correos
parched *adj* seco
parchment *n* pergamino
pardon *v* perdonar
pardon *n* perdón
pare *v* cortar
pare down *v* reducir
parenthesis *n* paréntesis
parents *n* padres
parish *n* parroquia
parishioner *n* parroquiano
parity *n* paridad
park *v* aparcar
park *n* parque
parking *n* aparcamiento
parliament *n* parlamento
parlor *n* salón
parochial *adj* parroquial
parrot *n* perico, loro
parsley *n* peregil
parsnip *n* remolacha
part *v* separarse

part *n* parte
partial *adj* parcial
partially *adv* parcialmente
participate *v* participar
participation *n* participación
participle *n* participio
particle *n* partícula
particular *adj* particular
particularly *adv* sobre todo
parting *n* separación
partisan *n* partidario
partition *n* tabique
partly *adv* en parte
partner *n* socio
partnership *n* sociedad
partridge *n* perdiz
party *n* grupo; fiesta
party *v* irse de juerga
pass *n* puerto; pase
pass *v* pasar; aprobar
pass around *v* repartir
pass away *v* fallecer
pass out *v* desmayarse
passage *n* travesía, pasillo
passenger *n* pasajero
passer-by *n* transeúnte
passion *n* pasión
passionate *adj* apasionado
passive *adj* pasivo
passport *n* pasaporte
password *n* contraseña
past *adj* pasado

P

paste v pegar
paste n engrudo
pasteurize v pausterizar
pastime n pasatiempo
pastor n párroco
pastoral adj pastoral
pastry n pastel
pasture n pasto
pat n palmada, caricia
pat v acariciar
patch v remendar, reparar
patch n remiendo, parche
patchy adj desigual
patent n patente
patent adj claro, evidente
paternity n paternidad
path n camino
pathetic adj patético
pathway v camino
patience n paciencia
patient adj paciente
patio n patio
patriarch n patriarca
patrimony n patrimonio
patriot n patriota
patriotic adj patriótico
patrol n patrulla
patrol v patrullar
patron n patrono; patrón
patronage n patrocinio
patronize v patrocinar
pattern n patrón, modelo

pause n pausa
pause v hacer una pausa
pavement n acera, calzada
pavilion n caseta
paw n pata, garra
pawn v empeñar
pawn n peón
pawnbroker n prestamista
pay n paga, sueldo
pay iv pagar
pay back v devolver
pay off v saldar, liquidar
payable adj pagadero
paycheck n sueldo
payee n portador
payment n pago
payroll n nómina
payslip n recibo
pea n guisante
peace n paz
peaceful adj pacífico
peach n melocotón
peacock n pavo real
peak n cumbre, cima
peal n tañido, repique
peanut n cacahuete
pear n pera
pearl n perla
peasant n campesino
pebble n guijarro
peck v picotear
peck n picotazo

peculiar *adj* peculiar
pedagogy *n* pedagogía
pedal *n* pedal
pedantic *adj* pedante
peddle *v* vender, traficar
pedestrian *n* peatón
peek *v* ojeada
peel *v* pelar; despegar
peel *n* cáscara
peep *v* mirar a escondidas
peer *n* compañero
pelican *n* pelícano
pellet *n* perdigón, bolita
pen *n* pluma
penalize *v* penalizar
penalty *n* multa; penalti
penance *n* penitencia
penchant *n* predilección
pencil *n* lápiz
pendant *n* pendiente
pending *adj* pendiente
pendulum *n* péndulo
penetrate *v* penetrar
penguin *n* pinguino
penicillin *n* penicilina
penicillin *v* penicilina
peninsula *n* península
penitent *n* penitente
penniless *adj* indigente
penny *n* penique
pension *n* pensión
pensioner *v* pensionista

pentagon *n* pentágono
penthouse *v* ático
pent-up *adj* reprimido
people *n* gente
pep *v* animar
pepper *n* pimienta
per *pre* por
perceive *v* percibir
percent *adv* por ciento
percentage *n* porcentage
perception *n* percepción
perch *v* percha
perennial *adj* perenne
perfect *adj* perfecto
perfection *n* perfección
perforate *v* perforar
perforation *n* perforación
perform *v* realizar; actuar
performance *n* actuación;
  resultado
perfume *n* perfume
perfunctory *adj* superficial
perhaps *adv* quizás
peril *n* peligro
perilous *adj* peligroso
perimeter *n* perímetro
period *n* periodo
periodic *v* periódico
periphery *n* periferia
perish *v* perecer
perishable *adj* perecedero
perjury *n* perjurio

P

perks *n* ventajas
permanent *adj* permanente
permeate *v* penetrar
permission *n* permiso
permit *v* permitir
permit *n* pemiso, licencia
pernicious *adj* pernicioso
perpetrate *v* perpetrar
perpetual *adj* perpetuo
perplex *v* dejar perplejo
persecute *v* perseguir
persecution *n* persecución
persevere *v* perseverar
persist *v* persistir
persistence *n* persistencia
persistent *adj* persistente
person *n* persona
personal *adj* personal
personality *n* personalidad
personify *v* personificar
personnel *n* personal
perspective *n* perspectiva
perspiration *n* sudor
perspire *v* sudar
persuade *v* persuadir
persuasion *n* persuasión
persuasive *adj* persuasivo
pertain *v* pertenecer
pertinent *adj* pertinente
perturb *v* perturbar
perverse *adj* perverso
perversion *n* distorsión

pervert *v* pervertir
pervert *adj* pervertido
pessimism *n* pesimismo
pessimistic *adj* pesimista
pest *n* molestia
pester *v* molestar, dar la lata
pesticide *n* pesticida
pet *n* animal doméstico
petal *n* pétalo
petite *adj* pequeño
petition *n* petición
petrified *adj* petrificado
petroleum *n* petróleo
pettiness *n* mezquindad
petty *adj* mezquino, pequeño
pew *n* banco de iglesia
phantom *n* fantasma
pharmacist *n* farmacéutico
pharmacy *n* farmacia
phase *n* fase
pheasant *n* faisán
phenomenon *n* fenómeno
philosopher *n* filósofo
philosophy *n* filosofía
phobia *n* fobia
phone *n* teléfono
phone *v* telefonear
phoney *adj* falso, fingido
phosphorus *n* fósforo
photo *n* fotografía
photocopy *n* fotocopia
photograph *v* fotografiar**

place

photographer *n* fotógrafo
photography *n* fotografía
phrase *n* frase
physically *adj* físicamente
physician *n* médico
physics *n* física
pianist *n* pianista
piano *n* piano
pick *v* elegir; recoger
pick up *v* recoger
pickpocket *n* ratero
pickup *n* furgoneta
picture *n* cuadro, dibujo, foto
picture *v* imaginar(se)
picturesque *adj* pintoresco
pie *n* tarta, pastel
piece *n* pieza
piecemeal *adv* por partes
pier *n* muelle
pierce *v* perforar
piercing *n* perforación
piety *n* piedad, devoción
pig *n* cerdo
pigeon *n* paloma
piggy bank *n* hucha
pile *v* acumular
pile *n* montón
pile up *v* amontonarse
pilfer *v* robar, saquear
pilgrim *n* peregrino
pilgrimage *n* peregrinación
pill *n* pastilla

pillage *v* saquear
pillar *n* columna
pillow *n* almohada
pillowcase *n* funda
pilot *n* piloto
pimple *n* grano
pin *n* alfiler
pincers *n* tenazas
pinch *v* pellizcar
pinch *n* pellizco, pizca
pine *n* pino
pineapple *n* piña
pink *adj* rosado
pinpoint *v* precisar
pint *n* pinta
pioneer *n* pionero
pious *adj* piadoso
pipe *n* tubo, caño
pipeline *n* oleoducto
piracy *n* piratería
pirate *n* pirata
pistol *n* pistola
pit *n* hoyo; fosa
pitch-black *adj* muy negro
pitchfork *n* horca
pitfall *n* escollo; riesgo
pitiful *adj* lastimoso
pity *n* compasión
pity *v* sentir lástima
placard *n* letrero, pancarta
placate *v* apaciguar
place *n* lugar, sitio

P

place *v* colocar

placement *n* colocación

placid *adj* apacible

plague *n* plaga

plain *n* llanura

plain *adj* claro, simple; liso

plainly *adv* claramente

plaintiff *n* demandante

plan *v* hacer planes

plan *n* plan, plano

plane *n* avión

planet *n* planeta

plank *n* tabla de madera

plant *v* plantar, sembrar

plant *n* planta

plaque *n* placa

plaster *n* yeso

plaster *v* enyesar

plastic *n* plástico

plate *n* plato

plateau *n* meseta

platform *n* plataforma

platinum *n* platino

platoon *n* pelotón

plausible *adj* verosímil

play *v* jugar; tocar

play *n* juego; obra

player *n* jugador

playful *adj* juguetón

playground *n* lugar de recreo

plea *n* súplica, apelación

plead *v* suplicar, defender

pleasant *adj* agradable

please *v* agradar

pleasing *adj* agradable

pleasure *n* placer

pleat *n* pliegue

pleated *adj* doblado

pledge *v* prometer

pledge *n* promesa

plentiful *adj* abundante

plenty *n* mucho

pliable *adj* flexible

pliers *n* alicates

plot *v* tramar

plot *n* complot

plow *v* arar

ploy *n* estratagema

pluck *v* coger

plug *v* enchufar; tapar

plug *n* enchufe; tapón

plum *n* ciruela

plumber *n* fontanero

plumbing *n* fontanería

plummet *v* caer en picado

plump *adj* rechoncho

plunder *v* saquear

plunge *v* lanzarse; hundir

plunge *n* caida, salto

plural *n* plural

plus *adv* más

plush *adj* lujoso

plutonium *n* plutonio

pneumonia *n* pulmonía**

pocket *n* bolsillo
pocket *v* embolsarse
poem *n* poema
poet *n* poeta
poetry *n* poesía
poignant *adj* conmovedor
point *n* punto; cuestión
point *v* señalar
pointed *adj* afilado; mordaz
pointless *adj* sin sentido
poise *n* elegancia
poison *v* envenenar
poison *n* veneno
poisoning *n* envenenamiento
poisonous *adj* venenoso
Poland *n* Polonia
polar *adj* polar
pole *n* poste; polo
police *n* policía (la)
policeman *n* policía (el)
policy *n* póliza
Polish *adj* polaco
polish *n* betún, brillo
polish *v* pulir, sacar brillo
polite *adj* cortés
politeness *n* cortesía
politician *n* político
politics *n* política
poll *n* encuesta, votación
poll *v* encuestar
pollen *n* polen
pollute *v* ensuciar

pollution *n* polución
polygamist *adj* polígamo
polygamy *n* poligamia
pomegranate *n* granada
pomposity *n* pomposidad
pond *n* estanque
ponder *v* ponderar
pontiff *n* pontífice
pool *n* piscina; billar
pool *v* juntar
poor *n* pobre
poorly *adv* mal, pobremente
popcorn *n* palomitas
Pope *n* Papa
poppy *n* amapola
popular *adj* popular
popularize *v* popularizar
populate *v* poblar
population *n* población
porcelain *n* porcelana
porch *n* pórtico
porcupine *n* puercoespín
pore *n* poro
pork *n* carne de cerdo
porous *adj* poroso
port *n* puerto
portable *adj* portátil
portent *n* augurio
porter *n* maletero, mozo
portion *n* porción
portrait *n* retrato
portray *v* describir

P

portrayal *n* actuación
Portugal *n* Portugal
Portuguese *adj* portugués
pose *v* posar; plantear
posh *adj* elegante
position *n* posición
positive *adj* positivo
possess *v* poseer
possession *n* posesión
possessive *adj* posesivo
possibility *n* posibilidad
possible *adj* posible
post *n* puesto; poste
post office *n* correos
postage *n* sello
postcard *n* tarjeta postal
poster *n* cartel, póster
posterity *n* posteridad
posthumous *adj* póstumo
postman *n* cartero
postmark *n* matasellos
postpone *v* aplazar
postponement *n* aplazamiento
posture *n* postura
pot *n* olla; tiesto
potato *n* patata
potent *adj* potente
potential *adj* potencial
pothole *n* bache
poultry *n* aves de corral
pound *v* golpear
pound *n* libra

pour *v* echar, verter
poverty *n* pobreza
powder *n* polvo
power *n* poder
powerful *adj* poderoso
powerless *adj* impotente
practical *adj* práctico
practice *v* ejercicio
practise *v* practicar
practising *adj* practicante
pragmatist *adj* pragmático
prairie *n* pradera
praise *v* alabar
praise *n* alabanza
praiseworthy *adj* loable
prank *n* travesura
prawn *n* gamba
pray *v* rezar
prayer *n* oración
preach *v* predicar
preacher *n* predicador
preaching *n* predicación
preamble *n* preámbulo
precarious *adj* precario, débil
precaution *n* precaución
precede *v* preceder
precedent *n* precedente
preceding *adj* anterior
precept *n* mandato
precious *adj* precioso
precipice *n* precipicio
precipitate *v* precipitar(se)

precise *adj* preciso, exacto
precision *n* precisión
preclude *v* descartar
precocious *adj* precoz
precursor *n* precursor
predecessor *n* antecesor
predicament *n* apuro
predict *v* pronosticar
prediction *n* predicción
predilection *n* predilección
predisposed *adj* predispuesto
predominate *v* predominar
preempt *v* adelantarse
pre-emptive *adj* preventivo
prefabricate *v* prefabricar
preface *n* prefacio
prefer *v* preferir
preference *n* preferencia
prefix *n* prefijo
pregnancy *n* embarazo
pregnant *adj* embarazada
prehistoric *adj* prehistórico
prejudice *n* prejuicio
prejuditial *adj* perjudiciar
preliminary *adj* preliminar
prelude *n* preludio
premature *adj* prematuro
premeditate *v* premeditar
premeditation *n* premeditación
premier *adj* estreno
premise *n* premisa
premises *n* local

premonition *n* premonición
preoccupation *n* preocupación
preoccupy *v* preocuparse
preparation *n* preparación
prepare *v* preparar
preposition *n* preposición
prerequisite *n* prerequisito
prerogative *n* prerrogativa
presage *n* presagio
prescribe *v* recetar
prescription *n* prescripción
presence *n* presencia
present *adj* presente
present *v* presentar
presentation *n* presentación
preserve *v* preservar
preset *v* programar
preside *v* presidir
presidency *n* presidencia
president *n* presidente
press *n* prensa, imprenta
press *v* insistir; apretar
pressing *adj* apremiante
pressure *v* presionar
pressure *n* presión
prestige *n* prestigio
presume *v* suponer
presumption *n* presunción
presuppose *v* presuponer
presupposition *n* suposición
pretend *v* pretender
pretense *n* excusa; farsa

pretension *n* pretensión
pretentious *adj* pretencioso
pretext *n* pretesto
pretty *adj* lindo, bonito
prevail *v* prevalecer
prevalent *adj* extendido
prevent *v* impedir
prevention *n* prevención
preventive *adj* preventivo
preview *n* preestreno
previous *adj* anterior
previously *adv* antes
prey *n* presa
price *n* precio
pricey *adj* caro
prick *v* pinchar, picar
prickle *n* pincho
pride *n* orgullo
priest *n* sacerdote
priestess *n* sacerdotisa
priesthood *n* sacerdocio
primacy *n* primacía
primarily *adv* ante todo
prime *adj* primordial
primitive *adj* primitivo
prince *n* príncipe
princess *n* princesa
principal *adj* principal
principle *n* principio
print *v* imprimir
print *n* huella
printer *n* impresor

printing *n* imprenta
prior *adj* previo, anterior
priority *n* prioridad
prism *n* prisma
prison *n* prisión
prisoner *n* prisionero
privacy *n* intimidad
private *adj* privado
privation *n* privación
privilege *n* privilegio
prize *n* premio
probability *n* probabilidad
probable *adj* probable
probe *v* investigar
probe *n* investigación
probing *n* investigación
problem *n* problema
problematic *adj* problemático
procedure *n* procedimiento
proceed *v* continuar
proceedings *n* proceso
proceeds *n* ganancias
process *v* tramitar, procesar
process *n* proceso
procession *n* desfile
proclaim *v* proclamar
proclamation *n* proclamación
procrastinate *v* demorar
procreate *v* procrear
procure *v* conseguir
prod *v* empujar, forzar
prodigious *adj* prodigioso

P

prodigy n prodigio
produce v producir
produce n vegetales
producer n productor
product n producto
production n producción
productive adj productivo
profane adj profano
profess v profesar
profession n profesión
professional adj profesional
professor n profesor
proficiency n competencia
proficient adj competente
profile n perfil
profit v aprovechar
profit n beneficio
profitable adj rentable
profound adj profundo
prognosis n pronóstico
program n programa
programmer n programador
progress v avanzar
progress n progreso
progressive adj progresista
prohibit v prohibir
prohibition n prohibición
project v proyectar
project n proyecto
projectile n proyectil
projection n proyección
proliferate v proliferar

prologue n prólogo
prolong v prolongar
promenade n paseo
prominent adj prominente
promiscuous adj promiscuo
promise n promesa
promising adj prometedor
promote v fomentar
promotion n ascenso
prompt adj puntual, rápido
prone adj propenso
pronoun n pronombre
pronounce v pronunciar
proof n prueba
propaganda n propaganda
propagate v propagar
propel v propulsar
propensity n propensión
proper adj apropiado
properly adv correctamente
property n propiedad
prophecy n profecía
prophet n profeta
proportion n proporción
proposal n propuesta
propose v proponer
proposition n proposición
prose n prosa
prosecute v procesar
prosecutor n fiscal
prospect n probabilidad
prosper v prosperar

P

prosperity *n* prosperidad
prosperous *adj* próspero
prostate *n* próstata
prostrate *adj* prostrado
protect *v* proteger
protection *n* protección
protein *n* proteína
protest *v* protestar
protest *n* protesta
protocol *n* protocolo
prototype *n* prototipo
protract *v* prolongar
protracted *adj* prolongado
protrude *v* sobresalir
proud *adj* orgulloso
proudly *adv* orgullosamente
prove *v* probar
proven *adj* probado
proverb *n* proverbio
provide *v* proveer
providence *n* providencia
providing that *c* siempre que
province *n* provincia
provision *n* suministro
provisional *adj* provisional
provocation *n* provocación
provoke *v* provocar
prow *n* proa
prowl *v* merodear
proximity *n* proximidad
proxy *n* poder
prudence *n* prudencia

prudent *adj* prudente
prune *v* podar
prune *n* ciruela seca
prurient *adj* lascivo
pry *v* entrometerse
pseudonym *n* seudónimo
psychiatrist *n* psiquiatra
psychiatry *n* psiquiatría
psychic *adj* psíquico
psychology *n* psicología
psychopath *n* psicópata
psycosis *n* psicosis
puberty *n* pubertad
public *adj* público
publication *n* publicación
publicity *n* publicidad
publicly *adv* públicamente
publish *v* publicar
publisher *n* editor
pudding *n* pudín
puerile *adj* infantil
puff *n* soplo, bocanada
puffed *adj* hinchado
pull *v* tirar, arrastrar
pull ahead *v* adelantar
pull down *v* derribar; bajar
pull out *v* sacar
pulley *n* polea
pulp *n* pulpa
pulpit *n* púlpito
pulsate *v* latir, pulsar
pulse *n* pulso

P

pulverize *v* pulverizar
pump *v* bombear
pump *n* bomba
pumpkin *n* calabaza
punch *v* golpear, agujerear
punch *n* puñetazo, golpe
punctual *adj* puntual
punctuation *n* puntuación
puncture *n* pinchazo
punish *v* castigar
punishable *adj* castigable
punishment *n* castigo
puny *adj* insignificante
pupil *n* alumno
puppet *n* títere
puppy *n* cachorro
purchase *v* comprar
purchase *n* compra
purchaser *n* comprador
pure *adj* puro, limpio
puree *n* puré
purgatory *n* purgatorio
purge *n* purga
purge *v* purgar
purification *n* purificación
purify *v* purificar
purity *n* pureza
purple *adj* morado
purpose *n* fin, propósito
purposely *adv* adrede
purse *n* bolso
pursue *v* perseguir; buscar

pursuit *n* búsqueda; logro
pus *n* pus
push *v* empujar
pushy *adj* insistente
put *iv* poner
put aside *v* separar
put away *v* guardar
put off *v* aplazar
put out *v* apagar
put up *v* levantar
put up with *v* aguantar
putrefy *v* pudrir(se)
putrid *adj* pútrido
puzzle *n* rompecabezas
puzzle *v* desconcertar
puzzled *adj* perplejo
puzzling *adj* desconcertante
pyramid *n* pirámide
python *n* serpiente pitón

P
Q

Q

quagmire *n* pantano, atolladero
quail *n* codorniz
quake *v* terremoto
qualify *v* calificar
quality *n* calidad
qualm *n* reparo, escrúpulo

quandary _n_ dilema
quantity _n_ cantidad
quarentine _n_ cuarentena
quarrel _v_ reñir, pelear
quarrel _n_ riña, pelea
quarrelsome _adj_ peleón
quarry _n_ cantera
quarter _n_ cuarto; barrio
quarterly _adj_ trimestral
quarters _n_ alojamiento
quash _v_ aplastar; anular
queen _n_ reina
queer _adj_ raro
quell _v_ sofocar
quench _v_ saciar, sofocar
quest _n_ búsqueda
question _v_ preguntar
question _n_ pregunta
questionable _adj_ dudoso
questionnaire _n_ cuestionario
queue _n_ cola
quick _adj_ rápido
quicken _v_ apresurar
quickly _adv_ rápidamente
quicksand _n_ arena movediza
quiet _adj_ quieto, callado
quietness _n_ silencio, quietud
quilt _n_ colcha
quince _n_ membrillo
quirk _n_ rareza
quit _iv_ dejar, abandonar
quite _adv_ bastante

quiver _v_ estremecerse
quiz _v_ interrogar
quotation _n_ cita
quote _v_ citar
quotient _n_ cociente

R

rabbi _n_ rabino
rabbit _n_ conejo
rabies _n_ rabia
raccoon _n_ racún
race _v_ correr
race _n_ carrera; raza
racism _n_ racismo
racist _adj_ racista
racket _n_ raqueta; estafa
racketeering _n_ extorsión
radar _n_ radar
radiation _n_ radiación
radiator _n_ radiador
radical _adj_ radical
radio _n_ radio
radish _n_ rábano
radius _n_ radio
raffle _n_ sorteo, rifa
raft _n_ balsa
rag _n_ trapo

Q
R

rage *n* rabia
ragged *adj* harapiento
raid *n* asalto; redada
raid *v* asaltar, atacar
raider *n* asaltante
rail *n* carril; baranda
railroad *n* ferrocarril
rain *n* lluvia
rain *v* llover
rainbow *n* arco iris
raincoat *n* impermeable
rainfall *n* lluvia
rainstorm *n* chaparrón
rainy *adj* lluvioso
raise *n* aumento
raise *v* aumentar; levantar
raisin *n* pasa
rake *n* rastrillo
rally *n* mitin, reunión
ram *n* carnero
ram *v* embestir
ramble *v* divagar
rambling *adj* confuso
ramification *n* ramificación
ramp *n* rampa
rampage *v* arrasar
rampant *adj* extendido
ranch *n* rancho
rancor *n* rencor
randomly *adv* al azar
range *n* alcance, gama
rank *n* rango; tropa

rank *v* clasificar
ransack *v* desvalijar
ransom *v* rescatar
ransom *n* rescate
rape *v* violar
rape *n* violación
rapid *adj* rápido
rapist *n* violador
rapport *n* relacción
rare *adj* poco común, raro
rarely *adv* raramente
rascal *n* pícaro, pillo
rash *v* precipitarse
rash *n* prisa
rash *adj* precipitado
rasp *v* raspar
raspberry *n* mora
rat *n* rata
rate *n* tarifa; ritmo, tipo
rather *adv* más bien
ratification *n* ratificación
ratify *v* ratificar
ratio *n* proporción
ration *v* racionar
ration *n* ración
rational *adj* racional
rationalize *v* justificar
rattle *v* traquetear
ravage *v* arrasar
ravage *n* estragos
raven *n* cuervo
ravine *n* barranco**

R

raw *adj* crudo
ray *n* rayo
raze *v* arrasar
razor *n* cuchilla
reach *v* alcanzar
reach *n* alcance
react *v* reaccionar
reaction *n* reacción
reactivate *v* reactivar
read *iv* leer
reader *n* lector
readiness *n* preparación
reading *n* lectura
readjust *v* reajustar
ready *adj* preparado
real *adj* real, genuino
realism *n* realismo
reality *n* realidad
realize *v* darse cuenta
really *adv* de verdad
realm *n* reino
realty *n* inmobiliaria
reap *v* cosechar
reappear *v* reaparecer
rear *v* criar
rear *n* retaguardia
rear *adj* trasero, último
reason *v* razonar
reason *n* razón
reasonable *adj* razonable
reasoning *n* razonamiento
reassure *v* tranquilizar

rebate *n* reembolso
rebel *v* rebelarse
rebel *n* rebelde
rebellion *n* rebelión
rebirth *n* renacimiento
rebound *v* rebotar
rebound *n* rebote
rebuff *v* rechazar, desairar
rebuff *n* desaire, rechazo
rebuild *v* reconstruir
rebuke *v* reprender
rebuke *n* reprimenda
rebut *v* rebatir
recalcitrant *adj* obstinado
recall *v* recordar
recant *v* desdecirse
recap *v* resumir
recapture *v* reconquistar
recede *v* retroceder
receipt *n* recibo
receive *v* recibir
recent *adj* reciente
receptacle *n* recipiente
reception *n* recepción
receptionist *n* recepcionista
receptive *adj* acogedor
recess *n* descanso, hueco
recession *n* recesión
recharge *v* recargar
recipe *n* receta
reciprocal *adj* recíproco
recital *n* recital**

recite *v* recitar
reckless *adj* imprudente
reckon *v* estimar, creer
reckon on *v* contar con
reclaim *v* reclamar
recline *v* reclinar
recluse *n* solitario
recognition *n* reconocimiento
recognize *v* reconocer
recollect *v* recordar
recollection *n* recuerdo
recommend *v* recomendar
recompense *v* recompensar
recompense *n* recompensa
reconcile *v* reconciliar
reconsider *v* reconsiderar
reconstruct *v* reconstruir
record *v* grabar; registrar
record *n* disco; récord
recorder *n* grabadora
recording *n* grabación
recount *n* recuento
recount *v* relatar
recoup *v* recuperar
recourse *v* recurrir
recourse *n* recurso
recover *v* recobrar
recovery *n* recuperación
recreate *v* recrear
recreation *n* recreación
recruit *v* reclutar
recruit *n* recluta

recruitment *n* reclutamiento
rectangle *n* rectángulo
rectangular *adj* rectangular
rectify *v* rectificar
rector *n* rector
rectum *n* recto
recuperate *v* reponerse
recur *v* repetirse
recurrence *n* repetición
recycle *v* reciclar
red *adj* rojo
red tape *n* papeleo
redden *v* enrojecer(se)
redeem *v* redimir
redemption *n* redención
redhead *adj* pelirojo
red-hot *adj* candente
redo *v* rehacer
redouble *v* redoblar
redress *v* reparar
reduce *v* reducir
redundant *adj* superfluo
reed *n* junco
reef *n* arrecife
reel *n* carrete; rollo
reelect *v* reelegir
reenactment *n* recreación
reentry *n* vuelta
refer to *v* referirse a
referee *n* árbitro
reference *n* referencia
referendum *n* referendum

R

refill *v* rellenar
refinance *v* refinanciar
refine *v* refinar
refinery *n* refinería
reflect *v* reflexionar
reflection *n* reflexión
reflexive *adj* reflexivo
reform *v* reformar
reform *n* reforma
refrain *v* abstenerse
refresh *v* refrescar
refreshing *adj* refrescante
refreshment *n* refresco
refrigerate *v* refrigerar
refuel *v* repostar
refuge *n* refugio
refugee *n* refugiado
refund *v* devolver
refund *n* reembolso
refurbish *v* restaurar
refusal *n* negativa
refuse *v* rehusar
refuse *n* basura
refute *v* refutar
regain *v* recobrar
regal *adj* regio
regard *v* considerar
regarding *pre* con respecto a
regardless *adv* sin reparar en
regards *n* saludos
regeneration *n* regeneración
regent *n* regente

regime *n* régimen
regiment *n* regimiento
region *n* región
regional *adj* regional
register *v* registrarse
registration *n* matrícula
regret *v* lamentar
regret *n* pena, pesar
regrettable *adj* lamentable
regularity *n* regularidad
regularly *adv* regularmente
regulate *v* regular
regulation *n* regla, norma
rehabilitate *v* rehabilitar
rehearsal *n* ensayo
rehearse *v* ensayar
reign *v* reinar
reign *n* reinado
reimburse *v* reembolsar
reimbursement *n* reembolso
rein *v* frenar, controlar
rein *n* rienda
reindeer *n* reno
reinforce *v* reforzar
reinforcements *n* refuerzos
reinstate *v* readmitir
reiterate *v* reiterar
reject *v* rechazar
rejection *n* rechazo
rejoice *v* regocijarse
rejoin *v* juntarse
rejuvenate *v* rejuvenecer

rekindle v reavivar
relapse n recaída
relapse v reincidir
relate v referirse
related adj relacionado
relation n relación
relationship n relación
relative adj relativo
relative n pariente
relax v descansar
relax n descanso
relaxation n relajación
relaxed adj relajado
relaxing adj relajante
relay v transmitir
release v soltar
relegate v relegar
relent v ceder
relentless adj implacable
relevant adj pertinente
reliable adj fiable
reliance n confianza
relic n reliquia
relief n alivio
relieve v aliviar, relevar
religion n religión
religious adj religioso
relinquish v abandonar
relish v saborear
relive v revivir
relocate v mudarse
relocation n translado

reluctance n aversión
reluctant adj reacio
reluctantly adv de mala gana
rely on v contar con
remain v permanecer
remainder n resto
remaining adj restante
remains n restos
remake v rehacer
remark v comentar, observar
remark n comentario
remarkable adj notable
remarry v casarse de nuevo
remedy v remediar
remedy n remedio
remember v acordarse
remembrance n recuerdo
remind v recordar
reminder n recordatorio
remiss adj negligente
remission n remisión, perdón
remit v remitir, perdonar
remittance n envío
remnant n resto
remodel v remodelar
remorse n remordimiento
remorseful adj arrepentido
remote adj remoto
removal n eliminación
remove v eliminar, quitar
remunerate v recompensar
renew v renovar

R

renewal *n* renovación
renounce *v* renunciar
renovate *v* renovar
renovation *n* renovación
renowned *adj* famoso
rent *v* rentar
rent *n* renta
renunciation *n* renuncia
reopening *n* reapertura
reorganize *v* reorganizar
repair *v* reparar
reparation *n* reparación
repatriate *v* repatriar
repay *v* devolver, pagar
repayment *n* reembolso
repeal *v* revocar
repeal *n* revocación
repeat *v* repetir
repeat *n* repetición
repel *v* rechazar
repellent *adj* repelente
repent *v* arrepentirse
repentance *n* arrepentimiento
repetition *n* repetición
replace *v* reemplazar
replacement *n* sustituto
replay *n* repetición
replenish *v* reponer
replete *adj* repleto
replica *n* réplica
replicate *v* reproducir
reply *v* contestar

reply *n* respuesta
report *v* reportar
report *n* reporte
reportedly *adv* según dicen
reporter *n* periodista
repose *v* descansar
repose *n* reposo
represent *v* representar
repress *v* reprimir
repression *n* represión
reprieve *n* indulto, alivio
reprimand *n* reprimenda
reprint *v* reimprimir
reprint *n* reimpresión
reprisal *n* represalia
reproach *v* reprochar(se)
reproach *n* reproche
reproduce *v* reproducir
reproduction *n* reproducción
reptile *n* reptil
republic *n* república
repudiate *v* repudiar, rechazar
repugnant *adj* repugnante
repulse *v* rechazar
repulse *n* rechazo
repulsion *n* repulsión
repulsive *adj* repulsivo
reputation *n* reputación
repute *n* reputación
reputedly *adv* según dicen
request *v* solicitar
request *n* petición

R

require _v_ requerir
requirement _n_ requisito
requisite _n_ requisito
re-rout _v_ desviar
rescind _v_ rescindir
rescue _v_ rescatar
rescue _n_ rescate
research _v_ investigar
research _n_ investigación
resemblance _n_ parecido
resemble _v_ parecerse
resent _v_ resentirse
resentment _n_ resentimiento
reservation _n_ reservación
reserve _v_ reservar
reservoir _n_ pantano
reset _v_ reajustar
reside _v_ residir
residence _n_ residencia
residue _n_ residuo
resign _v_ dimitir, resignar(se)
resignation _n_ resignación
resilient _adj_ resistente
resist _v_ resistir
resistance _n_ resistencia
resistant _adj_ resistente
resolute _adj_ resuelto
resolution _n_ resolución
resolve _v_ resolver
resort _v_ recurrir
resound _v_ resonar
resounding _adj_ sonoro

resource _n_ recurso
respect _v_ respetar
respect _n_ respeto
respectful _adj_ respetuoso
respective _adj_ respectivo
respiration _n_ respiración
respite _n_ respiro
respond _v_ responder
response _n_ respuesta
responsibility _n_ responsabilidad
responsible _adj_ responsable
responsive _adj_ sensible, atento
rest _v_ descansar
rest _n_ reposo
rest room _n_ aseos
restaurant _n_ restaurante
restful _adj_ descansado
restitution _n_ restitución
restive _adj_ intranquilo
restless _adj_ inquieto
restoration _n_ restauración
restore _v_ restaurar
restrain _v_ contener
restraint _n_ moderación
restrict _v_ restringir
result _n_ resultado
resume _v_ reanudar
resumption _n_ reanudación
resurface _v_ reaparecer
resurrection _n_ resurrección
resuscitate _v_ resucitar
retain _v_ retener, conservar

R

retaliate *v* retaliar
retaliation *n* represalia
retarded *adj* retrasado
retention *n* retención
retire *v* jubilarse; retirar(se)
retirement *n* jubilación, retiro
retouch *v* retocar
retract *v* retractarse
retreat *v* retirarse
retreat *n* retiro, retirada
retrieval *n* recuperación
retrieve *v* recobrar
retroactive *adj* retroactivo
retrograde *adj* retrógado
return *v* volver
return *n* regreso
reunion *n* encuentro
revamp *v* renovar
reveal *v* revelar
revealing *adj* revelador
revel *v* gozar
revelation *n* revelación
revenge *v* vengarse
revenge *n* venganza
revenue *n* ingresos
reverbarate *v* resonar
revere *v* venerar
reverence *n* reverencia
reversal *n* cambio
reverse *n* el reverso
reversible *adj* reversible
revert *v* volver a

review *v* repasar, revisar
review *n* revista; crítica
revise *v* revisar, cambiar
revision *n* revisión
revive *v* revivir
revoke *v* revocar
revolt *v* sublevarse
revolt *n* sublevación
revolting *adj* desagradable
revolve *v* dar vueltas, girar
revolver *v* revólver
revue *n* revista
revulsion *n* repugnancia
reward *v* recompensar
reward *n* recompensa
rewarding *adj* agradable
rheumatism *n* reumatismo
rhinoceros *n* reinoceronte
rhyme *n* rima
rhythm *n* ritmo
rib *n* costilla
ribbon *n* cinta
rice *n* arroz
rich *adj* rico
rid of *iv* deshacerse
riddle *n* acertijo
ride *iv* viajar; montar
ridge *n* cresta
ridicule *v* burlarse
ridicule *n* burla
ridiculous *adj* ridículo
rife *adj* plagado

rifle *n* fusil

rift *n* grieta

right *adv* bien

right *adj* correcto; derecho

right *n* derecho

rightful *adj* legítimo

rightous *adj* honrado

rigid *adj* rígido

rigor *n* rigor

rigorous *adj* riguroso

rim *n* borde, llanta

ring *iv* sonar

ring *n* anillo; timbrazo

ringleader *n* cabecilla

rinse *v* enjuagar

riot *v* amotinarse

riot *n* disturbio, motín

rip *v* rasgar

rip apart *v* destrozar

rip off *v* timar, engañar

ripe *adj* maduro

ripen *v* madurar

ripple *n* onda

rise *iv* levantarse

risk *v* arriesgar

risk *n* riesgo

risky *adj* arriesgado

rite *n* rito

rival *n* rival

rivalry *n* rivalidad

river *n* río

rivet *v* remachar; captar

riveting *adj* fascinante

road *n* carretera

roam *v* vagar

roar *v* rugir

roar *n* rugido

roast *v* asar

roast *n* carne asada

rob *v* robar

robber *n* ladrón

robbery *n* robo

robe *n* albornoz, bata

robe *n* bata, toga

robust *adj* robusto

rock *n* roca, peñasco

rocket *n* cohete

rocky *adj* rocoso

rod *n* vara, caña

rodent *n* roedor

roll *v* enrollar

rolling *adj* ondulado

romance *n* romance

romantic *adj* romántico

roof *n* tejado, techo

room *n* cuarto; lugar

roomy *adj* amplio

rooster *n* gallo

root *n* raíz

root *v* arraigar

rope *n* cuerda

rosary *n* rosario

rose *n* rosa

rosy *adj* prometedor

R

rot *v* pudrirse
rot *n* podredumbre
rotate *v* girar
rotation *n* rotación
rotten *adj* podrido
rough *adj* áspero
round *adj* redondo
roundup *n* redada
rouse *v* excitar
rousing *adj* caluroso
rout *v* derrotar
route *n* ruta, camino
routine *n* rutina
row *v* remar
row *n* remo; fila; bronca
rowdy *adj* ruidoso
royal *adj* real
royalty *n* realeza
rub *v* frotar
rubber *n* goma
rubbish *n* basura
rubble *n* escombros
ruby *n* rubí
rudder *n* timón
rude *adj* rudo, tosco
rudeness *n* descortesía
rudimentary *adj* rudimentario
rug *n* alfombra
ruin *v* arruinar
ruin *n* ruina
rule *v* gobernar, regir
rule *n* norma, regla

ruler *n* regla, gobernante
rum *n* ron
rumble *v* retumbar
rumble *n* sonido sordo
rumor *n* rumor
run *iv* correr
run away *v* huir
run into *v* tropezar con
run out *v* agotarse
run over *v* atropellar
run up *v* acumular
runner *n* corredor
runway *n* pista de aterrizaje
rupture *n* ruptura
rupture *v* romperse
rural *adj* rural
ruse *n* artimaña
rush *v* apresurar
Russia *n* Rusia
Russian *adj* ruso
rust *v* oxidarse
rust *n* herrumbre
rustic *adj* rústico
rust-proof *adj* inoxidable
rusty *adj* oxidado
ruthless *adj* despiadado
rye *n* centeno

R

S

sabotage *v* sabotear
sabotage *n* sabotaje
sack *v* saquear; despedir
sack *n* saco; saqueo
sacrament *n* sacramento
sacred *adj* sagrado
sacrifice *n* sacrificio
sacrilege *n* sacrilegio
sad *adj* triste
sadden *v* entristecer
saddle *n* silla de montar
sadist *n* sadista
sadness *n* tristeza
safe *adj* seguro
safeguard *n* protección
safety *n* seguridad
sail *v* navegar
sail *n* vela
sailboat *n* velero
sailor *n* marinero
saint *n* santo
salad *n* ensalada
salary *n* salario
sale *n* venta
sale slip *n* recibo
salesman *n* vendedor
saliva *n* saliva
salmon *n* salmón
saloon *n* bar, salón

salt *n* sal
salty *adj* salado
salvage *v* recuperar
salvation *n* salvación
same *adj* mismo, igual
sample *n* muestra
sanctify *v* santificar
sanction *v* sancionar, aprobar
sanction *n* sanción, multa
sanctity *n* santidad
sanctuary *n* santuario
sand *n* arena
sandal *n* sandalia
sandpaper *n* papel de lijar
sandwich *n* bocadillo
sane *adj* cuerdo
sanity *n* sensatez
sap *n* savia
sap *v* chupar
saphire *n* safiro
sarcasm *n* sarcasmo
sarcastic *adj* sarcástico
sardine *n* sardina
satanic *adj* satánico
satellite *n* satélite
satire *n* sátira
satisfaction *n* satisfacción
satisfactory *adj* satisfactorio
satisfy *v* satisfacer
saturate *v* saturar
Saturday *n* sábado
sauce *n* salsa

S

saucepan n cacerola
saucer n platillo
sausage n salchicha
savage adj feroz
savagery n salvajismo
save v ahorrar; salvar
savings n ahorros
savior n salvador
savor v saborear
saw iv serrar
saw n sierra
say iv decir
saying n dicho, proverbio
scaffolding n andamio
scald v escaldar
scale v trepar
scale n balanza; escama
scalp n cabellera
scam n timo
scan v otear
scandal n escándalo
scandalize v escandalizar
scapegoat n chivo expiatorio
scar n cicatriz
scarce adj escaso
scarcely adv apenas
scarcity n escasez
scare v asustar
scare n susto
scare away v ahuyentar
scarf n bufanda
scary adj de miedo

scatter v desparramar
scenario n situación
scene n escena; bastidor
scenery n escenario
scenic adj pintoresco
scent n perfume; pista
sceptic adj escéptico
schedule v programar
schedule n horario; programa
scheme n plan; intriga
schism n cisma
scholar n erudito
scholarship n beca
school n escuela
science n ciencia
scientific adj científico
scientist n científico
scissors n tijeras
scoff v mofarse
scold v regañar
scolding n regaño
scooter n moto
scope n ámbito
scorch v quemar
score n resultado
score v marcar
scorn v despreciar
scornful n despreciativo
scorpion n escorpión
scoundrel n canalla
scour v fregar; rastrear
scourge n tormento**

scout *n* explorador
scramble *v* darse prisa
scrambled *adj* revueltos
scrap *n* chatarra
scrap *v* descartar
scrape *v* raspar; rozar
scratch *v* rascarse
scratch *n* rasguño
scream *v* chillar
scream *n* chillido
screech *v* chirriar
screen *n* pantalla; mampara
screen *v* proyectar; bloquear
screw *v* atornillar, arruinar
screw *n* tornillo
screwdriver *n* atornillador
scribble *v* hacer garabatos
script *n* guión
scroll *n* manuscrito
scrub *v* restregar
scruples *n* escrúpulos
scrupulous *adj* escrupuloso
scrutiny *n* escrutinio
scuffle *n* refriega
sculptor *n* escultor
sculpture *n* escultura
sea *n* mar
seafood *n* pescado
seagull *n* gaviota
seal *v* sellar
seal *n* foca; sello
seal off *v* acordonar, aislar

seam *n* costura
seamless *adj* sin junturas
seamstress *n* modista
search *v* buscar
search *n* búsqueda
seashore *n* orilla del mar
seasick *adj* mareado
seaside *adj* costero
season *n* estación
seasonal *adj* temporal
seasoning *n* condimento
seat *n* asiento
seated *adj* sentado
secede *v* separarse
secluded *adj* retirado
seclusion *n* aislamiento
second *n* segundo
secondary *adj* secundario
secrecy *n* secreto
secret *n* secreto
secretary *n* secretario
secretly *adv* en secreto
sect *n* secta
section *n* sección, parte
sector *n* sector
secure *v* asegurar
secure *adj* seguro
security *n* seguridad
sedate *v* calmar
sedation *n* sedación
seduce *v* seducir
seduction *n* seducción

S

see *iv* ver
seed *n* semilla
seedless *adj* sin pepitas
seedy *adj* de mala fama
seek *iv* buscar
seem *v* parecer
see-through *adj* transparente
segment *n* segmento
segregate *v* segregar
segregation *n* segregación
seize *v* agarrar; incautar
seizure *n* ataque
seldom *adv* raramente
select *v* seleccionar
selection *n* selección
self-concious *adj* tímido
self-esteem *n* autoestima
self-evident *adj* obvio
self-interest *n* interés propio
selfish *adj* egoísta
selfishness *n* egoísmo
self-respect *n* amor propio
sell *iv* vender
seller *n* vendedor
sellout *n* liquidación
semblance *n* apariencia
semester *n* semestre
seminary *n* seminario
senate *n* senado
senator *n* senador
send *iv* enviar
sender *n* remitente

senile *adj* senil
senior *adj* de mayor edad
seniority *n* antiguedad
sensation *n* sensación
sense *v* sentir, notar
sense *n* sentido; sensatez
senseless *adj* sin sentido
sensible *adj* sensato
sensitive *adj* sensible
sensual *adj* sensual
sentence *v* sentenciar
sentence *n* sentencia; frase
sentiment *n* sentimiento
sentimental *adj* sentimental
sentry *n* centinela
separate *v* separar
separate *adj* separado
separation *n* separación
September *n* septiembre
sequel *n* continuación
sequence *n* secuencia
serenade *n* serenata
serene *adj* sereno
serenity *n* serenidad
sergeant *n* sargento
series *n* serie
serious *adj* serio; grave
seriousness *n* seriedad; gravedad
sermon *n* sermón
serpent *n* serpiente
serum *n* suero
servant *n* siervo, sirviente**

S

serve _v_ servir; atender

service _n_ servicio; saque

service _v_ revisar

session _n_ sesión

set _n_ juego

set _iv_ poner

set about _v_ ponerse a

set off _v_ partir; causar

set out _v_ partir, marchar

set up _v_ establecer

setback _n_ contratiempo

setting _n_ marco

settle _v_ resolver; calmar

settle down _v_ establecerse

settle for _v_ conformarse

settlement _n_ acuerdo; colonia

settler _n_ colono

setup _n_ trampa, situación

seven _adj_ siete

seventeen _adj_ diecisiete

seventh _adj_ séptimo

seventy _adj_ setenta

sever _v_ cortar, romper

several _adj_ varios

severance _n_ ruptura

severe _adj_ severo; grave

severity _n_ gravedad

sew _v_ coser

sewage _n_ aguas sucias

sewer _n_ alcantarilla

sewing _n_ costura

sex _n_ sexo

sexuality _n_ sexualidad

shabby _adj_ raído, gastado

shack _n_ chabola

shackle _n_ grillos, cadenas

shade _n_ matiz; sombra

shadow _n_ sombra

shady _adj_ sombreado

shake _iv_ sacudir

shaken _adj_ conmovido

shaky _adj_ inestable

shallow _adj_ superficial

sham _n_ farsa

shambles _n_ caos

shame _v_ avergonzar

shame _n_ verguenza

shameful _adj_ vergonzoso

shameless _adj_ sinverguenza

shape _v_ dar forma

shape _n_ forma

share _v_ compartir

share _n_ porción; acción

shareholder _n_ accionista

shark _n_ tiburón

sharp _adj_ afilado, definido

sharpen _v_ afilar; sacar punta

sharpener _n_ sacapuntas

shatter _v_ hacer añicos

shattering _adj_ demoledor

shave _v_ afeitarse

she _pro_ ella

shear _iv_ esquilar

shed _iv_ derramar

S

sheep *n* oveja
sheets *n* sábanas
shelf *n* estante
shell *n* concha
shellfish *n* mariscos
shelter *v* acoger
shelter *n* refugio
shelves *n* estanterías
shepherd *n* pastor
sherry *n* jerez
shield *v* proteger
shield *n* escudo
shift *n* cambio; turno
shift *v* mover, cambiar
shine *iv* resplandecer
shiny *adj* brillante
ship *n* barco
shipment *n* envío
shipwreck *n* naufragio
shipyard *n* astillero
shirk *v* eludir
shirt *n* camisa
shiver *v* tiritar
shiver *n* escalofrío
shock *v* dar un susto
shock *n* susto; descarga
shocking *adj* espantoso
shoddy *adj* de pacotilla
shoe *n* zapato
shoelace *n* cordón
shoepolish *n* betún
shoestore *n* zapatería

shoot *iv* disparar; rodar
shoot down *v* derribar
shop *v* ir de compras
shop *n* tienda
shoplifting *n* robo
shopping *n* compras
shore *n* orilla
short *adj* corto; bajo
shortage *n* escasez
shortcoming *n* defecto
shortcut *n* atajo
shorten *v* acortar
shorthand *n* taquigrafía
shortlived *adj* efímero
shortly *adv* enseguida
shorts *n* pantalón corto
shortsighted *adj* miope
shot *n* disparo; inyección
shotgun *n* escopeta
shoulder *n* hombro
shout *v* gritar
shout *n* grito
shouting *n* griterío
shove *v* empujar
shove *n* empujón
shovel *n* pala
show *iv* mostrar
show off *v* presumir
show up *v* aparecer
showdown *n* enfrentamiento
shower *n* ducha
shrapnel *n* metralla**

shred *v* desmenuzar

shred *n* triza, trozo

shrewd *adj* astuto

shriek *v* chillar

shriek *n* alarido, chillido

shrimp *n* camarón

shrine *n* santuario

shrink *iv* encogerse

shroud *n* sudario

shrouded *adj* envuelto

shrub *n* arbusto

shrug *v* encoger (hombros)

shudder *n* escalofrío

shudder *v* estremecerse

shuffle *v* barajar

shun *v* esquivar

shut *iv* cerrar

shut off *v* cortar

shut up *v* callarse

shuttle *v* conectar

shy *adj* tímido

shyness *n* timidez

sick *adj* enfermo

sicken *v* enfermarse

sickening *adj* repugnante

sickle *n* hoz

sickness *n* enfermedad

side *n* lado

sideburns *n* patillas

sidestep *v* evadir

sidewalk *n* acera

sideways *adv* de lado

siege *n* cerco, sitio

siege *v* sitiar

sift *v* cribar

sigh *n* suspiro

sigh *v* suspirar

sight *n* vista

sightseeing *n* visita de lugares

sign *v* firmar

sign *n* señal; letrero

signal *n* señal

signature *n* firma

significance *n* importancia

significant *adj* significativo

signify *v* significar

silence *n* silencio

silence *v* acallar

silent *adj* callado

silhouette *n* silueta

silk *n* seda

silly *adj* estúpido

silver *n* plata

silverplated *adj* plateado

silversmith *n* platero

silverware *n* cubiertos

similar *adj* semejante

similarity *n* semejanza

simmer *v* hervir despacio

simple *adj* simple

simplicity *n* simplicidad

simplify *v* simplificar

simply *adv* simplemente

simulate *v* simular

S

simultaneous *adj* simultáneo

sin *v* pecar

sin *n* pecado

since *c* ya que

since *pre* desde

since then *adv* desde entonces

sincere *adj* sincero

sincerity *n* sinceridad

sinful *adj* pecaminoso

sing *iv* cantar

singer *n* cantante

single *n* soltero

single *adj* solo, único, sencillo

singlehanded *adj* sin ayuda

singleminded *adj* firme

singular *adj* singular

sinister *adj* siniestro

sink *iv* hundir

sinking *n* hundimiento

sink in *v* penetrar

sinner *n* pecador

sip *v* sorber

sip *n* sorbito

sir *n* señor

siren *n* sirena

sirloin *n* solomillo

sissy *adj* afeminado

sister *n* hermana

sister-in-law *n* cuñada

sit *iv* sentarse

site *n* sitio, lugar

sitting *n* sesión

situated *adj* situado

situation *n* situación

six *adj* seis

sixteen *adj* dieciséis

sixth *adj* sexto

sixty *adj* sesenta

sizable *adj* considerable

size *n* tamaño, talla

size up *v* evaluar, medir

skate *v* patinar

skate *n* patín

skeleton *n* esqueleto

skeptic *adj* escéptico

sketch *v* esbozar

sketch *n* bosquejo

sketchy *adj* incompleto

ski *v* esquiar

skill *n* destreza

skillful *adj* diestro

skim *v* desnatar

skin *v* despellejar

skin *n* piel

skinny *adj* flaco

skip *v* saltarse

skip *n* salto, brinco

skirmish *n* escaramuza

skirt *n* falda

skull *n* cráneo

sky *n* firmamento

skylight *n* claraboya

skyscraper *n* rascacielos

slab *n* losa

S

slack *adj* flojo
slacken *v* aflojar
slacks *n* pantalones
slam *v* cerrar con golpe
slander *n* calumnia
slanted *adj* parcial, inclinado
slap *n* bofetada
slap *v* dar un cachete
slash *n* corte, raja
slash *v* acuchillar, cortar
slate *n* pizarra
slaughter *v* matar
slaughter *n* matanza
slave *n* esclavo
slavery *n* esclavitud
slay *iv* matar
sleazy *adj* de mala fama
sleep *iv* dormir
sleep *n* sueño
sleeve *n* manga
sleeveless *adj* sin mangas
sleigh *n* trineo
slender *adj* esbelto; remoto
slice *v* cortar
slice *n* tajada, rodaja
slide *iv* deslizarse
slightly *adv* un poco
slim *adj* delgado; remoto
slip *v* resbalar
slip *n* resbalón, desliz
slipper *n* zapatilla
slippery *adj* resbaladizo

slit *iv* rajar
slob *adj* sucio, dejado
slogan *n* lema
slope *n* ladera, cuesta
sloppy *adj* descuidado
slot *n* ranura, hueco
slow *adj* lento
slow down *v* ir despacio
slow motion *n* cámara lenta
slowly *adv* despacio
sluggish *adj* lento
slum *n* arrabal
slump *v* desplomarse
slump *n* desplome, bajón
slur *v* pronunciar mal
sly *adj* astuto
smack *n* bofetada
smack *v* abofetar
small *adj* pequeño
small print *n* letra pequeña
smallpox *n* viruela
smart *adj* listo, vivo
smash *v* chocar, estrellarse
smear *n* borrón, mancha
smear *v* difamar; untar
smell *iv* oler
smelly *adj* maloliente
smile *v* sonreír
smile *n* sonrisa
smith *n* herrero
smoke *v* fumar
smoked *adj* ahumado

S

smoker *n* fumador
smoking gun *n* prueba
smooth *v* allanar, suavizar
smooth *adj* suave, liso
smoothly *adv* suavemente
smoothness *n* suavidad
smother *v* sofocar
smuggler *n* contrabandista
snail *n* caracol
snake *n* serpiente
snapshot *n* foto instantánea
snare *v* engañar
snare *n* trampa
snatch *v* agarrar
sneak *v* entrar a escondidas
sneeze *v* estornudar
sneeze *n* estornudo
sniff *v* olfatear
sniper *n* francotirador
snitch *v* delatar
snooze *v* dormitar
snore *v* roncar
snore *n* ronquido
snow *v* nevar
snow *n* nieve
snowfall *n* nevada
snowflake *n* copo de nieve
snub *v* desairar
snub *n* desaire
soak *v* empapar, remojar
soak in *v* penetrar
soak up *v* absorber

soar *v* remontarse
sob *v* sollozar
sob *n* sollozo
sober *adj* sobrio
so-called *adj* llamado
sociable *adj* sociable
socialism *n* socialismo
socialist *adj* socialista
socialize *v* alternar
society *n* sociedad
sock *n* calcetín
sod *n* césped
soda *n* refresco
sofa *n* sofá
soft *adj* blando
soften *v* ablandar
softly *adv* suavemente
softness *n* suavidad
soggy *adj* remojado
soil *v* ensuciar
soil *n* tierra
soiled *adj* manchado
solace *n* alivio
solar *adj* solar
solder *v* soldar
soldier *n* soldado
sold-out *adj* agotado
sole *n* suela
sole *adj* único
solely *adv* solamente
solemn *adj* solemne
solicit *v* solicitar

S

solid *adj* sólido, duro
solidarity *n* solidaridad
solitary *adj* solitario
solitude *n* soledad
soluble *adj* soluble
solution *n* solución
solve *v* solucionar
solvent *adj* solvente
somber *adj* sombrío
some *adj* algunos
somebody *pro* alguien
someday *adv* algún día
somehow *adv* de algún modo
someone *pro* alguien
something *pro* algo
sometimes *adv* a veces
someway *adv* de algún modo
somewhat *adv* algo
son *n* hijo
song *n* canción
son-in-law *n* yerno
soon *adv* pronto
soothe *v* aliviar
sorcerer *n* hechicero
sorcery *n* hechicería
sore *n* llaga
sore *adj* doloroso
sorrow *n* pena, dolor
sorrowful *adj* triste
sorry *adj* arrepentido
sort *n* especie de
sort out *v* clasificar

soul *n* alma
sound *n* sonido
sound *v* sonar; parecer
sound out *v* sondear
soup *n* sopa
sour *adj* amargo, agrio
source *n* fuente
south *n* sur
southbound *adv* hacia el sur
southeast *n* sudeste
southern *adj* sureño
southerner *n* del sur
southwest *n* suroeste
souvenir *n* recuerdo
sovereign *adj* soberano
sovereignty *n* soberanía
soviet *adj* soviético
sow *iv* sembrar
spa *n* balneario
space *n* espacio, sitio
space out *v* espaciar
spacious *adj* espacioso, amplio
spade *n* pala
Spain *n* España
span *v* extenderse
span *n* espacio; tramo
Spaniard *n* español
Spanish *adj* español
spank *v* zurrar, azotar
spanking *n* azote
spare *v* librar; perdonar
spare *adj* sobrante

S

spare part *n* repuesto
sparingly *adv* con moderación
spark *n* chispa
spark off *v* desencadenar
spark plug *n* bujía
sparkle *v* destellar
sparrow *n* gorrión
sparse *adj* escaso, esparcido
spasm *n* espasmo
speak *iv* hablar
speaker *n* altavoz; orador
spear *n* lanza
spearhead *v* encabezar
special *adj* especial
specialize *v* especializarse
specialty *n* especialidad
species *n* especies
specific *adj* específico
specimen *n* muestra, ejemplar
speck *n* mota, grano
spectacle *n* espectáculo
spectator *n* espectador
speculate *v* especular
speculation *n* especulación
speech *n* discurso
speechless *adj* mudo
speed *iv* acelerar
speed *n* rapidez
speedily *adv* rápidamente
speedy *adj* veloz
spell *iv* deletrear
spell *n* hechizo

spelling *n* ortografía
spend *iv* gastar
spending *n* gastos
sperm *n* esperma
sphere *n* esfera
spice *n* especia
spicy *adj* picante
spider *n* araña
spiderweb *n* telaraña
spill *iv* derramar
spill *n* derrame
spin *iv* dar vueltas; hilar
spine *n* espina dorsal
spineless *adj* débil
spinster *n* solterona
spirit *n* espíritu, ánimo
spiritual *adj* espiritual
spit *iv* escupir
spite *n* rencor
spiteful *adj* rencoroso
splash *v* salpicar
splendid *adj* espléndido
splendor *n* esplendor
splint *n* tablilla
splinter *n* astilla
splinter *v* astillarse
split *n* separación
split *iv* partir, repartir
split up *v* separarse
spoil *v* estropear
spoils *n* despojos, botín
sponge *n* esponja**

S

sponsor *n* patrocinador
spontaneity *n* espontaneidad
spontaneous *adj* espontáneo
spooky *adj* horripilante
spool *n* carrete
spoon *n* cuchara
spoonful *n* cucharada
sporadic *adj* esporádico
sport *n* deporte
sportsman *n* deportista
sporty *adj* deportista
spot *v* ver, notar
spot *n* lugar; mancha
spotless *adj* inmaculado
spotlight *n* foco
spouse *n* cónyuge
sprain *v* torcerse
sprawl *v* extenderse
spray *v* rociar
spread *iv* extender; untar
spring *iv* brotar; brincar
spring *n* primavera; muelle
springboard *n* trampolín
sprinkle *v* rociar
sprout *v* brotar
spruce up *v* dejar limpio
spur *v* estimular
spur *n* espuela; incentivo
spy *v* espiar
spy *n* espía
squalid *adj* muy sucio
squander *v* despilfarrar

square *adj* cuadrado
square *n* plaza; cuadrado
squash *v* aplastar
squeak *v* rechinar
squeaky *adj* chirriante
squeamish *adj* miedoso
squeeze *v* apretar; exprimir
squeeze in *v* hacer lugar
squeeze up *v* apretarse
squid *n* calamar
squirrel *n* ardilla
stab *v* apuñalar
stab *n* puñalada
stability *n* estabilidad
stable *adj* estable
stable *n* establo
stack *v* amontonar
stack *n* montón
staff *n* personal
stage *n* escenario; etapa
stage *v* organizar
stagger *v* tambalearse
staggering *adj* asombroso
stagnant *adj* estancado
stagnate *v* estancarse
stagnation *n* estancamiento
stain *v* manchar, teñir
stain *n* mancha, tinte
stair *n* escalón
staircase *n* escalera
stairs *n* escalera
stake *n* riesgo; poste

S

stake v arriesgar

stale adj rancio

stalemate n empate

stalk v acechar, seguir

stalk n tallo

stall n puesto, casilla

stall v ganar tiempo

stammer v tartamudear

stamp v sellar; patear

stamp n estampilla, sello

stamp out v eliminar

stampede n estampido

stand iv estar de pie

stand n puesto

stand for v defender

stand out v destacar

stand up v ponerse de pie

standard n norma, estandarte

standardize v estandarizar

standing n reputación

standpoint n punto de vista

standstill adj paralizado

staple v grapar

staple n grapa

stapler n grapadora

star n estrella

starch n almidón

starchy adj almidonado

stare v mirar fijo

stark adj desolador

start v empezar

start n comienzo

startle v sobresaltar

startled adj sobrecogido

starvation n hambre

starve v pasar hambre

state n estado; nación

state v decir, declarar

statement n declaración

station n estación

stationary adj parado, fijo

stationery n papelería

statistic n estadística

statue n estatua

status n posición; estado

statute n estatuto

staunch adj fiel, leal

stay v quedarse

stay n estancia

steady adj firme; continuo

steak n chuleta

steal iv robar

stealthy adj sigiloso, callado

steam n vapor

steel n acero

steep adj empinado

stem n tallo

stem v contener

stench n hedor

step n paso; escalón

step down v dimitir

step out v salir un rato

step up v aumentar

stepbrother n hermanastro

step-by-step *adv* paso a paso
stepdaughter *n* hijastra
stepfather *n* padrastro
stepladder *n* escalera
stepmother *n* madrastra
stepsister *n* hermanastra
stepson *n* hijastro
sterile *adj* estéril
sterilize *v* esterilizar
stern *n* popa
stern *adj* severo, firme
sternly *adv* con firmeza
stew *n* guisado
stewardess *n* azafata
stick *n* palo, bastón
stick *iv* pegar, fijar
stick around *v* quedarse
stick out *v* sobresalir
stick to *v* seguir
sticker *n* etiqueta
sticky *adj* pegajoso
stiff *adj* tieso, duro
stiffen *v* endurecerse
stiffness *n* rigidez
stifle *v* reprimir; ahogar
stifling *adj* sofocante
still *adj* inmóvil
still *adv* todavía
stimulant *n* estimulante
stimulate *v* estimular
stimulus *n* estímulo
sting *iv* picar

sting *n* picadura; aguijón
stinging *adj* punzante
stingy *adj* tacaño
stink *iv* apestar
stink *n* hedor, peste
stinking *adj* hediondo
stipulate *v* estipular
stir *v* menear; mover
stir up *v* agitar
stitch *v* coser, suturar
stitch *n* puntada
stock *v* almacenar
stock *n* provisiones, acciones
stocking *n* media
stockpile *n* reservas
stockroom *n* almacén
stoic *adj* estoico
stomach *n* estómago
stone *n* piedra
stone *v* apedrear
stool *n* taburete
stop *v* parar(se), detener
stop *n* parada
stop by *v* visitar
stop over *v* hacer escala
storage *n* almacén
store *v* almacenar
store *n* tienda
stork *n* cigüeña
storm *n* tormenta
stormy *adj* tempestuoso
story *n* cuento; planta, piso

S

stove *n* estufa
straight *adj* recto
straighten out *v* enderezar
strain *v* colar, escurrir
strain *n* tensión, agobio
strained *adj* tirante, tenso
strainer *n* colador
strait *n* estrecho
stranded *adj* sin recursos
strange *adj* raro
stranger *n* extraño
strangle *v* estrangular
strap *n* correa
strategy *n* estrategia
straw *n* paja
strawberry *n* fresa
stray *adj* extraviado
stray *v* extraviarse
stream *n* arroyo; riada
street *n* calle
streetcar *n* tranvía
streetlight *n* farol
strength *n* fuerza
strengthen *v* reforzar
strenuous *adj* agotador
stress *n* estrés, énfasis
stressful *adj* estresante
stretch *n* tramo
stretch *v* estirar
stretcher *n* camilla
strict *adj* estricto
stride *iv* dar zancadas

strife *n* lucha
strike *n* huelga
strike *iv* pegar
strike back *v* atacar
strike out *v* tachar
strike up *v* entablar
striking *adj* sorprendente
string *n* cuerda; hilera
stringent *adj* riguroso
strip *n* tira, franja
strip *v* desnudar
stripe *n* raya
striped *adj* rayado
strive *iv* esforzarse, luchar por
stroke *n* golpe; embolia
stroll *v* pasear
strong *adj* fuerte
structure *n* estructura
struggle *v* luchar
struggle *n* lucha
stub *n* colilla; resguardo
stubborn *adj* testarudo
student *n* estudiante
study *v* estudiar
stuff *n* cosas; materia
stuff *v* llenar, rellenar
stuffing *n* relleno
stuffy *adj* mal ventilado
stumble *v* tropezar
stun *v* dejar atónito
stunning *adj* imponente
stupendous *adj* estupendo

S

stupid *adj* estúpido
stupidity *n* estupidez
sturdy *adj* firme, fuerte
stutter *v* tartamudear
style *n* estilo
subdue *v* dominar
subdued *adj* sumiso
subject *v* someter
subject *n* asignatura; tema
sublime *adj* sublime
submerge *v* sumergir
submissive *adj* sumiso
submit *v* presentar
subpoena *v* citar
subpoena *n* citación
subscribe *v* suscribir
subscription *n* subscripción
subsequent *adj* posterior
subsidiary *adj* filial
subsidize *v* subvencionar
subsidy *n* subvención
subsist *v* subsistir
substance *n* sustancia
substandard *adj* deficiente
substantial *adj* sustancial
substitute *v* sustituir
substitute *n* suplente
subtitle *n* subtítulo
subtle *adj* sutil
subtract *v* restar
subtraction *n* resta
suburb *n* suburbio

subway *n* metro
succeed *v* tener éxito
success *n* éxito
successful *adj* exitoso
successor *n* sucesor
succulent *adj* suculento
succumb *v* sucumbir
such *adj* tal
suck *v* chupar
sucker *adj* bobo, ingenuo
sudden *adj* repentino
suddenly *adv* de repente
sue *v* demandar
suffer *v* sufrir
suffer from *v* padecer
suffering *n* sufrimiento
sufficient *adj* suficiente
suffocate *v* sofocar
sugar *n* azúcar
suggest *v* sugerir
suggestion *n* sugerencia
suggestive *adj* sugestivo
suicide *n* suicidio
suit *n* traje
suitable *adj* apropiado
suitcase *n* maleta
sullen *adj* malhumorado
sulphur *n* sulfuro
sum *n* suma
sum up *v* resumir
summarize *v* resumir
summary *n* resumen

S

summer *n* verano

summit *n* cumbre

summon *v* convocar

sumptuous *adj* suntuoso

sun *n* sol

sunblock *n* crema antisolar

sunburn *n* quemadura

Sunday *n* domingo

sundown *n* atardecer

sunglasses *n* gafas de sol

sunken *adj* hundido

sunny *adj* soleado

sunrise *n* amanecer

sunset *n* crepúsculo

superb *adj* magnífico

superfluous *adj* superfluo

superior *adj* superior

superiority *n* superioridad

supermarket *n* supermercado

superpower *n* superpotencia

supersede *v* suplantar

superstition *n* superstición

supervise *v* supervisar

supervision *n* supervisión

supper *n* cena

supple *adj* flexible

supplier *n* distribuidor

supplies *n* suministros

supply *v* suministrar

support *v* apoyar

supporter *n* partidiario

suppose *v* suponer

supposing *c* suponiendo que

supposition *n* suposición

suppress *v* suprimir

supremacy *n* supremacía

supreme *adj* supremo

surcharge *n* recargo

sure *adj* seguro

surely *adv* seguramente

surf *v* navegar

surface *n* superficie

surge *n* aumento

surgeon *n* cirujano

surgical *adv* quirúrgico

surname *n* apellido

surpass *v* superar

surplus *n* excedente

surprise *v* sorprender

surprise *n* sorpresa

surrender *v* rendirse

surrender *n* rendición

surround *v* rodear

surroundings *n* alrededores

surveillance *n* vigilancia

survey *n* encuesta, estudio

survival *n* supervivencia

survive *v* sobrevivir

survivor *n* superviviente

susceptible *adj* susceptible

suspect *v* sospechar

suspect *n* sospechoso

suspend *v* suspender

suspenders *n* tirantes

suspense n duda, suspense
suspension n suspensión
suspicion n sospecha
suspicious adj sospechoso
sustain v sostener
sustenance n sustento
swallow v tragar
swamp n pantano
swamped adj abrumado
swan n cisne
swap v cambiar
swap n intercambio
swarm n enjambre
sway v mover, influir
swear iv jurar
sweat n sudor
sweat v sudar
sweater n suéter
Sweden n Suecia
Sweedish adj sueco
sweep iv barrer
sweet adj dulce
sweeten v endulzar
sweetheart n novio
sweetness n dulzura
sweets n dulces
swell iv hinchar
swelling n hinchazón
swift adj rápido
swim iv nadar
swimmer n nadador
swimming n natación

swindle v estafar
swindle n estafa
swindler n estafador
swing iv balancear, oscilar
swing n columpio; vaivén
Swiss adj suizo
switch v cambiar
switch n interruptor; cambio
switch off v apagar
switch on v encender
Switzerland n Suiza
swivel v girar
swollen adj hinchado
sword n espada
swordfish n pez espada
syllable n sílaba
symbol n símbolo
symbolic adj simbólico
symmetry n simetría
sympathize v simpatizar
sympathy n compasión
symphony n sinfonía
symptom n síntoma
synagogue n sinagoga
synchronize v sincronizar
synod n sínodo
synonym n sinónimo
synthesis n síntesis
syphilis n sífilis
syringe n jeringa
syrup n jarabe
system n sistema

S

systematic *adj* sistemático

T

table *n* mesa
tablecloth *n* mantel
tablespoon *n* cuchara
tablet *n* pastilla, tableta
tacit *adj* tácito
tack *n* tachuela
tackle *v* abordar
tact *n* tacto
tactful *adj* discreto
tactical *adj* táctico
tactics *n* táctica
tag *n* etiqueta
tail *n* cola, rabo
tail *v* seguir a alguien
tailor *n* sastre
taint *n* mancha
tainted *adj* manchado
take *iv* tomar
take apart *v* desmontar
take away *v* quitar
take back *v* devolver
take in *v* acoger
take off *v* despegar
take out *v* sacar

take over *v* apoderarse
tale *n* cuento
talent *n* talento
talented *adj* dotado
talk *v* hablar
talkative *adj* hablador
tall *adj* alto
tame *v* domesticar
tan *adj* bronceado
tangent *n* tangente
tangerine *n* mandarina
tangible *adj* tangible
tangle *n* lío
tank *n* tanque
tantamount to *adj* equivalente a
tantrum *n* rabieta
tap *n* grifo, llave
tap into *v* utilizar
tape *n* cassette, cinta
tape recorder *n* grabadora
tapestry *n* tapiz
tar *n* brea, alquitrán
tarantula *n* tarántula
tardy *adv* tardío
target *n* blanco; meta
tariff *n* tarifa
tarnish *v* manchar
tart *n* tarta
tartar *n* sarro
task *n* tarea
taste *v* probar; saber a
taste *n* gusto; sabor

S
T

tasteful *adj* de buen gusto

tasteless *adj* soso

tasty *adj* sabroso

tavern *n* taberna

tax *n* impuesto

tea *n* té

teach *iv* enseñar

teacher *n* maestro

team *n* equipo

teapot *n* tetera

tear *iv* rasgar; romper

tear *n* lágrima

tearful *adj* lloroso

tease *v* tomar el pelo

teaspoon *n* cucharita

technical *adj* técnico

technicality *n* formalidad

technician *n* técnico

technique *n* técnica

technology *n* tecnología

tedious *adj* aburrido

tedium *n* aburrimiento

teenager *n* adolescente

teeth *n* dientes

teeth *v* salir los dientes

telegram *n* telegrama

telepathy *n* telepatía

telephone *n* teléfono

telescope *n* telescopio

televise *v* televisar

television *n* televisión

tell *iv* decir

teller *n* cajero

telling *adj* indicador

temper *n* mal humor

temperate *adj* moderado

temperature *n* temperatura

tempest *n* tempestad

temple *n* templo; sien

temporary *adj* temporal

tempt *v* tentar

temptation *n* tentación

tempting *adj* tentador

ten *adj* diez

tenacity *n* tenacidad

tenant *n* inquilino

tenacious *adj* tenaz

tend *v* tender; atender

tendency *n* tendencia

tender *adj* tierno; sensible

tender *v* ofrecer

tenderness *n* ternura; blandura

tendon *n* tendón

tenet *n* principio

tennis *n* tenis

tenor *n* tenor

tense *adj* tenso

tension *n* tensión

tent *n* tienda de campaña

tentacle *n* tentáculo

tentative *adj* provisional

tenth *n* décimo

tenuous *adj* tenue

tepid *adj* tibio

T

term *n* mandato, plazo
terminate *v* terminar
terminology *n* terminología
termite *n* termita
terms *n* condiciones
terrace *n* terraza
terrain *n* terreno
terrestrial *adj* terrestre
terrible *adj* terrible
terrific *adj* fantástico
terrify *v* aterrorizar
terrifying *adj* espantoso
territory *n* territorio
terror *n* terror
terrorism *n* terrorismo
terrorist *n* terrorista
terrorize *v* aterrorizar
terse *adj* rígido
test *v* probar, examinar
test *n* prueba, examen
testament *n* testamento
testify *v* testificar
testimony *n* testimonio
testing *adj* duro
text *n* texto
textbook *n* libro de texto
textile *adj* testil
texture *n* textura
thank *v* agradecer
thankful *adj* agradecido
thanks *n* gracias
that *adj* ese, aquel

thaw *v* descongelar
thaw *n* deshielo
theater *n* teatro
theft *n* robo
theme *n* tema
themselves *pro* ellos mismos
then *adv* entonces
theologian *n* teólogo
theology *n* teología
theoretical *adj* teórico
theory *n* teoría
therapeutic *adj* terapéutico
therapist *n* terapeuta
therapy *n* terapia
there *adv* allí
thereby *c* por eso
therefore *adv* por lo tanto
thermometer *n* termómetro
thermostat *n* termostato
these *adj* estos, estas
thesis *n* tesis
they *pro* ellos
thick *adj* espeso; grueso
thicken *v* espesar
thickness *n* grosura, espesor
thief *n* ladrón
thigh *n* muslo
thin *adj* delgado; claro
thin *v* adelgazar
thing *n* cosa
think *iv* pensar
thinly *adv* ligeramente

third *adj* tercero
thirst *v* tener sed
thirsty *adj* sediento
thirteen *adj* trece
thirty *adj* treinta
this *adj* este, esta
thorax *n* tórax
thorn *n* espina
thorny *adj* espinoso
thorough *adj* ninucioso, perfecto
those *adj* esos, aquellos
though *c* aunque
thought *n* pensamiento
thoughtful *adj* atento
thousand *adj* mil
thread *v* enhebrar
thread *n* hilo, rosca
threat *n* amenaza
threaten *v* amenazar
three *adj* tres
thresh *v* trillar
threshold *n* umbral
thrifty *adj* económico
thrill *v* emocionar
thrill *n* emoción
thrilling *adj* emocionante
thrive *v* prosperar
throat *n* garganta
throb *n* latido, punzada
throb *v* latir
thrombosis *n* trombosis
throne *n* trono

throng *n* muchedumbre
through (thru) *pre* a través de
throughout *pre* por todo
throw *iv* tirar, lanzar
throw away *v* derrochar
throw up *v* vomitar
throwback *n* retroceso
thrust *n* impulso
thrust *v* empujar, clavar
thug *n* gamberro
thumb *n* dedo pulgar
thumbs-up *n* aprobación
thumbtack *n* chincheta
thunder *n* trueno
thunderbolt *n* rayo
thunderstorm *n* tormenta
Thursday *n* jueves
thus *adv* así
thwart *v* frustrar, impedir
thyroid *n* tiroides
ticket *n* entrada
tickle *v* hacer cosquillas
tickle *n* cosquillas
ticklish *adj* cosquilloso
tidal wave *n* maremoto
tide *n* marea
tidy *adj* arreglado
tie *v* empatar; atar
tie *n* corbata; empate
tiger *n* tigre
tight *adj* apretado; estricto
tighten *v* apretar

T

tile *n* teja; azulejo

till *adv* hasta

till *v* cultivar, labrar

tilt *v* inclinar

timber *n* madera

time *n* tiempo

time *v* medir el tiempo

timeless *adj* eterno

timely *adj* oportuno

times *n* veces

timetable *n* horario

timid *adj* tímido

timidity *n* timidez

tin *n* estaño

tinge *n* tono, matiz

tinker *v* jugar con

tiny *adj* muy pequeño

tip *n* punta; propina

tip *v* dar propina; inclinar

tip off *v* advertir, avisar

tip over *v* volcar

tiptoe *n* andar de puntillas

tired *adj* cansado

tiredness *n* cansancio

tireless *adj* incansable

tiresome *adj* pesado, cansado

tiring *adj* cansado

tissue *n* tejido, kleenex

title *n* título

to *pre* a

toad *n* sapo

toast *v* tostar; brindar

toast *n* tostada, brindis

toaster *n* tostador

tobacco *n* tabaco

today *adv* hoy

toddler *n* niño pequeño

toe *n* dedo del pie

toenail *n* uña del pie

together *adv* juntos

toil *v* trabajar duro

toilet *n* retrete

token *n* muestra

tolerable *adj* tolerable

tolerance *n* tolerancia

tolerate *v* tolerar

toll *n* peaje; victimas

toll *v* tañar, tocar

tomato *n* tomate

tomb *n* tumba

tombstone *n* lápida

tomorrow *adv* mañana

ton *n* tonelada

tone *n* tono

tongs *n* tenazas

tongue *n* lengua

tonic *n* tónica

tonight *adv* esta noche

tonsil *n* amígdala

too *adv* también

tool *n* herramienta

tooth *n* diente

toothache *n* dolor de muelas

toothpick *n* palillo de dientes

top *n* cumbre, cima
topic *n* tema
topple *v* derrocar
torch *n* antorcha
torment *v* atormentar
torment *n* tormento
torpedo *n* torpedo
torpedo *v* torpedear
torrent *n* torrente
torrid *adj* tórrido
torso *n* espalda
tortoise *n* tortuga
tortuous *adj* tortuoso
torture *v* torturar
torture *n* tortura
toss *v* tirar, echar
total *adj* total
totalitarian *adj* totalitario
totality *n* totalidad
totter *v* tambalearse
touch *n* tacto; contacto
touch *v* tocar
touch on *v* aludir
touch up *v* retocar
touchdown *n* aterrizaje
touching *adj* sentimental
touchy *adj* delicado
tough *adj* duro, fuerte
toughen *v* endurecer
tour *n* viaje
tourism *n* turismo
tourist *n* turista

tournament *n* torneo
tow *v* remolcar
tow truck *n* grúa
towards *pre* hacia
towel *n* toalla
tower *n* torre
towering *adj* imponente
town *n* ciudad
town hall *n* ayuntamiento
toxic *adj* tóxico
toxin *n* toxina
toy *n* juguete
trace *v* calcar; localizar
track *n* rastro, pista
track *v* seguir el rastro
traction *n* tracción
tractor *n* tractor
trade *n* comercio
trade *v* comerciar
trademark *n* marca de fábrica
trader *n* comerciante
tradition *n* tradición
traffic *n* tráfico
traffic *v* traficar
tragedy *n* tragedia
tragic *adj* trágico
trail *v* rastrear; arrastrar
trail *n* senda, rastro
trailer *n* remolque
train *n* tren
train *v* adiestrar
trainee *n* aprendiz

T

trainer *n* entrenador
training *n* entrenamiento
trait *n* rasgo
traitor *n* traidor
trajectory *n* trajectoria
tram *n* tranvía
trample *v* pisotear
trance *n* trance
trancript *n* transcripción
tranquility *n* tranquilidad
transaction *n* transacción
transcend *v* transcender
transcribe *v* transcribir
transfer *v* transladar, transferir
transfer *n* traslado
transform *v* transformar
transformation *n* transformación
transfusion *n* transfusión
transient *adj* transitorio
transient *n* viajero
transit *n* tránsito
transition *n* transición
transitive *adj* transitivo
translate *v* traducir
translator *n* traductor
transmit *v* transmitir
transparency *n* transpariencia
transparent *adj* transparente
transpire *v* indicar
transplant *v* trasplantar
transport *v* transportar
trap *n* trampa

trap *v* atrapar
trash *n* basura
trash can *n* cubo de basura
traumatic *adj* traumático
traumatize *v* traumatizar
travel *v* viajar
traveler *n* viajero
tray *n* bandeja
treacherous *adj* traicionero
treachery *n* traición
tread *iv* pisar
treason *n* traición
treasure *n* tesoro
treasurer *n* tesorero
treat *v* tratar
treat *n* regalo
treatment *n* trato; tratamiento
treaty *n* tratado
tree *n* árbol
tremble *v* temblar
tremendous *adj* tremendo
tremor *n* temblor
trench *n* zanja
trend *n* tendencia
trendy *adj* de moda
trespass *v* entrar sin permiso
trial *n* juicio; dificultad
triangle *n* triángulo
tribe *n* tribu
tribulation *n* tribulación
tribunal *n* tribunal
tribute *n* tributo, homenaje

trick *v* engañar
trick *n* engaño; truco
trickle *v* gotear
tricky *adj* difícil
trifle *n* tontería
trigger *v* desencadenar
trigger *n* gatillo
trim *v* recortar
trimester *n* trimestre
trimmings *n* guarnición
trip *n* viaje, tropezón
trip *v* tropezar, caerse
triple *adj* triple
triplicate *v* triplicar
tripod *n* trípode
triumph *n* triunfo
triumphant *adj* triunfante
trivial *adj* insignificante
trivialize *v* trivializar
trolley *n* tranvía
troop *n* tropa
trophy *n* trofeo
tropic *n* trópico
tropical *adj* tropical
trouble *n* problema, molestia
trouble *v* inquietar, molestar
troublesome *adj* problemático
trousers *n* pantalones
trout *n* trucha
truce *n* tregua
truck *n* camión
trucker *n* camionero

true *adj* verdadero
truly *adv* sinceramente
trumped-up *adj* falso
trumpet *n* trompeta
trunk *n* tronco; baúl
trust *v* confiar
trust *n* confianza
truth *n* verdad
truthful *adj* veraz
try *v* tratar, probar
trying *adj* difícil, duro
tub *n* bañera
tube *n* tubo, conducto
tuberculosis *n* tuberculosis
Tuesday *n* martes
tug *v* remolcar
tuition *n* matrícula
tulip *n* tulipán
tumble *v* caer en picado
tummy *n* barriga
tumor *n* tumor
tumult *n* tumulto
tumultuous *adj* tumultuoso
tuna *n* atún
tune *n* melodía, aire
tune *v* sintonizar
tune up *v* afinar
tunic *n* túnica
tunnel *n* túnel
turbine *n* turbina
turbulence *n* turbulencia
turbulent *n* turbulento

T

turf *n* césped

Turk *adj* turco

Turkey *n* Turquía

turmoil *n* alboroto

turn *n* vuelta; turno

turn *v* girar; volver

turn back *v* volverse atrás

turn down *v* rechazar

turn in *v* entregar

turn off *v* apagar

turn on *v* encender

turn out *v* resultar

turn over *v* volcar

turn up *v* aparecer

turnout *n* asistencia total

turret *n* torreón

turtle *n* tortuga

tusk *n* colmillo

tutor *n* tutor

tweezers *n* pinzas

twelfth *adj* duodécimo

twelve *adj* doce

twentieth *adj* vigésimo

twenty *adj* veinte

twice *adv* dos veces

twilight *n* crepúsculo

twin *n* gemelo

twinkle *v* brillar

twist *v* torcer

twist *n* torcedura; giro

twisted *adj* torcido

twister *n* tornado

two *adj* dos

tycoon *n* magnate

type *n* clase; tipo

type *v* escribir a máquina

typhoon *n* tifón

typical *adj* típico

tyranny *n* tiranía

tyrant *n* tirano

U

ugliness *n* fealdad

ugly *adj* feo

ulcer *n* úlcera

ultimate *adj* último

ultimatum *n* ultimatum

ultrasound *n* ultrasonido

umbrella *n* paraguas

umpire *n* árbitro

unable *adj* incapaz

unanimity *n* unanimidad

unarmed *adj* desarmado

unassuming *adj* sin pretensiones

unattached *adj* soltero

unavoidable *adj* inevitable

unaware *adj* inconsciente

unbearable *adj* insoportable

unbeatable *adj* invencible

unbelievable *adj* increíble
unbiased *adj* imparcial
unbroken *adj* intacto
unbutton *v* desabrochar
uncertain *adj* incierto
uncle *n* tío
uncomfortable *adj* incómodo
uncommon *adj* raro
unconscious *adj* sin sentido
uncover *v* descubrir
undecided *adj* indeciso
undeniable *adj* innegable
under *pre* debajo
undercover *adj* secreto
underdog *n* el más débil
undergo *v* sufrir
underground *adj* subterráneo
underlie *v* sostentar
underline *v* subrayar
underlying *adj* subyacente
undermine *v* socavar
underneath *pre* debajo
underpass *n* paso subterráneo
understand *v* comprender
understandable *adj* comprensible
understanding *adj* comprensivo
undertake *v* emprender
underwear *n* ropa interior
underwrite *v* asegurar
undeserved *adj* inmerecido
undesirable *adj* indeseable
undisputed *adj* indiscutible

undo *v* deshacer
undoubtedly *adv* indudablemente
undress *v* desnudarse
undue *adj* excesivo
unearth *v* desenterrar
uneasiness *n* inseguridad
uneasy *adj* inseguro
uneducated *adj* inculto
unemployed *adj* sin empleo
unemployment *n* desempleo
unending *adj* interminable
unequal *adj* desigual
unequivocal *adj* claro
uneven *adj* desigual
uneventful *adj* sin incidentes
unexpected *adj* inesperado
unfailing *adj* exitoso
unfair *adj* injusto
unfairly *adv* injustamente
unfairness *n* injusticia
unfaithful *adj* infiel
unfamiliar *adj* desconocido
unfasten *v* desatar
unfavorable *adj* desfavorable
unfit *adj* no apto
unfold *v* desdoblar
unforeseen *adj* imprevisto
unforgettable *adj* inolvidable
unfounded *adj* sin fundamento
unfriendly *adj* antipático
unfurnished *adj* sin amueblar
ungrateful *adj* desagradecido

unhappiness *n* tristeza
unhappy *adj* descontento
unharmed *adj* ileso
unhealthy *adj* malsano
unheard-of *adj* inaudito
unhurt *adj* ileso
unification *n* unificación
uniform *n* uniforme
uniformity *n* uniformidad
unify *v* unificar
unilateral *adj* unilateral
union *n* unión
unique *adj* único
unit *n* unidad
unite *v* unir
unity *n* unidad
universal *adj* universal
universe *n* universo
university *n* universidad
unjust *adj* injusto
unjustified *adj* injustificado
unknown *adj* desconocido
unlawful *adj* ilegal
unleaded *adj* sin plomo
unleash *v* desatar
unless *c* a no ser que
unlike *adj* distinto
unlikely *adj* improbable
unlimited *adj* ilimitado
unload *v* descargar
unlock *v* abrir
unlucky *adj* desafortunado

unmarried *adj* soltero
unmask *v* desenmascarar
unmistakable *adj* inconfundible
unnecessary *adj* innecesario
unnoticed *adj* desapercibido
unoccupied *adj* desocupado
unofficially *adv* sin confirmar
unpack *v* deshacer
unpleasant *adj* desagradable
unplug *v* desenchufar
unpopular *adj* impopular
unpredictable *adj* imprevisible
unprofitable *adj* no rentable
unprotected *adj* desprotegido
unravel *v* desenredar
unreal *adj* irreal
unrealistic *adj* poco realista
unreasonable *adj* irrazonable
unrelated *adj* no relacionado
unreliable *adj* incierto
unrest *n* malestar
unsafe *adj* peligroso
unselfish *adj* generoso
unspeakable *adj* indecible
unstable *adj* inestable
unsteady *adj* inseguro
unsuccessful *adj* sin éxito
unsuitable *adj* inapropiado
unsuspecting *adj* confiado
unthinkable *adj* inconcebible
untie *v* desatar
until *pre* hasta

untimely *adj* inoportuno
untouchable *adj* intocable
untrue *adj* falso
unusual *adj* insólito
unveil *v* desvelar
unwillingly *adv* de mala gana
unwind *v* relajarse
unwise *adj* imprudente
unwrap *v* desenvolver
upbringing *n* educación
upcoming *adj* venidero
update *v* poner al día
upgrade *v* mejorar
upheaval *n* convulsión
uphill *adv* cuesta arriba
uphold *v* defender
upholstery *n* tapicería
upkeep *n* mantenimiento
upon *pre* sobre
upper *adj* superior
upright *adj* derecho
uprising *n* sublevación
uproar *n* escándalo
uproot *v* desarraigar
upset *v* molestar
upside-down *adv* al revés
upstairs *adv* arriba
uptight *adj* tenso
up-to-date *adj* moderno
upturn *n* mejora
upwards *adv* hacia arriba
urban *adj* urbano

urge *n* impulso
urge *v* animar
urgency *n* urgencia
urgent *adj* urgente
urinate *v* orinar
urine *n* orina
urn *n* urna
us *pro* nosotros
usage *n* uso
use *v* usar, utilizar
use *n* uso, utilización
used to *adj* acostumbrado
useful *adj* útil
usefulness *n* utilidad
useless *adj* inservible, inútil
user *n* usuario
usher *n* ujier
usual *adj* normal
usurp *v* usurpar
utensil *n* utensilio
uterus *n* útero
utilize *v* utilizar
utmost *adj* sumo, máximo
utter *v* decir, pronunciar

vacancy n libre
vacant adj desocupado
vacate v desocupar
vacation n vacación
vaccinate v vacunar
vaccine n vacuna
vacillate v vacilar, dudar
vagrant n vagabundo
vague adj impreciso
vain adj vano
vainly adv en vano
valiant adj valiente
valid adj válido, vigente
validate v validar
validity n validez
valley n valle
valuable adj valioso
value n valor
valve n válvula
vampire n vampiro
van n furgoneta
vandal n vándalo
vandalism n vandalismo
vandalize v destruir
vanguard n vanguardia
vanish v desaparecer
vanity n vanidad
vanquish v vencer
vapor n vapor

vaporize v vaporizar
variable adj variable
varied adj variado
variety n variedad
various adj varios
varnish v barnizar
varnish n barniz
vary v variar
vase n jarrón
vast adj enorme
vault n bóveda
veal n ternera
veer v torcer, girar
vegetable v legumbre
vegetarian v vegetariano
vegetation n vegetación
vehicle n vehículo
veil n velo
vein n vena
velocity n velocidad
velvet n terciopelo
vendor n vendedor
venerate v venerar
venereal adj venéreo
vengeance n venganza
venison n carne de venado
venom n veneno
vent n respiradero
ventilate v ventilar
ventilation n ventilación
venture v arriesgarse
venture n riesgo; negocio

verb _n_ verbo
verbally _adv_ de palabra
verbatim _adv_ literalmente
verdict _n_ veredicto
verge _n_ borde
verification _n_ verificación
verify _v_ verificar
versatile _adj_ versátil
verse _n_ verso
versed _adj_ versado
version _n_ versión
versus _pre_ contra
vertebra _n_ vértebra
very _adv_ muy
vessel _n_ barco
vest _n_ chaleco
vestige _n_ vestigio
veteran _n_ veterano
veterinarian _n_ veterinario
veto _v_ vetar
viable _adj_ viable
viaduct _n_ viaducto
vibrant _adj_ vibrante
vibrate _v_ vibrar
vibration _n_ vibración
vicar _n_ párroco, vicario
vice _n_ vicio
viceversa _adv_ al revés
vicinity _n_ cercanías
vicious _adj_ feroz
victim _n_ víctima
victimize _v_ tratar mal

victor _n_ vencedor
victorious _adj_ victorioso
victory _n_ victoria
view _n_ vista, opinion
view _v_ ver, mirar
viewpoint _n_ punto de vista
vigil _n_ vigilia
vigorous _adj_ vigoroso
vile _adj_ vil
village _n_ pueblo, aldea
villager _n_ aldeano
villain _n_ villano
vindicate _v_ justificar
vindictive _adj_ vengativo
vine _n_ vid, parra
vinegar _n_ vinagre
vineyard _n_ viña, viñedo
violate _v_ violar
violence _n_ violencia
violent _adj_ violento
violet _n_ violeta
violin _n_ violín
violinist _n_ violinista
viper _n_ víbora
virgin _n_ virgen
virginity _n_ virginidad
virile _adj_ viril
virility _n_ virilidad
virtually _adv_ prácticamente
virtue _n_ virtud
virtuous _adj_ virtuoso
virulent _adj_ virulento

virus *n* virus
visa *n* visado
visibility *n* visibilidad
visible *adj* visible
vision *n* visión, sentido
visit *n* visita
visit *v* visitar
visitor *n* visitante
visual *adj* visual
visualize *v* visualizar
vital *adj* vital, decisivo
vitality *n* vitalidad
vitamin *n* vitamina
vivacious *adj* vivaz
vivid *adj* gráfico
vocabulary *n* vocabulario
vocation *n* vocación
vogue *n* moda
voice *n* voz
void *adj* vacío; nulo
volatile *adj* inestable
volcano *n* volcán
volleyball *n* vólibol
volt *n* voltio
voltage *n* voltaje
volume *n* volumen; capacidad
volunteer *n* voluntario
vomit *v* vomitar
vomit *n* vómito
vote *v* votar
vote *n* voto
voting *n* votación

vouch for *v* responder por
voucher *n* vale
vow *v* jurar
vow *n* voto, promesa
vowel *n* vocal
voyage *n* viaje por mar
voyager *n* pasajero
vulgar *adj* vulgar
vulgarity *n* vulgaridad
vulnerable *adj* vulnerable
vulture *n* buitre

wafer *n* barquillo
wag *v* menear
wage *n* sueldo, salario
wagon *n* vagón
wail *v* llorar
wail *n* lloriqueo, llanto
waist *n* cintura
wait *v* esperar
waiter *n* camarero
waiting *n* espera
waitress *n* camarera
waive *v* renunciar, suspender
wake up *iv* despertarse
walk *v* caminar

walk *n* paseo

walkout *n* huelga

wall *n* pared, muro

wallet *n* cartera

walnut *n* nuez

walrus *n* morsa

waltz *n* vals

wander *v* vagar, divagar

wanderer *n* vagabundo

wane *v* menguar

want *v* querer

war *n* guerra

ward *n* sala

ward off *v* parar, rechazar

warden *n* guardián

wardrobe *n* armario, ropero

warehouse *n* almacén

warfare *n* guerra

warm *adj* caliente

warm up *v* calentarse

warmth *n* calor

warn *v* avisar, advertir

warning *n* aviso

warp *v* doblarse

warped *adj* retorcido

warrant *v* justificar

warrant *n* orden judicial

warranty *n* garantía

warrior *n* guerrero

warship *n* barco de guerra

wart *n* verruga

wary *adj* cauteloso

wash *v* lavar

washable *adj* lavable

washer *n* lavadora

washing *n* lavado

wasp *n* avispa

waste *v* desperdiciar

waste *n* desperdicio

waste basket *n* papelera

wasteful *adj* derrochador

watch *n* reloj

watch *v* vigilar

watch out *v* tener cuidado

watchdog *n* inspector

watchful *adj* vigilante

watchmaker *n* relojero

water *n* agua

water *v* regar

water down *v* diluir

waterfall *n* cascada

waterheater *n* calentador

watermelon *n* sandía

waterproof *adj* impermeable

watershed *n* momento crítico

watertight *adj* hermético

watery *adj* aguado

watt *n* vatio

wave *n* onda; ola

waver *v* vacilar

wavy *adj* ondulado

wax *n* cera

way *n* camino; modo

way in *n* entrada

way out *n* salida

we *pro* nosotros

weak *adj* débil

weaken *v* debilitar

weakness *n* debilidad

wealth *n* riqueza

wealthy *adj* rico

weapon *n* arma

wear *n* uso; desgaste

wear *iv* usar; calzar; llevar

wear down *v* agotar

wear out *v* desgastar

weary *adj* cansado, agotado

weather *n* tiempo

weave *iv* tejer

web *n* telaraña; red

web site *n* sitio en la red

wed *iv* casarse

wedding *n* boda

wedge *n* cuña

Wednesday *n* miércoles

weed *n* hierba mala

weed *v* escardar

week *n* semana

weekday *adj* día laborable

weekend *n* fin de semana

weekly *adv* semanalmente

weep *iv* llorar

weigh *v* pesar

weight *n* peso

weighty *adj* pesado, serio

weird *adj* raro

welcome *v* acoger, recibir

welcome *n* bienvenida

weld *v* soldar

welder *n* soldador

welfare *n* bienestar

well *n* pozo

well-being *n* bienestar

well-known *adj* conocido

well-off *adj* rico

well-to-do *adj* acomodado

west *n* oeste

westbound *adv* hacia el oeste

western *adj* occidental

westerner *n* del occidente

wet *adj* mojado

whack *v* golpear, pegar

whale *n* ballena

wharf *n* muelle

what *adj* que

whatever *adj* lo que

wheat *n* trigo

wheel *n* rueda

wheelbarrow *n* carretilla

wheelchair *n* silla de ruedas

wheeze *v* silbar respirando

when *adv* cuando

whenever *adv* cada vez que

where *adv* donde

whereabouts *n* paradero

whereas *c* mientras que

whereupon *c* por lo tanto

wherever *c* dondequiera que

W

whether *c* si, aunque

which *adj* que

while *c* mientras que

whim *n* capricho

whine *v* quejarse

whip *v* azotar; batir

whip *n* látigo

whirl *v* dar vueltas, girar

whirlpool *n* remolino

whirlwind *n* torbellino

whisk away *v* transladar

whiskers *n* patillas

whisper *v* susurrar

whisper *n* susurro

whistle *v* silbar

whistle *n* silbato

white *adj* blanco

whiten *v* blanquear

whittle *v* tallar, rascar

whittle away *v* reducir

who *pro* quien

whoever *pro* cualquiera que

whole *adj* entero

wholehearted *adj* sincero

wholesale *n* al por mayor

wholesaler *n* mayorista

wholesome *adj* sano

whom *pro* quien

whooping *adj* enorme

why *adv* por qué

wicked *adj* malvado

wickedness *n* maldad

wide *adj* ancho, amplio

widely *adv* ampliamente

widen *v* ampliar

widespread *adj* extendido

widow *n* viuda

widower *n* viudo

width *n* anchura

wield *v* ejercer, blandir

wife *n* esposa

wig *n* peluca

wiggle *v* menear

wild *adj* salvaje

wild boar *n* jabalí

wilderness *n* desierto

wildlife *n* fauna

will *n* voluntad; testamento

willfully *adv* a sabiendas

willing *adj* dispuesto

willingly *adv* con gusto

willingness *n* buena voluntad

willow *n* sauce

wily *adj* astuto

wimp *adj* débil

win *iv* ganar

win back *v* recuperar

wind *n* viento

wind *iv* enrollar; serpentear

wind up *v* concluir

winding *adj* tortuoso

windmill *n* molino de viento

window *n* ventana

windpipe *n* tráquea

windshield *n* parabrisas
windy *adj* ventoso
wine *n* vino
winery *n* bodega de vino
wing *n* ala
wink *n* guiño
wink *v* guiñar
winner *n* ganador
winter *n* invierno
wipe *v* limpiar, borrar
wipe out *v* eliminar
wire *n* alambre, cable
wireless *adj* sin cable
wisdom *n* sabiduría
wise *adj* sensato; sabio
wish *v* desear
wish *n* deseo
wit *n* ingenio
witch *n* bruja
witchcraft *n* brujería
with *pre* con
withdraw *v* retirar(se); sacar
withdrawal *n* retirada
withdrawn *adj* retraído
wither *v* marchitarse
withhold *iv* retener
within *pre* dentro
without *pre* sin
withstand *v* resistir, aguantar
witness *n* testigo
witty *adj* ingenioso
wives *n* esposas

wizard *n* mago
wobble *v* temblar; vacilar
woes *n* desgracias
wolf *n* lobo
woman *n* mujer
womb *n* vientre; útero
women *n* mujeres
wonder *v* preguntarse
wonder *n* maravilla
wonderful *adj* maravilloso
wood *n* madera
wooden *adj* de madera
wool *n* lana
woolen *adj* de lana
word *n* palabra
wording *n* redacción
work *n* trabajo
work *v* trabajar; funcionar
work out *v* resolver
workable *adj* viable, factible
workbook *n* cuaderno
worker *n* trabajador
workout *n* ejercicio
workshop *n* taller
world *n* mundo
worldly *adj* mundano
worldwide *adj* mundial
worm *n* gusano
worn-out *adj* gastado
worring *adj* preocupante
worrisome *adj* alarmante
worry *v* preocupar(se)

W

worry *n* preocupación
worse *adj* peor
worsen *v* empeorar
worship *n* adoración, culto
worst *adj* el peor
worthless *adj* sin valor
worthwhile *adj* valioso
worthy *adj* digno
would-be *adj* presunto
wound *n* herida
wound *v* herir
woven *adj* tejido
wrap *v* envolver
wrap up *v* resumir
wrapping *n* envoltura
wrath *n* ira
wreath *n* corona de flores
wreck *v* destrozar
wreckage *n* escombros
wrench *n* llave inglesa
wrestle *v* luchar, forcejear
wrestler *n* luchador
wrestling *n* lucha libre
wretched *adj* desgraciado
wring *iv* exprimir; sacar
wrinkle *v* arrugar(se)
wrinkle *n* arruga
wrist *n* muñeca de mano
write *iv* escribir
write down *v* tomar nota
writer *n* escritor
writhe *v* retorcerse

writing *n* escritura
written *adj* escrito
wrong *adj* equivocado
wrongful *adj* ilegal

X-mas *n* Navidad
X-ray *n* radiografía

yacht *n* yate
yam *n* camote, boniato
yard *n* yarda
yarn *n* hilo
yawn *n* bostezo
yawn *v* bostezar
year *n* año
yearly *adv* anualmente
yearn *v* anhelar
yeast *n* levadura
yell *v* gritar
yellow *adj* amarillo

W
X
Y

yes *adv* sí
yesterday *adv* ayer
yet *c* sin embargo
yield *v* ceder; producir
yield *n* réditos
yoke *n* yugo
yolk *n* yema
you *pro* tú, usted
young *adj* joven
youngster *n* joven
your *adj* tu, su
yours *pro* tuyo
yourself *pro* tú mismo
youth *n* juventud
youthful *adj* juvenil

Z

zap *v* borrar, cambiar
zeal *n* celo
zealous *adj* entusiasta
zebra *n* cebra
zero *n* cero
zest *n* entusiasmo
zinc *n* cinc
zip code *n* código postal
zipper *n* cremallera
zone *n* zona
zoo *n* zoológico
zoology *n* zoología**

Spanish-English

Bilingual Dictionaries, Inc.

Abbreviations

English - Spanish

a – article – artículo
adj – adjective - adjetivo
adv – adverb – adverbio
c – conjunction - conjunctión
e – exclamation - exclamación
nf – feminine noun - nombre femenino *
nm – masculine noun - nombre masculino *
pre – preposition - preposición
pro – pronoun - pronombre
v – verb - verbo

*Feminine nouns use the article **la** in the singular form and **las** in the plural form.

*Masculine nouns use the article **el** in the singular form and **los** in the plural form.

a *pre* to
abadía *nf* abbey
abajo *adv* down, below
abandonar *v* abandon
abandono *nm* abandonment
abarcar *v* extend
abarrotar *adj* pack, crowd
abastecer *v* supply
abastecimiento *nm* supply
abatido *adj* downcast
abdicar *v* abdicate
abdomen *nm* abdomen
abdominal *adj* abdominal
abeja *nf* bee
aberración *nf* aberration
abertura *nf* opening
abierto *adj* open
abismo *nm* abyss
ablandar *v* soften
abnegación *nf* self-denial
abocado *adj* doomed
abochornar *v* embarrass
abofetear *v* slap, smack
abogado *nm* attorney, lawyer
abogar *v* defend
abolición *v* abolition
abolir *v* abolish
abolladura *nf* dent
abollar *v* dent

abominable *adj* abominable
abonar *v* pay, fertilize
abono *nm* compost; payment
abordar *v* board; tackle
aborrecer *v* detest, loathe
abortar *v* have an abortion
aborto *nm* abortion
abrasar *v* burn
abrazadera *nf* clamp
abrazar *v* embrace, hug
abrazo *nm* embrace, hug
abrelatas *nm* can opener
abreviar *v* shorten
abreviatura *nf* abbreviaton
abridor *n* opener
abrigar *v* keep warm
abrigo *mn* overcoat
abril *nm* April
abrir *v* open, unlock
abrirse *v* open up
abrochar *v* fasten
abrogar *v* repeal
abrumar *v* overwhelm
abrupto *adj* steep
absolución *nf* absolution
absoluto *adj* absolute
absolver *v* absolve, acquit
absorber *v* absorb
absorción *nf* absorption
absorto *adj* engrossed in
absorvente *adj* absorbent
abstenerse *v* abstain

abstinencia *nf* abstinence
abstracto *adj* abstract
absurdo *adj* absurd
abuchear *v* boo
abuela *nf* grandmother
abuelo *nm* grandfather
abuelos *nm* grandparents
abultado *adj* bulky
abultar *v* swell, be bulky
abundancia *nf* abundance, glut
abundante *adj* plentiful
abundar *v* abound
aburrido *adj* boring, dull
aburrimiento *nm* boredom, tedium
aburrirse *v* get bored
abusar *v* abuse
abusivo *adj* abusive
abuso *nm* abuse
acá *adv* here
acabar *v* finish
acabar en *v* end up
academia *nf* academy
académico *adj* academic
acaecer *v* occur
acallar *v* silence
acalorado *adj* heated
acampar *v* camp
acantilado *nm* cliff
acaparar *v* hoard
acariciar *v* caress, pat
acarrear *v* cause; carry

acaso *adv* perhaps
acatar *v* obey, comply
acatarrarse *v* catch a cold
accesible *adj* accessible
acceso *nm* access, entry
accesorio *nm* accessory
accidental *adj* accidental
accidente *nm* accident
acción *nf* action
accionista *nm* shareholder
acechar *v* lurk, stalk
aceite *nm* oil
aceituna *nf* olive
acelerador *nf* accelerator
acelerar *v* speed up
acento *nm* accent
acentuar *v* emphasize
aceptable *adj* acceptable
aceptación *nf* acceptance
aceptar *v* accept
acera *nf* sidewalk, pavement
acerca de *pre* about, concerning
acercar *v* bring closer
acercarse *v* approach
acero *nm* steel
acertado *adj* correct
acertar *v* get right
acertijo *nm* riddle
acesible *adj* accessible
aceso *nm* access
acesorio *nm* accessory
achacar *v* blame

achacoso *adj* sikly
achaque *nm* ailment
achatar *v* flatten
achicharrar *v* burn
acidez *nf* acidity, heartburn
ácido *adj* sour, acid
acierto *nm* good idea
aclamar *v* acclaim
aclarar *v* clarify, rinse
aclimatarse *v* acclimatize
acogedor *adj* cozy, homely
acoger *v* shelter, receive
acogida *nf* reception
acometer *v* attack, undertake
acomodado *adj* affluent
acomodarse *v* adapt, get used
acompañar *v* accompany
acongojar *v* grieve
aconsejable *adj* advisable
aconsejar *v* advise, counsel
acontecer *v* happen, occur
acontecimiento *nm* event
acorazado *nm* battleship
acordar *v* agree
acordarse *v* remember
acordeón *mn* accordion
acordonar *v* seal off, cordon off
acorralar *v* round up
acortar *v* shorten
acosar *v* harass, hound
acoso *nm* harassment
acostar *v* put to bed

acostarse *v* lie, go to bed
acostumbrar *v* accustom
acostumbrarse *v* get used
acre *nm* acre
acrecentar *v* increase
acreditación *nf* accreditation
acreedor *n* creditor
acróbata *nm* acrobat
actitud *nf* attitude
activación *nf* activation
activar *v* activate
actividad *nf* activity
activo *adj* active
actor *nm* actor
actriz *nf* actress
actuación *nf* performance
actual *adj* actual, current
actuar *v* act
acuaducto *nm* aqueduct
acuático *adj* aquatic
acudir *v* attend, come
acuerdo *nm* agreement, accord
acumulación *nf* accumulation
acumular *v* accumulate, hoard
acuñar *v* mint
acurrucarse *v* huddle
acusación *nf* accusation
acusado *nm* defendant
acusador *nm* accuser
acusar *v* accuse, charge
acústica *n* accoustics
acústico *adj* acoustic

adaptable *adj* adaptable

adaptación *nf* adaptation

adaptador *nm* adapter

adaptar *v* adapt

adecuado *adj* appropiate

adelantar *v* overtake, outrun

adelantarse *v* get ahead

adelante *adv* ahead, forward

adelgazar *v* lose weight

ademán *nm* gesture

además *adv* besides, also

adentro *adv* inland

aderezar *v* season

adherirse *v* join

adhesión *nf* adhesion

adhesivo *adj* adhesive

adicción *nf* addiction

adicional *adj* additional

adictivo *adj* addictive

adicto *adj* addicted

adiestrar *v* train

adinerado *adj* wealthy

adiós *e* good-bye

adivinar *v* guess

adjetivo *nf* adjective

adjuntar *v* attach

administrar *v* administer

administrar mal *v* mismanage

admirable *adj* admirable

admiración *fn* admiration, awe

admirador *nf* admirer

admirar *v* admire

admisible *adj* admissible

admisión *nf* admission

admitir *v* admit, accept

adoctrinar *v* indoctrinate

adolescencia *nf* adolescence

adolescente *nm* teenager

adopción *nf* adoption

adoptar *v* adopt

adoptivo *adj* adoptive

adoquín *nm* cobblestone

adorable *adj* adorable

adoración *nf* adoration

adorar *v* adore, worship

adornar *v* adorn

adorno *nm* ornament

adquirir *v* acquire

adquisición *nf* acquisition

adrede *adv* on purpose

aduana *nf* customs

adulación *nf* adulation

adular *v* flatter

adulterar *v* adulterate

adulterio *nm* adultery

adúltero *adj* adulterous

adulto *nm* adult, grown up

adverbio *nm* adverb

adversario *nm* adversary

adversidad *nf* adversity

adverso *adj* adverse

advertencia *nf* warning

advertir *v* warn, tip off

Adviento *nm* Advent

aeropuerto *nm* airport
afable *adj* affable
afán *nm* eagerness
afear *v* make ugly
afectar *v* affect
afectivo *adj* affectionate
afecto *nm* affection
afeitarse *v* shave
afeminado *adj* effeminate
aferrarse *v* cling, stick to
affirmar *v* assert
afianzar *v* strengthen
aficion *nf* love
aficionado *adj* fond
aficionado *nm* amateur
afilado *adj* pointed, sharp
afilar *v* sharpen
afiliación *nf* affiliation
afiliarse *v* affiliate
afinidad *nf* affinity
afirmación *nf* assertion
afirmar *v* affirm
afirmativo *adj* affirmative
aflicción *nf* grief, sorrow
afligido *adj* distressed
afligir *v* afflict, distress
aflojar *v* loosen
aflorar *v* surface
afluencia *nf* influx
afortunado *adj* fortunate, lucky
afrenta *nf* insult
africano *adj* African

afrodisiaco *adj* aphrodisiac
afrontar *v* confront
afuera *adv* out, outside
agacharse *v* bend down, crouch
agarradera *nf* handle
agarrado *adj* stingy
agarrar *v* grasp, seize
agarrarse *v* cling, take hold
agasajar *v* treat nicely
agencia *nf* agency
agenda *nf* agenda
agente *nm* officer, agent
ágil *adj* agile
agilidad *nf* agility
agitación *nf* agitation
agitado *adj* hectic
agitador *nm* agitator
agitar *v* shake
aglomeración *nf* agglomeration
agnosticismo *nm* agnosticism
agnóstico *nm* agnostic
agobiado *adj* stressed
agobiar *v* overwhelm
agonía *nf* agony
agonizar *v* agonize
agosto *nm* August
agotamiento *nm* exhaustion
agotar *v* exhaust, deplete
agradable *adj* pleasant, agreeable
agradar *v* please, delight
agradecer *v* thank
agradecido *adj* grateful, obliged

agrandar *v* enlarge
agravamiento *nm* aggravation
agravante *adj* aggravating
agravar *v* get worse
agravio *nm* grievance
agredir *v* attack
agregar *v* add
agresión *nf* aggression
agresivo *adj* aggressive
agresor *nm* aggressor, attacker
agricultor *nm* farmer
agricultura *nf* agriculture
agrietar *v* crack
agrupación *nf* cluster
agrupar *v* cluster, group
agua *nf* water
aguacate *nm* avocado
aguacero *nm* downpour
aguado *adj* watery
aguantar *v* endure, bear
aguar *v* spoil
aguardar *v* wait
agudo *adj* acute, sharp
aguijonear *v* goad
águila *nf* eagle
aguja *nf* needle
agujerear *v* make a hole, drill
agujero *nm* hole
ahí *adv* there
ahogar *v* drown
ahondar *v* go deep
ahora *adv* now

ahorcar *v* hang
ahorrar *v* save
ahorros *nm* savings
ahumado *adj* smoked
ahuyentar *v* chase away
aire *nm* air
airear *v* air
aislamiento *nm* seclusion, isolation
aislar *v* isolate
ajedrez *nm* chess
ajeno *adj* extraneous
ajetreado *adj* busy
ajo *nm* garlic
ajustable *adj* adjustable
ajustado *adj* tight
ajustar *v* adjust, fit
ajuste *nm* adjustment
al aire libre *adv* outdoors
al azar *adv* randomly
al lado de *pre* beside, alongside
al momento *adv* instantly
al otro lado *pre* across
al por mayor *adv* wholesale
al principio *adv* initially
al revés *adv* upside-down
ala *nf* wing
alabanza *nf* praise
alabar *v* praise
alacena *nf* cupboard
alambrada *nf* barbed wire
alambre *nm* wire

alardear *v* boast
alargar *v* lengthen
alarido *nm* shriek
alarma *nf* alarm
alarmante *adj* alarming
alarmista *nm* alarmist
albañil *nm* bricklayer, mason
albaricoque *nm* apricot
albergar *v* shelter
albergue *nm* shelter, hostel
albóndiga *nf* meatball
alborada *nf* dawn, sunrise
albornoz *nm* robe
alboroto *nm* commotion
alcachofa *nf* artichoke
alcalde *nm* mayor
alcance *nm* range
alcantarilla *nf* sewer
alcanzar *v* reach
alcazar *nm* fortress
alcoba *nf* bedroom
alcohólico *adj* alcoholic
alcoholismo *nm* alcoholism
aldea *nf* hamlet, village
aldeano *nm* villager
aleación *nf* alloy
alegar *v* allege
alegoría *n* allegory
alegórico *adj* allegoric
alegrar *v* make happy
alegre *adj* joyful, happy
alegría *nf* joy, happiness

alemán *adj* German
Alemania *nf* Germany
alentar *v* encourage
alergia *nf* allergy
alérgico *adj* allergic
alerta *nf* alert
aleta *nf* fin
aletear *v* flutter
alfabeto *nm* alphabet
alfalfa *nf* alfalfa
alfiler *nm* pin
alfombra *nf* carpet, rug
algas *nf* algae
álgebra *nf* algebra
algo *pro* something
algodón *nm* cotton
alguacil *nm* bailiff
alguien *pro* somebody
algún *adj* some
algunos *adj* some
alhaja *nf* jewel
aliado *adj* allied
aliado *nm* ally
alianza *nf* alliance
aliarse *v* ally
alicates *nm* pliers, cutter
aliento *nm* breath
aligerar *v* lighten, quicken
alimentar *v* feed
alimento *nm* nourishment
alimonia *nf* alimony
alineamiento *nm* alignment

alinear *v* align, line up
alisar *v* smooth
alistarse *v* enlist
aliviar *v* relieve, soothe
aliviarse *v* get well
alivio *nm* relief, solace
allanar *v* flatten, level
allí *adv* there
alma *nf* soul
almacén *nm* warehouse
almacenaje *nm* storage
almacenar *v* store, stock
almanaque *nm* almanac
almeja *nf* clam
almendra *nf* almond
almidón *nm* starch
almirante *nm* admiral
almohada *nf* pillow
almorzar *v* have lunch
almuerzo *nm* lunch, brunch
alojamiento *nm* lodging
alojarse *v* lodge, stay
alondra *nf* lark
alpinismo *nm* mountain climbing
alpinista *nm* mountain climber
alquilar *v* hire, rent
alquiler *nm* renting
alquitrán *nm* tar
alrededor *pro* around
alrededores *nm* outskirts
altamente *adv* highly
altanero *adj* haughty

altar *nm* altar
altavoz *nm* loudspeaker
alteración *nf* alteration
alterar *v* alter
altercado *nm* argument
alternador *n* alternator
alternar *v* alternate, socialize
alternativo *adj* alternative
Alteza *nf* Highness
altibajos *nm* ups and downs
altitud *nf* altitude
altivo *adj* proud
alto *adj* high, tall, loud
altura *nf* height, elevation
alubia *nf* bean
alucinante *adj* amazing
alucinar *v* amaze
aludir *v* refer
alumbrado *nm* lighting
alumbrar *v* brighten
aluminio *nm* aluminum
alumno *nm* pupil
alusión *nf* allusion
alzamiento *nm* uprising
alzar *v* lift, raise
amabilidad *nf* kindness
amable *adj* gracious, kind
amañarse *v* manage
amanecer *nm* dawn, sunrise
amante *nf* lover, mistress
amapola *nf* poppy
amar *v* love

amargado *adj* bitter

amargar *v* embitter

amargo *adj* bitter, sour

amargura *nf* bitterness

amarillo *adj* yellow

amarrar *v* moor, tie

amasar *v* amass

ambición *nf* ambition

ambiente *nm* environment

ambiguedad *nf* ambiguity

ambiguo *adj* ambiguous

ámbito *nm* scope

ambivalencia *nf* ambivalence

ambivalente *adj* ambivalent

ambos *adj* both

ambulancia *nf* ambulance

amedrentar *v* scare

amenaza *nf* threat

amenazador *adj* threatening

amenazar *v* threaten

amenizar *v* entertain

americano *adj* American

ametralladora *nf* machine gun

amígdala *nf* tonsil

amigo *nm* friend

aminorar *v* decrease

amistad *nf* friendship

amistoso *adj* friendly

amnesia *nf* amnesia

amnistía *nf* amnesty

amo *nm* owner

amoldarse *v* adapt

amonestar *v* admonish

amoniaco *nm* ammonia

amontonar *v* pile up, stack

amor *nm* love

amoral *adj* amoral

amoratado *adj* purple, bruised

amordazar *v* muzzle, gag

amorfo *adj* amorphous

amorío *nm* love affair

amoroso *adj* loving

amortajar *v* shroud

amortiguar *v* deaden, muffle

amortizar *v* pay off

amotinarse *v* riot, mutiny

amparar *v* protect

amparo *nm* protection

ampliación *nf* expansion

ampliamente *adv* widely

ampliar *v* broaden, widen

amplificador *nm* amplifier

amplificar *v* amplify

amplio *adj* spacious, ample

ampolla *nf* blister

amputación *nf* amputation

amputar *v* amputate

amueblar *v* furnish

anacronismo *nm* anachronism

añadir *v* add

analfabeto *adj* illiterate

análisis *nm* analysis

analizar *v* analyze

analogía *nf* analogy

anarquía *nf* anarchy
anarquista *nm* anarchist
anatomía *nf* anatomy
ancestral *adj* ancestral
ancho *adj* broad, wide
anchoa *nf* anchovy
anchura *nf* width, breadth
ancla *nf* anchor
andamio *nm* scaffold
andén *nm* platform
andrajo *nm* rag
anécdota *nf* anecdote
anemia *nf* anemia
anémico *adj* anemic
anestesia *nf* anesthesia
anestesiar *v* anesthesize
anestesista *nm* anesthetist
anexión *nf* annexation
anexionar *v* annex
anfibio *adj* amphibious
anfiteatro *nm* amphitheater
anfitrión *nm* host
anfitriona *nf* hostess
ángel *nm* angel
angélico *adj* angelic
angina *nf* angina
anglicano *adj* Anglican
angosto *adj* narrow
angular *adj* angular
ángulo *nm* angle
angustia *nf* anguish
angustiado *adj* distraught

angustiante *adj* distressing
angustiar *v* distress
angustiarse *v* agonize
angustioso *adj* agonising
anhelar *v* yearn, long for
anidar *v* nest
anillo *nm* ring
animación *nf* animation
animado *adj* lively
animal *nm* animal
animar *v* encourage
animosidad *nf* animosity
aniquilación *nf* annihilation
aniquilar *v* annihilate
aniversario *nm* anniversary
annual *adj* annual
anoche *adv* last night
anochecer *v* get dark
anochecer *nm* nightfall
anonimato *nm* anonymity
anónimo *adj* anonymous
anormal *adj* abnormal
anormalidad *nf* abnormality
anotación *nf* note
anotar *v* take notes
ansia *nf* yearning
ansiar *v* crave, yearn for
ansiedad *nf* anxiety
ansioso *adj* anxious
antagonismo *nm* antagonism
antagonizar *v* antagonize
ante todo *adv* primarily

antecedentes *nm* antecedents
anteceder *v* precede
antecesor *nm* predecessor
antelación *nf* advance
antemano (de) *adv* beforehand
antena *nf* antenna
anteojo *nm* eyeglass
antepasado *nm* ancestor
anterior *adj* previous, former
antes *adv* before
antesala *nf* lobby
anticipación *nf* anticipation
anticipar *v* anticipate
anticipo *nm* preview, advance
anticuado *adj* old-fashioned
antídoto *nm* antidote
antiguamente *adv* formerly
antiguedad *nf* antiquity
antiguo *adj* ancient, old
antipatía *nf* dislike
antipático *adj* unfriendly
antítesis *nf* antithesis
antojo *nm* whim
antorcha *nf* torch
antropología *nf* anthropology
anualmente *adv* yearly
anulación *nf* annulment
anular *v* annul, overrule
anunciar *v* announce
anuncio *nm* announcement
anzuelo *nm* hook
añejo *adj* old

año *nm* year
añoranza *nf* nostagia
añorar *v* miss
apacentar *v* graze
apacible *adj* gentle, placid
apaciguar *v* pacify
apagar *v* put out, turn off
apagón *nm* blackout
apalear *v* beat
apañarse *v* manage
aparato *nm* gadget, devise
aparcar *v* park
aparecer *v* appear, show up
aparentar *v* pretend
aparente *adj* apparent
aparición *nf* appearance
apariencia *nf* semblance
apartamento *nm* apartment
apartar *v* separate
aparte *adv* apart, besides
apasionado *adj* passionate
apasionar *v* excite
apatía *nf* apathy
apearse *v* get off
apechugar *v* cope with
apegado *adj* attached
apego *nm* attachment
apelación *nf* appeal
apelar *v* appeal
apellido *nm* surname
apenar *v* make sad
apenas *adv* barely, hardly

apéndice *nm* appendix
apendicitis *nf* appendicitis
aperitivo *nm* appetizer
apertura *nf* opening
apestar *v* stink
apestoso *adj* smelly, stinking
apetecer *v* feel like
apetito *nm* appetite
apiadarse *v* feel pity
apiñarse *v* crowd together
apio *nm* celery
aplacar *v* placate
aplastar *v* crush, squash
aplaudir *v* applaud, clap
aplauso *nm* applause
aplausos *nm* cheers
aplazamiento *nm* delay
aplazar *v* postpone, delay
aplicable *adj* applicable
aplicación *nf* application
aplicar *v* apply
apocado *adj* timid
apoderarse *v* take over
apodo *nm* nickname
apogeo *nm* climax
apología *nf* apology
aporrear *v* beat
aportación *nf* input
apostar *v* bet
apóstol *nm* apostle
apostólico *adj* apostolic
apóstrofe *nm* apostrophe

apoyar *v* back up, support
apoyarse *v* lean
apoyo *nm* backing, help
apreciar *v* appreciate
aprecio *nm* appreciation
apremiante *adj* urgent
apremio *nm* urgency
aprender *v* learn
aprendiz *nm* apprentice
aprensivo *adj* apprehensive
apresar *v* capture
apresurado *adj* hasty
apresurarse *v* hurry up
apretado *adj* tight
apretar *v* tighten, squeeze
aprieto *nm* difficulty
aprobación *nf* approval
aprobar *v* approve
apropiado *adj* suitable
aprovechar *v* make use
aprovecharse *v* take advantage
aproximarse *v* approach
aptitud *nf* aptitude
apto *adj* suitable
apuesta *nf* bet
apuñalar *v* stab
apuntar *v* point at, aim
apunte *nm* note
apurarse *v* worry
apuro *nm* worry, trouble
aquario *nm* aquarium
aquellos *adj* those

aquí *adv* here
árabe *adj* Arabic
arable *adj* arable
arado *nm* plough
araña *nf* spider
arañar *v* scratch
arañazo *nm* scratch
arar *v* plow, till
arbitrario *adj* arbitrary
árbitro *nm* umpire, referee
árbol *nm* tree
arbusto *nm* bush, shrub
arcaico *adj* archaic
arcángel *n* archangel
archiduque *n* archduke
archipiélago *nm* archipelago
archivar *v* file, shelve
archivo *nm* archive, file
arcilla *nf* clay
arco *nm* arc, arch
arco iris *nm* rainbow
arder *v* burn
ardiendo *adj* ablaze
ardiente *adj* ardent
arduo *adj* arduous
área *nf* area
arena *nf* sand
argumentar *v* argue
argumento *nm* argument
árido *adj* arid, dry
arisco *adj* surly
aristocracia *nf* aristocracy

aristócrata *adj* aristocrat
aritmética *nf* arithmetic
arma *nm* weapon
arma de fuego *nm* firearm
armada *nf* navy
armadura *nf* armor
armamento *nm* munitions
armar *v* assemble, arm
armario *nm* wardrobe, closet
armisticio *nm* armistice
armonía *nf* harmony
aro *n* hoop
aroma *nm* aroma
aromático *adj* aromatic
arpa *nf* harp
arpón *nm* harpoon
arqueología *nf* archaeology
arquitecto *nm* architect
arquitectura *nf* architecture
arraigado *adj* entrenched
arraigar *v* take root
arrancar *v* pull out
arrasar *v* ravage, raze
arrastrar *v* drag
arrastrarse *v* crawl
arrebatar *v* snatch, seize
arrebato *nm* outburst, fit
arrecife *nm* reef
arreglado *adj* tidy
arreglar *v* arrange, fix
arreglarse *v* groom
arreglárselas *v* cope, manage

arreglo *nm* solution; repair

arremeter *v* attack

arrendar *v* lease

arrendatario *v* tenant

arrepentido *adj* remorseful

arrepentirse *v* repent

arrestar *v* arrest

arresto *nm* arrest

arriba *adv* up, above

arribar *v* arrive

arriendo *nm* lease

arriesgado *adj* risky

arriesgar *v* gamble, risk

arriesgarse *v* venture

arritmia *nf* arrhythmia

arrodillarse *v* kneel down

arrogancia *nf* arrogance

arrogante *adj* arrogant

arrojar *iv* cast, throw

arrollar *v* run over

arroyo *nm* stream

arroz *nm* rice

arruga *nf* wrinkle

arrugar *v* wrinkle

arruinar *v* ruin

arsenal *nm* arsenal

arsénico *nm* arsenic

arson *nm* arson, fuego

arte *nm* art

artefacto *nm* artifact

arteria *nf* artery

artesano *nm* craftsman

ártico *nm* arctic

articular *v* articulate

artículo *nm* article, item

artificial *adj* artificial

artillería *nf* artillery

artista *nm* artist

artístico *adj* artistic

artritis *nf* arthritis

arzobispo *nm* archbishop

as *nm* ace

asa *nm* handle

asador *nm* broiler

asaltante *nm* attacker

asaltar *v* assault, raid

asalto *nm* holdup, raid

asamblea *nf* assembly

asar *v* broil, roast

ascender *v* ascend, rise

ascendiente *nm* ancestor

ascenso *nm* promotion

ascensor *nm* elevator

ascético *adj* ascetic

asco *nm* disgust

aseado *adj* neat, clean

asediar *v* siege

asedio *nm* siege

asegurar *v* insure, secure

asegurarse *v* make sure

asentir *v* agree

aseos *nm* restroom

asequible *adj* attainable

asesinar *v* assassinate

asesinato *nm* murder
asesino *nm* assassin, killer
asfalto *nm* asphalt
asfixia *nf* asphyxiation
asfixiar *v* asphyxiate
así *adv* thus
asiento *nm* seat
asignar *v* allocate, assign
asignatura *nf* subject
asilo *nm* asylum
asimilación *nf* assimilation
asimilar *v* assimilate
asimismo *adv* likewise
asir *v* grab
asistencia *nf* attendance, help
asistente *nm* attendant
asistir *v* attend, help
asma *nf* asthma
asmático *adj* asthmatic
asno *nm* donkey
asociación *nf* association
asociar *v* associate
asomarse *v* lean out
asombrar *v* astonish, amaze
asombro *nm* amazement
asombroso *adj* amazing
aspecto *nm* aspect, looks
áspero *adj* rough
aspiración *nf* aspiration
aspiradora *nf* vacuum cleaner
aspirar *v* inhale, aspire
aspirina *nf* aspirin

asqueroso *adj* nasty
asta *nf* flagpole
asterisco *nm* asterisk
asteroide *nm* asteroid
astilla *nf* splinter
astillero *nm* shipyard
astrología *nf* astrology
astrólogo *nm* astrologer
astronauta *nm* astronaut
astronomía *nf* astronomy
astrónomo *nm* astronomer
astuto *adj* shrewd, cunning
asumir *v* assume, accept
asunto *nm* affair, matter
asustar *v* frighten, scare
atacar *v* attack
atadura *nf* tie
atajo *nm* shortcut
atañer *v* concern
ataque *nm* seizure; attack
atar *v* tie
atardecer *nm* sundown
atareado *adj* busy
atascar *v* clog, block
atasco *nm* traffic jam
ataúd *nm* casket, coffin
ateísmo *nm* atheism
atemorizar *v* frighten
atención *nf* attention
atender *v* serve, care for
atenerse a *v* abide by
atentado *nm* attack

atento *adj* attentive
atenuar *v* minimize, lessen
ateo *nm* atheist
aterrador *adj* frightening
aterrar *v* frighten
aterrizaje *nm* landing
aterrizar *v* land
aterrorizar *v* terrorize
atestiguar *v* testify
ático *nm* attic, penthouse
atleta *nm* athlete
atlético *adj* athletic
atmósfera *nf* atmosphere
atmosférico *adj* atmospheric
atolladero *nm* quagmire
atollarse *v* get stuck
atómico *adj* atomic
átomo *nm* atom
atónito *adj* amazed
atontado *v* dazed
atorarse *v* get stuck
atormentar *v* torture
atornillador *nm* screwdriver
atornillar *v* screw
atracador *nm* mugger
atracción *nf* attraction
atraco *nm* mugging
atractivo *adj* attractive
atraer *v* lure, attract
atrapar *v* catch, trap
atrás *adv* at the back
atrasado *adj* backward

atrasar *v* postpone
atravesar *v* cross
atrayente *adj* appealing
atreverse *v* dare
atrevido *adj* daring
atribuir *v* attribute
atrocidad *nf* atrocity
atropellar *v* run over
atroz *adj* atrocious
atún *nm* tuna
aturdido *adj* dazed
aturdir *v* daze, stun
audacia *nf* boldness
audaz *adj* bold
audiencia *nf* audience
auditorio *nm* auditorium
auge *nm* boom, peak
augurar *v* augur
augurio *nm* omen
aula *nf* classroom
aullar *v* howl
aullido *nm* howl
aumentar *v* increase
aumento *nm* increase
aún *adv* still
aún si *c* even if
aunque *c* although
aura *nf* aura
auriculares *nm* earphones
ausencia *nf* absence
ausentarse *v* go away
ausente *adj* absent

auspicios *nm* auspices
austeridad *nf* austerity
austero *adj* austere
australiano *adj* Australian
austriaco *adj* Austrian
autenticidad *nf* authenticity
auténtico *adj* authentic
autentificar *v* authenticate
auto *nm* car
autobús *nm* bus
autocar *nm* coach
autoestima *nf* self-esteem
autógrafo *nm* autograph
automático *adj* automatic
automatizar *v* automate
automóvil *nm* automobile
autonomía *nf* autonomy
autónomo *adj* autonomous
autopista *nf* freeway
autopsia *nf* autopsy
autor *nm* author
autoridad *nf* authority
autoritario *adj* authoritarian
autorización *nf* authorization
autorizar *v* authorize
auxiliar *v* help
auxilio *nm* help
avalancha *nf* avalanche
avance *nm* advance
avanzar *v* advance
avaricia *nf* avarice, greed
avaricioso *adj* greedy

avaro *adj* greedy
avasallar *v* subjugate
ave *nm* bird
avellana *nf* hazelnut
avena *nf* oatmeal
avenida *nf* avenue
aventajar *v* surpass
aventura *nf* adventure
aventurero *nm* adventurer
avergonzado *adj* ashamed
avergonzar *v* embarrass
avería *nf* breakdown
averiarse *v* break down
averiguar *v* find out
aversión *nf* dislike
avestruz *nf* ostrich
aviación *nf* aviation
aviador *nm* aviator, flier
avidez *nf* eagerness
ávido *adj* eager
avión *nm* plane
avisar *v* warn, inform
aviso *nm* warning, notice
avispa *nf* wasp
avispón *nm* hornet
avocado *nm* avocado
ayer *adv* yesterday
ayuda *nf* aid, help
ayudante *nm/f* helper
ayudar *v* assist, help
ayunar *v* fast
ayuntamiento *nm* city

azada *nf* hoe
azafata *nf* stewardess
azar *nm* chance, fate
azotar *v* whip, spank
azote *nm* lash, spanking
azteca *adj* Aztec
azúcar *nm* sugar
azucarado *adj* sweetened
azucena *nf* lily
azufre *nm* sulphur
azul *adj* blue
azulejo *nm* tile

B

bacalao *nm* cod
bache *nm* pothole
bacteria *nf* bacteria
báculo *nm* staff
bahía *nf* bay
bailador *nm* dancer
bailarina *nf* ballerina
baile *nm* dance
bajar *v* go down, lower
bajo *adj* low
bajón *nm* drop
bala *nf* bullet
balada *nf* ballad

balancear *v* swing
balanza *nf* scale
balazo *nm* shot
balbucear *v* stammer
balcón *nm* balcony
balde *nm* pail, bucket
baldosa *nf* floor tile
ballena *nf* whale
ballet *nm* ballet
balneario *nm* spa
balompié *nm* football
balón *nm* ball
balsa *nf* raft
bálsamo *nm* balm
baluarte *nm* bulwark
bambú *nm* bamboo
bancarrota *nf* bankcrupcy
banco *nm* bank, bench, pew
banda *nf* band
bandeja *nf* tray
bandera *nf* flag
bandido *nm* bandit
banquero *nm* banker
banqueta *nf* sidewalk
banquete *nm* banquet
bañador *nm* siwmsuit
bañarse *v* bathe
bañera *nf* bathtub
baño *nm* bath, lavatory
bar *nm* bar, saloon
barajar *v* shuffle
barandilla *nf* handrail

barato *adj* cheap
barba *nf* beard
barbacoa *nf* barbecue
bárbaro *adj* barbaric
barbero *nm* barber
barbudo *adj* bearded
barca *nf* boat
barcaza *nf* barge
barco *nm* ship, boat
barniz *nm* varnish
barnizar *v* varnish
barómetro *nm* barometer
barón *nm* baron
barquillo *nm* wafer
barra de pan *nf* loaf
barranco *nm* gorge, ravine
barrer *v* sweep
barrera *nf* barrier
barriada *nf* district
barricada *nf* barricade
barriga *nf* belly
barril *nm* barrel
barrio *nm* neighborhood
barro *nm* mud
barrote *nm* bar
barullo *nm* uproar
báscula *nf* scales
base *nf* base, basis
básico *adj* basic
básketbol *nm* basketball
basta *e* enough, stop
bastante *adv* enough, quite

bastar *v* be sufficient
bastardo *nm* bastard
bastilla *nf* hem
basto *adj* coarse, rough
bastón *nm* stick
basura *nf* garbage, trash
basurero *nm* trash can
bata *nf* robe, gown
batalla *nf* battle
batallar *v* fight
batallón *nm* battalion
batear *v* bat
batería *nf* battery
batir *v* beat
batido *nm* shake
batidora *nf* blender
batuta *nf* baton
baúl *nm* trunk
bautismo *nm* baptism
bautizar *v* baptize
bautizo *nm* christening
bayoneta *nf* bayonet
bazar *nm* bazaar
beatificar *v* beatify
beato *adj* blessed, pious
bebé *nm* baby
bebedor *nm* drinker
beber *v* drink
bebida *nf* drink
beca *nf* grant
becerro *nm* calf
béisbol *nm* baseball

belga *adj* Belgian

Bélgica *nf* Belgium

belleza *nf* beauty

bellota *nf* acorn

bendecir *v* bless

bendición *nf* blessing

bendito *adj* blessed

beneficiar *v* benefit

beneficiario *nm* beneficiary

beneficio *nm* benefit

beneficioso *adj* beneficial

benévolo *adj* benevolent

bengala *nf* flare

benigno *adj* mild, benign

berrinche *nm* tantrum

berza *nf* cabbage

besar *v* kiss

beso *nm* kiss

bestia *nf* beast

bestialidad *nf* bestiality

betún *nm* shoe polish

biblia *nf* bible

bíblico *adj* biblical

bibliografía *nf* bibliography

biblioteca *nf* library

bibliotecario *nm* librarian

bicho *nm* bug

bicicleta *nf* bicycle

bien *adv* right, fine, okay

bidón *nm* drum

bienestar *nm* well-being

bienhechor *nm* benefactor

bienvenida *nf* welcome

bifurcarse *v* diverge

bigamia *nf* bigamy

bigote *nm* mustache

bikini *nm* bikini

bilateral *adj* bilateral

bilingue *adj* bilingual

bilis *nf* bile

billar *nm* billiards

billete *nm* bill, ticket

billón *adj* billion

billonario *nm* billionaire

bimestral *adj* bimonthly

binoculares *adj* binoculars

biografía *nf* biography

biología *nf* biology

biológico *adj* biological

biopsia *nf* biopsy

biquini *nm* bikini

bisagra *nf* hinge

bisiesto *adj* leap year

bisonte *nm* bison

bisturí *nm* scalpel

bizco *adj* cross-eyed

biznieto *nm* great-grandson

blanco *nm* target

blanco *adj* white

blanco (en) *adj* blank

blancura *nf* whiteness

blandir *v* wield

blando *adj* soft

blanquear *v* bleach, whiten

blasfemar *v* blaspheme, curse
blasfemia *nf* blasphemy
blasfemo *adj* blasphemous
blindado *adj* armored
bloquear *v* block, obstruct
bloqueo *nm* blockade
blusa *nf* blouse
bobada *nf* nonsence
bobo *adj* sucker
boca *nf* mouth
bocadillo *nm* sandwich
bocado *nm* bite, morsel
bocata *nf* sandwich
bochornoso *adj* embarrassing
bocina *nf* horn
boda *nf* wedding
bodega *nf* cellar
bofetada *nf* slap, smack
bofetear *v* slap
boicot *nm* boycott
boina *nf* beret
bola *nf* ball
boletín *nm* bulletin
boleto *nm* ticket
bollo *nm* bun
bolsa *nf* bag
bolsillo *nm* pocket
bolso *nm* handbag
bomba *nf* bomb; pump
bombardero *nm* bomber
bombazo *nf* explosion
bombear *v* pump

bombero *nm* fireman
bombilla *nf* light bulb
bondad *nf* goodness
bonificación *nf* bonus
bonito *adj* pretty
boquete *nm* hole
bordado *adj* embroidered
bordar *v* embroider
borde *nm* brink, curb
borrachera *nf* drunkenness
borracho *adj* drunk
borrador *nm* rough draft
borrar *v* delete, erase
borrasca *nf* storm
borrego *nm* lamb
borrón *nm* stain
borroso *adj* blurred
bosque *nm* forest, wood
bosquejar *v* outline, sketch
bosquejo *nm* outline, sketch
bostezar *v* yawn
bostezo *nm* yawn
bota *nf* boot
botar *v* bounce
bote *nm* boat
botella *nf* bottle
botica *nf* pharmacy
botín *nm* booty
botón *nm* button
bóveda *nf* vault
boxeador *nm* boxer
boxeo *nm* boxing

boya *nf* buoy
bozal *nm* muzzle
brasero *nm* brazier
brasileño *adj* Brazilian
bravo *adj* fierce
brazo *nm* arm
brea *nf* tar
brecha *nf* opening
brevaje *nm* concoction, drink
breve *adj* short
brevedad *nf* brevity
brigada *nf* brigade
brillante *adj* bright, shiny
brillar *v* gleam, glow
brillo *nm* brightness
brincar *v* jump
brinco *nm* jump, leap
brisa *nf* breeze
broca *nf* drill
brocha *nf* paintbrush
broche *nm* brooch
brócoli *nm* broccoli
broma *nf* joke
broma (en) *adv* jokingly
bromear *v* joke
bronce *nm* bronze
bronceado *adj* tan
bronco *adj* harsh
bronquitis *nf* bronchitis
brotar *v* germinate
brote *nm* bud, shoot
bruja *nf* witch

brujería *nf* witchcraft
brújula *nf* compass
bruma *nf* mist
brumoso *adj* misty, hazy
brusco *adj* sudden
Bruselas *nf* Brussels
brutal *adj* brutal
brutalidad *nf* brutality
bucear *v* dive
buceo *nm* diving
bueno *adj* fine, good
buey *nm* ox
bueyes *nm* oxen
búfalo *nm* buffalo
bufanda *nf* scarf
bufón *nm* buffoon
buho *nm* owl
buitre *nm* vulture
bujía *nf* spark plug
bulevar *nm* boulevard
bullicio *nm* bustle
bulto *nm* package; lump
buque *nm* ship
burbuja *nf* bubble
burgués *adj* bourgeois
burla *nf* mockery
burlarse *v* mock, make fun
burocracia *nf* bureaucracy
burócrata *nm* bureaucrat
burro *nm* donkey
burrada *nf* nonsense
buscar *v* look for, search

búsqueda *nf* search, quest
busto *nm* bust
butaca *nf* armchair
buzo *nm* diver
buzón *nm* mailbox

c

cabalgar *v* ride
caballería *nf* cavalry
caballero *nm* gentleman
caballo *nm* horse
cabaña *nf* hut, cabin
cabecear *v* nod
cabecilla *nf* ringleader
cabezonada *nf* stubborness
cabellera *nf* scalp
cabello *nm* hair
cabeza *nf* head
cabezada *nf* doze
cabida *nf* space
cabina *nf* booth, cabin
cabo *nm* cape; corporal
cabra *nf* goat
cabrearse *v* get mad
cabrito *nm* kid
cacahuete *nm* peanut
cacao *nm* cocoa

cacarear *v* crow
cacería *v* hunt
cacharro *nm* piece of junk
cachear *v* search
cachete *nm* cheek; slap
cacho *nm* bit
cachorro *nm* cub, puppy
cacto *nm* cactus
cada *adj* each, every
cada día *adv* everyday
cada hora *adv* hourly
cada uno *adv* apiece
cada uno *pro* everybody
cada vez que *adv* whenever
cadalso *nm* scafold
cadáver *nm* corpse
cadena *nf* chain
cadera *nf* hip
caducar *v* expire
caducado *adj* out of date
caer *v* fall
caerse *v* fall down
café *nm* coffee
cafeína *nf* caffeine
cafetería *nf* cafeteria
caída *nf* downfall, fall
caimán *nm* alligator
caja *nf* box
cajero *nm* cashier
cajón *nm* drawer
cal *nf* lime
calabacín *nm* zucchini

calabaza *nf* pumpkin
calabozo *nm* dungeon
calamar *nm* squid
calambre *nm* cramp
calamidad *nf* calamity
calamitoso *adj* dire
calar *v* soak
calavera *nm* skull
calcar *v* trace, copy
calcetín *nm* sock
calcinar *v* burn
calcio *nm* calcium
calculadora *nm* calculator
calcular *v* calculate
cálculo *nm* calculation
caldera *nf* boiler
caldo *nm* broth
calendario *nm* calendar
calentador *nm* heater
calentar *v* heat
calentura *nf* fever
calibrar *v* gauge
calibre *nm* caliber
calidad *nf* quality
cálido *adj* warm
caliente *adj* hot
calificar *v* describe
cáliz *nm* chalice
callado *adj* silent
callarse *v* keep silent
calle *nf* street
callejón *nm* alley

callejuela *nf* alley
callo *nm* corn; tripe
calma *nf* calm
calmante *nm* painkiller
calmar *v* calm
calor *nm* heat
caloría *nf* calorie
calumnia *nf* libel, slander
calvo *adj* bald
calzado *nm* footwear
calzar *v* wear
calzoncillos *nm* briefs
cama *nf* bed
cámara *nf* camera
camarada *nm* comrade
camarera *nf* waitress
camarero *nm* waiter
camarón *nm* shrimp
cambiar *v* change, switch
cambio *nm* change
camello *nm* camel
camilla *nf* stretcher
caminar *v* hike, walk
caminata *nf* long walk
camino *nm* journey, way
camión *nm* truck
camionero *nm* trucker
camisa *nf* shirt
camiseta *nf* T-shirt
camisón *nm* nightgown
campamento *nm* camp
campana *nf* bell

campaña *nf* campaign
campanada *nf* chime, stroke
campanario *nm* belfrey
campechano *adj* down-to-earth
campeón *nm* champion
campesino *nm* peasant
campo *nm* countryside
camuflar *v* camouflage
camuflage *nm* camouflage
canadiense *adj* Canadian
canal *nm* canal, channel
canalla *nm* scoundrel
canalón *nm* gutter
canario *nm* canary
canasto *nm* basket
cancelación *nf* cancellation
cancelar *v* cancel
cáncer *nm* cancer
canciller *nm* chancellor
canción *nf* song
candado *nm* padlock
candente *adj* red-hot
candidato *nm* candidate
candidatura *nf* candidacy
cándido *adj* naïve
candor *nm* frankness
candil *nm* oil lamp
cangrejo *nm* crab
canguro *nm* kangaroo
caníbal *nm* cannibal
canica *nf* márbol
canino *adj* canine

canjear *v* exchange
canoa *nf* canoe
canonizar *v* canonize
canoso *adj* grayish
cansado *adj* tired, tiring
cansancio *nm* tiredness
cansarse *v* get tired
cantante *nm/f* singer
cantar *v* sing
cántaro *nm* pitcher, jug
cantera *nf* quarry
cantidad *nf* amount
cantina *nf* canteen
canto *nm* chant, song
caña *nf* cane; glass of beer
cañería *nf* pipe
caño *nm* tube, pipe
cañon *nm* canyon; cannon
caos *nm* chaos
caótico *adj* chaotic
capa *nf* cape, cloak
capacidad *nf* capacity
capacitar *v* enable; prepare
caparazón *v* shell
capataz *nm* foreman
capaz *adj* able, capable
capellán *nm* chaplain
capilla *nf* chapel
capital *nf* capital
capitalismo *nm* capitalism
capitán *nm* captain
capitular *v* capitulate

capítulo *nm* chapter
capricho *nm* whim
cápsula *nf* capsule
captura *nf* capture
capturar *v* capture
capucha *nf* hood
cara *nf* face
caracol *nm* snail
carácter *nm* character
característica *nf* feature
característico *adj* characteristic
caracterizar *v* characterize
caramelo *nm* candy
caravana *nf* caravan
carbón *nm* charcoal, coal
carbonizado *adj* charred
carbonizar *v* char
carburador *nm* carburetor
carcajada *nf* loud laugh
cárcel *nf* jail
carcelero *nm* jailer
cardenal *nm* cardinal
cardiaco *adj* cardiac
cardiología *nf* cardiology
cardo *nm* thistle
carecer *v* lack
carencia *nf* lack
carestía *nf* shortage
carga *nf* burden, load
cargamento *nm* cargo
cargar *v* burden, load
caricatura *nf* caricature

caricia *nf* caress
caridad *nf* charity
caries *nm* decay
cariñoso *adj* affectionate
carisma *nm* charisma
carismático *adj* charismatic
caritativo *adj* charitable
carne *nf* flesh; meat
carne asada *nf* roast
carne de cerdo *nf* pork
carne de vaca *nf* beef
carne picada *nf* mincemeat
carnero *nm* ram
carnicería *nf* butchery
carnicero *nm* butcher
carnívoro *nm* carnivorous
caro *adj* expensive
carpeta *nf* folder
carpintería *nf* carpentry
carpintero *nm* carpenter
carrera *nf* race
carreta *nf* cart
carrete *nm* roll, reel
carretera *nf* road
carretilla *nf* wheelbarrow
carril *nm* lane
carta *nf* letter, epistle
cartel *nm* poster
cartera *nf* wallet
cartero *nm* mailman
cartílago *nm* cartilage
cartón *nm* cardboard

cartucho *nm* cartridge
casa *nf* house, home
casarse *v* marry, wed
cascada *nf* waterfall
cascarón *nm* shell
cascarrabias *nm* grouch
casco *nm* helmet; hull
casero *adj* homemade
caseta *nf* pavilion
casi *adv* almost, nearly
casino *nm* casino
casita *nf* cottage
caso *nm* case
caspa *nf* dandruff
cassette *nm* tape
castaña *nf* chestnut
castellano *adj* Castilian
castidad *nf* chastity
castigable *adj* punishable
castigar *v* punish
castigo *nm* punishment
castillo *nm* castle, chateau
castor *nm* beaver
cataclismo *nm* cataclysm
catalejo *nm* telescope
catalogar *v* rank, classify
catálogo *nm* catalog
catarata *nf* waterfall
catarro *nm* cold
catástrofe *nf* catastrophe
catear *v* fail, flunk
catecismo *nm* catechism

catedral *nf* cathedral
categoría *nf* category, class
categorizar *v* categorize
cateto *nm* peasant
catolicismo *nm* Catholicism
católico *adj* catholic
catorce *adj* fourteen
caudal *nm* flow, volume
caudillo *nm* leader
causa *nf* cause
cautela *nf* caution
cauteloso *adj* wary
cautivar *v* charm
cautiverio *nm* captivity
cautivo *nm* captive
cauto *adj* cautious
cavar *v* dig
caverna *nf* cavern, cave
cavidad *nf* cavity
cavilar *v* ponder
caza *nf* hunting
cazador *nm* hunter
cazar *v* hunt
cazuela *nf* casserole
cebada *nf* barley
cebar *v* fatten
cebo *nm* bait
cebolla *nf* onion
cebra *nf* zebra
ceder *v* yield; give up
cedro *nm* cedar
cegar *v* blind

C

ceguedad *nf* blindness

ceguera *nf* blindness

ceja *nf* eyebrow

celda *nf* cell

celebración *nf* celebration

celebrar *v* celebrate

célebre *adj* famoso

celestial *adj* heavenly

celibato *nm* celibacy

célibe *adj* celibate

celos *nm* jealousy

celoso *adj* jealous

célula *nf* cell

celular *adj* cellular

celulitis *nf* cellulite

cementerio *nm* cemetery

cemento *nm* cement, mortar

cena *nf* supper

cenar *v* dine

cenicero *nm* ashtray

ceniza *nf* ash, cinder

censo *nm* census

censor *nm* censor

censura *nf* censorship

censurar *v* censure

centenario *adj* centennial

centeno *nm* rye

centígrado *adj* centigrade

céntimo *nm* cent

centímetro *nm* centimeter

centinela *nm* sentry

central *adj* central

centralizar *v* centralize

centrar *v* centre

centro *nm* center

ceñido *adj* tight

cepillar *v* brush

cepillo *nm* brush

cera *nf* wax

cerámica *nf* ceramic

cerca *pre* near, close

cerca (de) *adv* closely

cerca de *pre* close to

cercanías *nf* vicinity

cercano *adj* close, nearby

cercar *v* encircle

cerciorarse *v* make sure

cerco *nm* siege

cerdo *nm* pig, hog

cereal *nm* cereal

cerebral *adj* cerebral

cerebro *nm* brain

ceremonia *nf* ceremony

ceremonial *adj* ceremonial

cereza *nf* cherry

cerilla *nf* match

cernerse *v* hang over

cero *nm* zero

cerradura *nf* lock

cerrar *v* close, lock, shut

cerro *nm* hill

cerrojo *nm* bolt

certamen *nm* competition

certeza *nf* certainty

certificado *nm* certificate
certificar *v* certify
cervecería *nf* brewery
cerveza *nf* beer, ale
cesar *v* cease
cesión *nf* transfer
césped *nm* grass, lawn
cesta *nf* basket, hamper
chabacano *adj* vulgar
chabola *nf* shack
chacal *nm* jackal
chalado *adj* crazy
chaleco *nm* vest
chalet *nm* chalet
chamaca *nf* girl
champán *nm* champagne
champiñón *nm* mushroom
chamuscar *v* scorch
chantaje *nm* blackmail
chantajear *v* blackmail
chaparrón *nm* downpour
chapotear *v* splash
chapuza *nf* shoddy work
chaqueta *nf* coat
charca *nf* pond
charlar *v* chat, chatter
charlatán *nm* charlatan
chasco *nm* disapointment
chasquear *v* click
chasquido *nm* flick
chatarra *nf* scrap
chato *adj* flat

chaval *nm* kid
cheque *nm* check
chequeo *nm* check-up
chequera *nf* checkbook
chica *nf* girl
chícharo *nm* pea
chicle *nm* bubble gum
chiflar *v* hiss, boo
chillar *v* scream, yell
chillido *nm* scream
chimenea *nf* fireplace
chimpancé *nm* chimpanzee
chincheta *nf* thumbtack
chinchón *nm* bump
chipirón *nm* squid
chiquillo *nm* kid
chirriar *v* squeak
chisme *nm* gossip
chispa *nf* spark
chiste *nm* joke
chivo *nm* goat
chocante *adj* odd, startling
chocar *v* crash, collide
chocolate *nm* chocolate
chófer *nm* chauffeur
choque *nm* collision, crash
chorizo *nm* sausage
chorrada *nf* stupidity
chorrear *v* drip
choza *nf* hut
chuleta *nf* steak; chop
chupar *v* suck, soak up

C

chusma *nf* mob

cianuro *nm* cyanide

cicatriz *nf* scar

ciclista *nm* cyclist

ciclo *nm* cycle

ciclón *nm* cyclone

ciegas (a) *adv* blindly

ciego *adj* blind

cielo *nm* heaven

cien *adj* hundred

ciencia *nf* science

cieno *nm* mud

científico *adj* scientific

científico *nm* scientist

cierre *nm* closing, closure

cierto *adj* certain

ciervo *nm* deer

cifra *nf* number

cigarrillo *nm* cigarette

cigarro *nm* cigar

cigüeña *nf* stork

cilindro *nm* cylinder

cima *nf* top, peak

cimiento *nm* foundation

cincel *nm* chisel

cinco *adj* five

cincuenta *adj* fifty

cine *nm* cinema

cínico *adj* cynic

cinismo *nm* cynicism

cinta *nf* ribbon, tape

cintura *nf* waist

cinturón *nm* seat belt

ciprés *nm* cypress

circo *nm* circus

circuito *nm* circuit

circulación *nf* circulation

circular *v* circulate, flow

círculo *nm* circle

circuncidar *v* circumcise

circunspecto *adj* circumspect

circunstancial *adj* circunstancial

circunvalación *nf* bypass

cirio *nm* candle

ciruela *nf* plum, prune

cirujano *nm* surgeon

cisma *nm* schism

cisne *nm* swan

cisterna *nf* cistern

cita *nf* appointment

citar *v* quote

ciudad *nf* city, town

ciudad natal *nf* hometown

ciudadanía *nf* citizenship

ciudadano *nm* citizen

cívico *adj* civic

civilización *nf* civilization

civilizar *v* civilize

clan *nm* clan, group

clandestino *adj* clandestine

clara *nf* egg white

claraboya *nf* skylight

claridad *nf* clarity

clarificación *nf* clarification

clarificar *v* clarify
clarinete *nm* clarinet
clarividente *nm/f* clairvoyant
claro *adj* clear, plainly
clase *nf* class
clásico *adj* classic
clasificado *adj* classified
clasificar *v* classify
claustro *nm* cloister
cláusula *nf* clause
clausura *nf* closing
clausurar *v* close
clavar *v* nail down
clave *nf* code
clavel *nm* carnation
clavícula *nf* collarbone
clavo *nm* nail
clemencia *nf* clemency
clerical *adj* clerical
clérigo *nm* cleric
clero *nm* clergy
cliente *nm* customer
clientela *nf* clientele
clima *nm* climate
climático *adj* climatic
clínica *nf* clinic
cloaca *nf* sewer
clonacion *n* cloning
clonar *v* clone
cloroformo *nm* choroform
club *nm* club
coacción *nf* coercion

coaccionar *v* coerce
coagular *v* coagulate
coágulo *nm* clot
coalición *nf* coalition
cobarde *adj* coward
cobarde *nm* coward
cobardía *nf* cowardice
cobertura *nf* coverage
cobija *nf* blanket
cobijarse *v* take shelter
cobre *nm* copper
cocaína *nf* cocaine
cocer *v* bake
coche *nm* car, auto
cochino *nm* hog
cochino *adj* filthy, dirty
cocido *nf* stew
cociente *nm* quotient
cocina *nf* kitchen
cocinar *v* cook
cocinero *nm* cook
coco *nm* coconut
cocodrilo *nm* crocodile
cóctel *nm* cocktail
codearse *v* rub shoulders
codicia *nf* greed
codiciar *v* covet
código *nm* code
código postal *nm* zip code
codo *nm* elbow
codorniz *nf* quail
coeficiente *nm* coefficient

C

coetáneo *adj* contemporary
coexistir *v* coexist
cofre *nm* chest
coger *v* catch, grab
cohabitar *v* cohabit
coherente *adj* coherent
cohesión *nf* cohesion
cohete *nm* rocket
cohibido *adj* shy
cohibir *v* inhibit
coincidencia *nf* coincidence
coincidir *v* coincide
cojear *v* limp
cojín *nm* cushion
cojo *adj* lame, crippled
col *nf* cabbage
cola *nf* tail
colaboración *n* collaboration
colaborador *nm* collaborator
colaborar *v* collaborate
colador *nm* strainer
colapsar *v* paralize
colapso *nm* collapse
colar *v* strain
colateral *adj* collateral
colcha *nf* bedspread
colchón *nm* mattress
colección *nf* collection
coleccionista *n* collector
colectar *v* collect
colectivo *adj* collective
colega *nm* colleague

colegio *nm* college
cólera *nf* cholera
colesterol *nm* cholesterol
colgar *v* hang
cólico *nm* colic
coliflor *nf* cauliflower
colina *nf* hill
colindante *adj* adjoining
colisión *v* collision
collar *nm* necklace
colmena *nf* beehive
colmillo *nm* tooth, fang
colmo *nm* limit
colocar *v* put, place
colonia *nf* cologne; colony
colonial *adj* colonial
colonizar *v* colonize
colono *nm* settler
color *nm* color
colorear *v* color
colorido *adj* colorful
colosal *adj* colossal
columna *nf* column, pillar
columpiar *v* swing
columpio *nm* swing
coma *nf* coma; comma
comadrona *nf* midwife
comandante *nm* commander
comando *nm* commando
comarca *nf* area, region
combate *nm* combat
combatiente *nm* combatant

combatir _v_ combat
combinación _nf_ combination
combinar _v_ combine
combustible _nm_ fuel
combustión _nf_ combustion
comedia _nf_ comedy
comediante _nm_ comedian
comedor _nm_ dining room
comentar _v_ comment
comentario _nm_ remark
comer _v_ eat
comercial _adj_ commercial
comerciante _nm_ merchant
comerciar _v_ trade
comercio _nm_ trade
comestible _adj_ edible
comestibles _nm_ groceries
cometa _nm_ comet; kite
cometer _v_ commit
comezón _nm_ itching
comicios _nm_ elections
cómico _adj_ comical
comida _nf_ meal, food
comienzo _nm_ beginning
comisaría _nf_ police station
comisión _nf_ commission
comité _nm_ committee
como _adv_ as, how
como _pre_ like
comodidades _nf_ amenities
cómoda _n_ chest of drawers
cómodo _adj_ comfortable

compacto _adj_ compact
compadre _nm_ buddy
compaginar _v_ combine
compañerismo _nm_ fellowship
compañero _nm_ companion
compañía _nf_ company
comparable _adj_ comparable
comparación _nf_ comparison
comparar _v_ compare
comparativo _adj_ comparative
comparecer _v_ appear
compartir _v_ share
compás _nm_ compass; rhythm
compasión _nf_ compassion
compasivo _adj_ merciful
compatible _adj_ compatible
compatriota _nm_ countryman
compendio _nm_ summary
compensar _v_ compensate
competencia _nf_ competence
competente _adj_ competent
competidor _nm_ competitor
competir _v_ compete
competitivo _adj_ competitive
compilar _v_ compile
complacer _v_ please
complejidad _nf_ complexity
complejo _adj_ complex
complemento _nm_ complement
completar _v_ complete
completo _adj_ complete
complicación _nf_ complication

complicar _v_ complicate
cómplice _nm_ accomplice
complicidad _nf_ complicity
complot _nm_ plot
componente _nm_ component
componer _v_ compose
comportarse _v_ behave
composición _nf_ composition
compositor _nm_ composer
compostura _nf_ composure
compra _nf_ purchase
comprador _nm_ buyer
comprar _v_ buy, purchase
comprender _v_ understand
comprensión _nf_ understanding
compresión _nf_ compression
compresor _nm_ compressor
comprimir _v_ compress
comprobar _v_ check, test
compromiso _nm_ commitment
compuerta _nf_ floodgate
compulsión _nf_ compulsion
compulsivo _adj_ compulsive
computadora _nf_ computer
comulgar _v_ take communion
común _adj_ common
comunicar _v_ communicate
comunidad _nf_ community
comunión _nf_ communion
comunismo _nm_ communism
comunista _adj_ communist
comúnmente _adv_ commonly

con _pre_ with
con cautela _adv_ cautiously
con confianza _adv_ confidently
con esperanza _adv_ hopefully
con fiebre _adv_ feverish
con firmeza _adv_ sternly
con fluidez _adv_ fluently
con gusto _adv_ willingly
con razón _adv_ justly
con respecto a _adv_ regarding
con tal que _c_ providing that
concebir _v_ conceive
conceder _v_ accord, grant
concentración _nf_ concentration
concentrar _v_ concentrate
concepto _nm_ concept
concernir _v_ concern
concesión _nf_ concession
concha _nf_ shell
conciencia _nf_ conscience
concierto _nm_ concert
conciliación _nf_ conciliation
conciliar _v_ conciliate
conciso _adj_ concise
concluir _v_ conclude
conclusión _nf_ conclusion
concordia _nf_ harmony
concreto _adj_ concrete
concursante _nm_ contestant
concursar _v_ compete
concurso _nm_ competition
condado _nm_ county

conde *nm* count
condenar *v* condemn
condensación *nf* condensation
condensar *v* condense
condesa *nf* countess
condición *nf* condition
condicional *adj* conditional
condiciones *nf* terms
condimentar *v* flavor
condimento *nm* seasoning
condonar *v* condone
cóndor *nm* condor
conducente *adj* conducive
conducir *v* drive, lead
conducta *nf* behavior
conductor *nm* driver, conductor
conectar *v* connect
conejo *nm* rabbit
conexión *nf* connection
conferencia *nf* conference
conferir *v* confer
confesar *v* confess
confesión *nf* confession
confiado *adj* confident
confianza *nf* trust
confiar *v* trust, confide
confidencial *adj* confidential
configurar *v* configure
confines *nm* confines
confirmación *nf* confirmation
confirmar *v* confirm
confiscación *nf* confiscation

confiscar *v* confiscate
conflicto *nm* conflict
conformarse *v* conform
conformidad *nf* compliance
confortable *adj* comfortable
confrontar *v* confront
confundir *v* confuse
confusión *nf* confusion
confuso *adj* confusing
congelación *nf* freezing
congelador *nm* freezer
congelar *v* freeze
congeniar *v* get along
congestionar *v* congest
congestión *nf* congestion
congoja *nf* anguish
congregar *v* congregate
congreso *nm* congress
conjetura *nf* conjecture
conjugar *v* conjugate
conjunción *nf* conjunction
conjunto *nm* outfit; collection
conjunto (en) *adv* overall
conmigo *pro* with me
conmoción *nf* fuss
conmovedor *adj* moving
conmutar *v* commute
cono *nm* cone
conocer *v* know
conocido *nm* acquaintance
conocimiento *nm* knowledge
conpadecer *v* pity

conquista *nf* conquest
conquistador *nm* conqueror
conquistar *v* conquer
consagración *nf* consecration
consagrar *v* consecrate
consciente *adj* aware, mindful
consecuencia *nf* fallout
consecuente *adj* consistent
consecutivo *adj* consecutive
conseguir *v* attain, achieve
consejero *nm* counselor
consejo *nm* advice
consenso *nm* consensus
consentir *v* consent
conserje *nm* concierge
conservación *nf* conservation
conservador *adj* conservative
conservar *v* conserve
considerable *adj* sizable
considerar *v* consider
consistencia *nf* consistency
consistir *v* consist
consolar *v* console
consolidar *v* consolidate
consonante *nf* consonant
consorcio *nm* consortium
conspiración *nf* conspiracy
conspirar *v* conspire
constante *adj* constant
constar *v* consist
constatar *v* verify
consternación *nf* dismay

consternar *v* dismay
constiparse *v* get a cold
constitución *nf* constitution
constructor *nm* builder
construir *v* build
consuelo *nm* solace
consulado *nm* consulate
consulta *nf* consultation
consultar *v* consult
consumidor *nm* consumer
consumir *v* consume
consumo *nm* consumption
contabilidad *nf* bookkeeping
contable *nm* bookkeeper
contacto *nm* contact
contados *adj* few
contagioso *adj* contagious
contaminación *nf* contamination
contaminar *v* contaminate
contar *v* count
contar con *v* rely on
contemplar *v* contemplate
contemporáneo *adj* contemporary
contendiente *nm* contender
contenedor *nm* container
contener *v* contain
contenido *nm* contents
contentar *v* please
contento *adj* content, glad
contestar *v* reply
contexto *nm* context
contigo *pro* with you

contiguo *adj* adjoining
continental *adj* continental
continente *nm* continent
contingencia *nf* contingency
continuación *nf* sequel
continuar *v* continue
continuidad *nf* continuity
continuo *adj* ongoing
contorno *nm* outline
contra *pre* against
contrabandista *nm* smuggler
contrabando *nm* contraband
contracción *nf* contraction
contradecir *v* contradict
contrapeso *n* counterweight
contrario *adj* contrary
contrarrestar *v* counteract
contraseña *nf* password
contrastar *v* contrast
contraste *nm* contrast
contratiempo *nm* setback
contratista *n* contractor
contrato *nm* contract
contribuir *v* contribute
contrición *nf* contrition
contrincante *nm* opponent
control *nm* control
controversia *nf* controversy
contundente *adj* compelling
convalecencia *nf* convalescense
convalecer *v* convalesce
convaleciente *adj* convalecent

convencer *v* convince
convención *nf* convention
convencional *adj* coventional
conveniencia *nf* convenience
conveniente *adj* convenient
convenio *nm* agreement
convento *nm* convent
convergir *v* converge
conversación *nf* conversation
conversar *v* converse, talk
conversión *nf* conversion
converso *nm* convert
convertir *v* convert
convidar *v* invite
convincente *adj* convincing
convite *nm* banquet
convivir *v* live together
convocar *v* summon
convoy *nm* convoy
convulsión *nf* convulsion
conyugal *adj* conjugal
cónyuge *nm* spouse
coñac *nm* cognac
cooperación *n* cooperation
cooperar *v* cooperate
coordinación *nf* coordination
coordinador *nm* coordinator
coordinar *v* coordinate
copa *nf* cup
copia *nf* copy
copiadora *nf* copier
copiar *v* copy

C

C

copioso *adj* plentiful
coquetear *v* flirt
coraje *nm* courage
corazón *nm* heart
corbata *nf* necktie
corcho *nm* cork
cordero *nm* lamb
cordial *adj* cordial
cordón *nm* shoelace
cordura *nf* sanity
cornear *v* gore
corneta *nf* cornet
coro *nm* choir
corona *nf* crown, wreath
coronación *nf* coronation
coronel *nm* colonel
corporación *nf* corporation
corporal *adj* corporal
corpulento *adj* corpulent
corral *nm* farmyard
correa *nf* belt, strap
corrección *nf* correction
correctamente *adv* properly
correcto *adj* correct, right
corredor *nm* runner
corregir *v* correct
correo *nm* mail
correos *nm* post office
correr *v* run, race
corresponder *v* correspond
corresponsal *nm* journalist
corrida *nf* bullfight

corriente *adj* ordinary
corroborar *v* corroborate
corroer *v* corrode, eat up
corromper *v* corrupt
corrosión *nf* corrosion
corrupción *nf* corruption
cortada *nf* cut
cortar *v* cut, slice, chop
cortauñas *nf* nail clippers
corte *nf* cut, court
cortejar *v* court
cortés *adj* polite
cortesía *nf* courtesy
corteza *nf* crust, bark
cortina *nf* curtain, drape
corto *adj* short
cosa *nf* thing
cosecha *nf* crop
cosechar *v* reap, harvest
coser *v* sew, stitch
cosmético *adj* cosmetic
cósmico *adj* cosmic
cosmonauta *nm* cosmonaut
cosquilloso *adj* ticklish
costa *nf* coast
costado *nm* side
costar *v* cost
costear *v* pay for
costero *adj* coastal
costilla *nf* rib, sparerib
costo *nm* cost
costoso *adj* costly

costra *nf* crust
costumbre *nf* custom, habit
costura *nf* sewing
cotidiano *adj* daily
cotillear *v* gossip
cotorra *nf* parrot
cráneo *nm* skull
cráter *nm* crater
creación *nf* creation
creador *nm* creator
crear *v* create
creatividad *nf* creativity
creativo *adj* creative
crecer *v* grow
crecimiento *nm* growth
credibilidad *nf* credibility
crédito *nm* credit
credo *nm* creed
crédulo *adj* credulous
creencia *nf* belief
creer *v* believe
creíble *adj* believable
crema *nf* cream
cremallera *nf* zipper
crematorio *nm* crematorium
crepúsculo *nm* sunset, twilight
cresta *nf* crest, ridge
creyente *nm* believer
criada *nf* maid
criadero *nm* nursery
criar *iv* breed, rear
criatura *nf* creature

crimen *nm* crime
criminal *adj* criminal
cripta *nf* crypt
crisis *nf* crisis
cristal *nm* glass, crystal
cristalería *nf* glassware
Cristiandad *nf* Christianity
cristianizar *v* christianize
cristiano *adj* christian
criterio *nm* criterion
crítica *nf* critique
criticar *v* criticize
crítico *nm* critic
crítico *adj* critical
crónica *nf* chronicle
crónico *adj* chronic
cronología *nf* chronology
cruce *nm* junction
crucero *nm* cruise ship
crucial *adj* crucial
crucificar *v* crucify
crucifijo *nm* crucifix
crucifixión *nf* crucifixion
crucigrama *nm* crossword
crudo *adj* raw
cruel *adj* cruel, harsh
crueldad *nm* cruelty
crujido *nm* creak
crujiente *adj* crispy, crunchy
cruz *nf* cross
cruzada *nf* crusade
cruzado *nm* crusader

C

C

cruzar *v* cross
cuaderno *nm* notebook
cuadra *nf* stable; block
cuadrado *adj* square
cuadrilla *nf* group
cuadro *nm* picture
cuajarse *v* curdle
cualquier *adj* whichever
cualquier cosa *pro* everything
cualquiera *pro* anybody
cualquiera que *pro* whoever
cuando *adv* when
cuantioso *adj* substantial
cuarenta *adj* forty
cuaresma *nf* Lent
cuarta parte *nf* quarter
cuartel *nm* barracks
cuarto *adj* fourth
cuarto *nm* room
cuatro *adj* four
cuba *nf* barrel
Cuba *nf* Cuba
cubano *adj* Cuban
cubículo *nm* cubicle
cubierta *nf* cover; deck
cubiertos *nm* silverware
cúbico *adj* cubic
cubo *nm* bucket
cubrir *v* cover
cucaracha *nf* cockroach
cuchara *nf* spoon
cucharada *nf* spoonful

cucharita *nf* teaspoon
cuchichear *v* whisper
cuchilla *nf* blade, razor
cuchillo *nm* knife
cuello *nm* neck; collar
cuenta *nf* account, bill
cuento *nm* tale, story
cuerda *nf* rope, string
cuerdo *adj* sensible, sane
cuerno *nm* horn
cuero *nm* leather
cuerpo *nm* body
cuervo *nm* crow
cuesta *nf* slope
cuesta abajo *adv* downhill
cuesta arriba *adv* uphill
cuestión *nf* issue, matter
cuestionario *nm* questionnaire
cueva *nf* cave
cuidado *nm* care
cuidadoso *adj* careful
cuidar *v* care, look after
culata *nf* butt
culebra *nf* snake
culminante *adj* climatic
culminar *v* culminate
culpa *nf* blame, fault
culpabilidad *nf* guilt
culpable *adj* guilty
culpar *v* blame
cultivar *v* cultivate, grow
culto *nm* worship

culto *adj* literate, learned
cultura *nf* culture
cultural *adj* cultural
cumbre *nf* summit, apex
cumpleaños *nm* birthday
cumplido *nm* compliment
cumplir *v* comply, fulfil
cúmulo *nm* pile
cuna *nf* cradle, crib
cuña *nf* wedge
cuñado *n* brother-in-law
cuneta *nf* gutter
cuota *nf* dues, fee
cupón *nm* coupon
cúpula *nf* dome
cura *nm* priest; cure
curable *adj* curable
curación *nf* cure
curandero *nm* healer
curar *v* cure, heal
curiosidad *nf* curiosity
curioso *adj* curious
cursiva *adj* italics
curso *nm* course
curtir *v* harden
curva *nf* curve
cúspide *nf* peak, top
custodia *nf* custody
cutis *nm* complexion
cuyo *pro* whose

D

dadivoso *adj* generous
dado *nm* dice
daga *nf* dagger
dama *nf* lady
danés *adj* Dannish
danza *nf* dance
danzar *v* dance
dañar *v* harm, damage
dañino *adj* harmful
daño *nm* damage, harm
dar *v* give
dar cuerda *v* wind
dar forma *v* shape
dar la lata *v* nag
dar la vuelta *v* turn, flip
dar pasos *v* pace
dar patadas *v* kick
dar vueltas *v* spin
dar zancadas *v* stride
dardo *n* dart
darse cuenta *v* realize
darse prisa *v* hasten
datos *nm* data
de *pre* from, of
debajo *adv* below
debajo de *pre* under, beneath
debate *nm* debate
debatir *v* debate
deber *v* owe

C
D

deber *nm* duty
debídamente *adv* duly
debido *adj* due
débil *adj* feeble, weak
debilidad *nf* weakness
debilitar *v* weaken
década *nf* decade
decadencia *nf* decadence
decaer *v* decline
decapitar *v* behead
decencia *nf* decency
decente *adj* decent
decepcionante *adj* disappointing
decepcionar *v* disappoint
decidido *adj* determined
decidir *v* decide
decimal *adj* decimal
décimo *adj* tenth
decir *v* say, tell
decisión *nf* decision
decisivo *adj* decisive
declaración *nf* statement
declarar *v* declare
decline *v* decline
declive *nm* slope
decoración *nf* decor
decorar *v* decorate
decorativo *adj* decorative
decoro *n* dignity
decrecer *v* decrease
decrépito *adj* decrepit
decretar *v* decree, order

decreto *nm* decree
dedal *nm* thimble
dedicar *v* dedicate
dedicarse *v* devote
dedo *nm* finger
dedo del pie *nm* toe
deducción *nf* deduction
deducible *adj* deductible
deducir *v* deduce, infer
defección *nf* defection
defecto *nm* fault, flaw
defectuoso *adj* defective
defender *v* defend
defensa *nf* defense
defensor *nm* defender
deficiente *adj* deficient
definición *nf* definition
definir *v* define
definitivo *adj* definitive
deformación *nf* deformity
deformar *v* deform
deforme *adj* deformed
defraudar *v* defraud
defunción *nf* death
degeneracion *nf* degeneration
degenerar *v* degenerate
degollar *v* behead
degradacion *n* degradation
degradante *adj* demeaning
degradar *v* demote, degrade
degradarse *v* demean
degustar *v* taste

deidad *nf* deity
dejadez *nf* neglect
dejar *v* quit, leave
dejar atónito *v* stun
dejar atrás *v* outgrow
dejar caer *v* drop
dejar entrar *v* let in
dejar perplejo *v* mystify
dejar salir *v* let out
dejar sitio *v* move over
dejo *nm* accent
del norte *adj* northern
del occidente *adj* western
del oriente *adj* eastern
del sur *adj* southern
delantal *nm* apron
delante *adv* in front, ahead
delatar *v* betray, snitch
delegar *v* delegate
deleitar *v* delight
deletrear *v* spell
delfín *nm* dolphin
delgado *adj* slim, thin
deliberar *v* deliberate
delicadeza *nf* delicacy
delicado *adj* delicate
delicia *nf* delight
delicioso *adj* delicious
delincuencia *nf* delinquency
delincuente *nm* criminal
delineante *nm* draftsman
delirar *v* be delirious

delito *nm* ofensa
demacrado *adj* emaciated
demandante *nm* plaintiff
demanda *nf* claim, lawsuit
demandar *v* sue
demasiado *adj* too much
demencia *nf* insanity
demente *adj* insane
democracia *nf* democracy
democrático *adj* democratic
demoler *v* demolish
demolición *nf* demolition
demonio *nm* demon, devil
demora *nf* delay
demorar *v* delay, be late
demostración *nf* demonstration
demostrar *v* prove
demostrativo *adj* demonstrative
denegar *v* refuse
denigrar *v* denigrate
denominador *nm* denominator
denotar *v* indicate
densidad *nf* density
denso *adj* thick, dense
dental *adj* dental
dentista *nm* dentist
dentro *pre* inside, within
denuncia *nf* accusation
denunciar *v* denounce
deodorante *nm* deodorant
departamento *nm* department
dependencia *nf* dependence

depender v depend, hinge
dependiente nm sales clerk
deplorable adj deplorable
deplorar v deplore
deportar v deport
deporte nm sport
deportista adj sporty
deportista nm sportsman
depositar v put, place
depósito nm deposit
depravado adj deprave
depreciación nf depreciation
depreciar(se) v depreciate
depresión nf depression
deprimente adj depressing
deprimir v depress
deprisa adv quickly
depurar v purify, purge
derecho adj straight, honest
derecho nm right
derivado nm by-product
derivado adj derived
derivar v derive
derogar v repeal
derramar v spill, shed
derrame nm spilling; stroke
derribar v demolish; topple
derritir v melt
derrocar v overthrow
derrochar v squander
derroche nm waste
derrota nf defeat

derrotar v defeat
derrumbar v knock down
derrumbarse v collapse
desabrido adj tasteless
desabrochar v unfasten, untie
desacato nm disrespect
desacierto nm mistake
desacreditar v discredit
desactivar v defuse
desacuerdo nm disagreement
desafiante adj defiant
desafiar v defy, challenge
desafinado adj out of tune
desafío nm challenge
desagradable adj unpleasant
desagradar v dislike
desagradecido adj ungrateful
desagrado nm displeasure
desahogo nm relief
desahuciar v give up hope
desairar v snub
desaire nm rebuff, snub
desalentador adj descouraging
desalentar v discourage
desalojamiento nm ouster
desalojar v oust, vacate
desamparado adj destitute
desamparar v abandon
desangrarse v bleed
desanimar v discourage
desaparecer v disappear
desaparición nf disappearance

desapego *nm* indiference
desapercibido *adj* unnoticed
desaprobación *nf* disapproval
desaprobar *v* disapprove
desaprovechar *v* waste
desarmado *adj* unarmed
desarme *nm* disarmament
desarmar *v* disarm
desarraigar *v* uproot
desarrollar *v* develop
desarrollo *nm* development
desarticular *v* break up
desastre *nm* disaster
desastroso *adj* disastrous
desatar *v* unfasten, untie
desatascar *v* clear, unplug
desatender *v* neglect
desatento *adj* inattentive
desatornillar *v* unscrew
desaugarse *v* relieve
desaveniencia *nf* disagreement
desayunar *v* have breakfast
desayuno *nm* breakfast
desbarajuste *nm* mess
desbaratar *v* ruin
desbocado *adj* amok
desbordar *v* overflow
descabellado *adj* crazy
descalabro *nm* disaster
descalificar *v* disqualify
descalzo *adj* barefoot
descansado *adj* restful

descansar *v* relax, rest
descanso *nm* recess, rest
descapotable *adj* convertible
descarado *adj* insolent, rude
descarga *nf* unloading
descargar *v* unload
descaro *nm* nerve
descarrilar *v* derail
descartar *v* discard; rule out
descendencia *nf* offspring
descender *v* descend
descendiente *nm* descendant
descenso *nm* descent, drop
descifrar *v* decipher
descolgar *v* take down
descolorido *adj* faded
descomponerse *v* rot; break down
desconcertado *adj* lost
desconcertante *adj* puzzling
desconcertar *v* baffle
desconcierto *nm* uncertainty
desconectar *v* disconnect
desconfiado *adj* distrustful
desconfianza *nf* mistrust
desconfiar *v* distrust
descongelar *v* defrost, thaw
desconocido *adj* unknown
desconsolado *adj* distressed
descontar *v* deduct
descontento *adj* unhappy
descontinuar *v* discontinue

descortés *adj* impolite
descortesía *n* rudeness
descoser *v* unstitch
descremar *v* skim
describir *v* describe
descripción *nf* description
descuartizar *v* cut up
descubrimiento *nm* discovery
descubrir *v* discover
descuento *nm* discount
descuidado *adj* careless
descuidar *v* neglect
descuido *nm* neglect, mistake
desde *pre* from, since
desdecirse *v* retract, recant
desdén *nm* contempt
desdeñar *v* scorn, despise
desdicha *nf* misfortune
desdichado *adj* unhappy
desdoblar *v* unfold
deseable *adj* desirable
desear *v* wish, desire
desecar *v* dry up
desechable *adj* disposable
desechar *v* throw
desecrar *v* desecrate
desegregar *v* desegregate
desembarcar *v* disembark
desembolsar *v* disburse
desempacar *v* unpack
desempeñar *v* play; exercise
desempleado *adj* unemployed

desempleo *nm* unemployment
desencadenar *v* trigger
desencantado *adj* disenchanted
desenchufar *v* unplug
desengaño *nm* disappointment
desenlace *nm* outcome
desenmascarar *v* unmask
desenredar *v* untangle
desenroscar *v* unscrew
desenterrar *v* exhume
desenvoltura *nf* ease
desenvolver *v* unwrap
desenvuelto *adj* self-confident
deseo *nm* wish, longing
deseoso *adj* eager
desequilibrado *adj* unbalanced
desequilibrio *nm* imbalance
desertar *v* defect
desértico *adj* desert
desertor *nm* deserter
desesperar *v* despair
desesperado *adj* desperate
desfalco *nm* embezzlement
desfavorable *adj* unfavorable
desfigurar *v* disfigure
desfilar *v* parade
desfilaredo *nm* gorge
desfile *nm* parade
desgana *nf* lack of interest
desgarrar *v* tear up
desgastar *v* wear down
desgracia *nf* misfortune

desgraciado *adj* unlucky
desgracias *nf* woes
desgravar *v* deduct
deshacer *v* undo
deshacerse de *v* get rid
deshecho *adj* exhausted
desheredar *v* desinherit
deshidratar *v* dehydrate
deshielo *nm* thaw
deshonestidad *n* dishonesty
deshonesto *adj* dishonest
deshonra *nf* dishonor
deshora *adv* wrong time
desierto *nm* desert
designar *v* designate, name
designio *nm* plan
desigual *adj* unequal; uneven
desigualdad *nf* inequality
desilusión *nf* disillusion
disolusionar *v* disappoint
desinfectar *v* disinfect
desinflar *v* deflate
desintegrar *v* disintegrate
desinteresado *adj* desinterested
desistir *v* give up
desleal *adj* disloyal
deslealtad *n* disloyalty
desligar *v* separate
desliz *nm* lapse
deslizar *v* slip, slide
deslumbrante *adj* dazzling
deslumbrar *v* dazzle

desmadre *nm* chaos
desmantelar *v* dismantle
desmayarse *v* faint, pass out
desmembrar *v* dismember
desmenuzar *v* shred
desmontar *v* take apart
desmoralizar *v* demoralize
desmoronado *adj* dilapidated
desmoronarse *v* crumble
desnatar *v* skim
desnudarse *v* undress, strip
desnudez *nf* nudity
desnudo *adj* nude, naked
desnutrición *nf* malnutrition
desobedecer *v* disobey
desobediencia *nf* disobedience
desobediente *adj* disobedient
desocupado *adj* vacant, empty
desocupar *v* vacate
desolación *nf* desolation
desolador *adj* bleak
desorden *nm* disorder, mess
desorientado *adj* disoriented
despabilado *adj* alert
despacho *nm* office
despacio *adv* slowly
desparramar *v* scatter
despavorido *v* terrified
despedazar *v* tear apart
despedida *nf* farewell
despedir *v* dismiss
despegar *v* take off; peel off

despegue *nm* takeoff
despejado *adj* clear
despellejar *v* skin
despensa *nf* pantry
desperdiciar *v* waste
desperdicio *nm* waste
desperdigarse *v* scatter
desperezarse *v* stretch
despertador *nm* alarm clock
despertar *v* wake up
despertar *nm* awakening
despiadado *adj* ruthless
despido *nm* dismissal
despierto *adj* awake
despilfarrar *v* squander
despistado *adj* clueless; lost
despiste *nm* mistake
desplazar *v* displace
desplegar *v* deploy
despliegue *nm* deployment
despojar *v* deprive, rob
despojos *nm* spoils
desposar *v* marry
déspota *nm* despot
despreciable *adj* despicable
despreciar *v* despise
desprecio *nm* contempt
despreocupado *adj* carefree
desprevenido *adj* unprepared
desprovisto *adj* lacking in
después de *pre* after
después *adv* afterwards

desquiciado *adj* deranged
desquite *nm* revenge
destacar *v* stand
destapar *v* open
destartalado *adj* dilapidated
desteñirse *v* fade
desterrar *v* banish
destiempo (a) *adv* out of turn
destierro *nm* exile
destinar *v* assign
destinatario *nm* addressee
destino *nm* fate; destination
destituir *v* dismiss
destornillador *nm* screwdriver
destornillar *v* unscrew
destreza *nf* skill
destrozar *v* wreck
destrucción *nf* destruction
destructor *nm* destroyer
destruir *v* destroy
desuso (en) *adj* not in use
desvalido *adj* destitude
desvalijar *v* rob
desván *nm* attic
desvanecer *v* fade, vanish
desvelar *v* stay awake
desventaja *nf* disadvantage
desviación *nf* detour
desviar *v* divert, re-rout
desvío *nm* diversion
detallar *v* detail, itemize
detalle *nm* detail

D

detectar *v* detect
detective *nm* detective
detector *nm* detector
detención *nf* detention
detener *v* detain, arrest
detergente *nm* detergent
deteriorar *v* deteriorate
determinar *v* determine
detonar *v* detonate
detrás *adv* behind
detrás de *pre* behind
deuda *nf* debt
deudor *nm* debtor
devaluar *v* devalue
devastador *adj* devastating
devastar *v* devastate
devoción *nf* devotion
devolver *v* refund, repay
devorar *v* devour
devoto *adj* devout
día *nm* day
día de fiesta *nm* holiday
diabético *adj* diabetic
diablo *nm* devil
diácono *nm* deacon
diagnosticar *v* diagnose
diagnóstico *nm* diagnosis
diagonal *adj* diagonal
diagrama *nm* diagram
dialecto *nm* dialect
diálogo *nm* dialogue
diamante *nm* diamond

diámetro *nm* diameter
diariamente *adv* daily
diario *nm* diary
diarrea *nf* diarrhea
dibujar *v* draw
dibujo *nm* drawing
diccionario *nm* dictionary
dicho *nm* saying
diciembre *nm* December
dictador *nm* dictator
dictadura *nf* dictatorship
dictar *v* dictate
diecinueve *adj* nineteen
dieciocho *adj* eighteen
dieciséis *adj* sixteen
diecisiete *adj* seventeen
diente *nm* tooth
dientes *nm* teeth
diestro *adj* skillful
dieta *nf* diet
diez *adj* ten
diezmar *v* decimate
difamar *v* defame
diferencia *nf* difference
diferir *v* defer
difícil *adj* difficult
dificultad *nf* difficulty
dificultades *nf* trials
difundir *v* broadcast
difunto *adj* deceased, late
digerir *v* digest
digestión *nf* digestion

dígito *nm* digit

dignarse *v* deign

dignidad *nf* dignity

digno *adj* worthy

dilación *nf* delay

dilapidar *v* waste

dilatar *v* prolong

dilema *nf* dilemma

diligencia *nf* diligence

diluir *v* dilute

diluvio *nm* deluge, flood

dimensión *nf* dimension

dimitir *v* resign

Dinamarca *nf* Denmark

dinamita *nf* dynamite

dinastía *nf* dynasty

dineral *nm* fortune

dinero *nm* money

diócesis *nf* diocese

Dios *nm* God

diosa *nf* goddess

diploma *n* diploma

diplomacia *nf* diplomacy

diplomático *nm* diplomat

diputado *nm* deputy

dique *nm* dike

dirección *nf* address; direction

directo *adj* direct

director *nm* director

discernir *v* discern

disciplina *nf* discipline

discípulo *nm* disciple

disco *nm* disk, record

discordia *nf* discord

discreción *nf* discretion.

discrepancia *nf* discrepancy

discrepar *v* disagree

discreto *adj* discreet

discriminar *v* discriminate

disculpa *nf* apology

disculparse *v* apologize

discurso *nm* speech

discusión *nf* discussion

discutible *adj* debatable

discutir *v* argue, discuss

diseminar *v* spread

disentir *v* disagree

diseño *nm* design

disfigurar *v* deface

disfrazarse *v* disguise

disgustar *v* upset

disimular *v* pretend

disipar *v* dispel

dislocar *v* dislocate

dislocarse *v* sprain

disminuir *v* decrease

disolución *nf* dissolution

disolver *v* dissolve

disparar *v* shoot, fire

disparate *nm* nonsense

disparo *nm* shot

disparos *nm* gunfire

dispensar *v* dispense

dispersar *v* disperse

dispersión *nf* dispersal
disponer *v* dispose
disponible *adj* available
disposición *nf* disposal
disputa *nf* dispute
distancia *nf* distance
distante *adj* aloof, distant
distinguir *v* distinguish
distinto *adj* unlike, distinct
distorsión *nf* distortion
distorsionar *v* distort
distracción *nf* distraction
distraer *v* distract
distribución *nf* distribution
distribuidor *nm* supplier
distribuir *v* distribute
distrito *nm* district
disturbio *nm* disturbance
disuadir *v* dissuade
disyuntiva *nf* dilemma
divagar *v* ramble
diván *nm* couch
diversidad *nf* diversity
diversificar *v* diversify
diversión *nf* fun, pastime
diverso *adj* diverse
divertidísimo *adj* hilarious
divertido *adj* amusing
divertir *v* amuse
dividir *v* divide
divino *adj* divine
divisa *nf* currency

división *nf* division
divorciar *v* divorce
divorcio *nm* divorce
divorciado *nm* divorcee
divulgar *v* spread
dobladillo *nm* hem
doblado *adj* pleated
doblar *v* bend, fold
doble *adj* double
doblegar *v* break
doblez *nf* fold, deceit
doce *adj* twelve
docena *nf* dozen
dócil *adj* docile
doctor *nm* doctor
doctrina *nf* doctrine
documental *nm* documentary
documento *nm* document
dólar *nm* dollar
doler *v* hurt
dolor *nm* pain, ache
doloroso *adj* painful
domar *v* tame
domesticado *adj* tamed
domesticar *v* domesticate
doméstico *adj* domestic
dominar *v* dominate
domingo *nm* Sunday
dominio *nm* dominion
don *nm* gift
donante *nm* donor
donar *v* donate

donativo *nm* donation
doncella *nf* maid
donde *adv* where
dondequiera *adv* wherever
dorado *adj* golden
dormido *adj* asleep
dormir *v* sleep
dormitar *v* doze
dormitorio *nm* bedroom
dorso *nm* back
dos *adj* two
dos veces *adv* twice
dosis *nf* dosage
dotado *adj* gifted, talented
dotar *v* endow
dote *nf* dowry
dragón *nm* dragon
dramático *adj* dramatic
drástico *adj* drastic
drenaje *nm* drainage
droga *nf* drug, dope
drogarse *v* drug
ducha *nf* shower
duda *nf* doubt
dudar *v* doubt
dudoso *adl* doubtful
duelo *nm* duel; mourning
dueño *nm* owner
dulce *adj* sweet
dulces *nm* sweets
dulzura *nf* sweetness
duodécimo *adj* twelfth

duplicación *nf* duplication
duplicar *v* duplicate
duque *nm* duke
duquesa *nf* duchess
duración *nf* duration
duradero *adj* lasting
durante *pre* during
durar *v* last
durazno *nm* peach
duro *adj* hard, tough

ebrio *adj* drunk
echar *v* pour, throw
echar a correos *v* mail
echar abajo *v* bring down
echar siesta *v* take a nap
echarse *v* lie down
echarse atrás *v* back down
eclipsar *v* outshine
eclipse *nm* eclipse
eco *nm* echo
ecología *nf* ecology
economía *nf* economy
económico *adj* inexpensive
ecuación *nf* equation
ecuador *nm* equator

edad *nf* age
edificar *v* build
edificio *nm* building
editar *v* edit
editor *nm* publisher
editorial *nf* editorial
edredón *nm* comforter
educación *nf* education
educar *v* educate
educativo *adj* educational
efectuar *v* effect
eficacia *nf* efficiency
eficaz *adj* effective
efigie *nf* effigy
efusión *nf* outpouring
efusivo *adj* effusive
egoísmo *nm* selfishness
egoísta *adj* selfish
eje *nm* axis, axle
ejecutar *v* execute
ejecutivo *nm* executive
ejemplar *adj* exemplary
ejemplificar *v* exemplify
ejemplo *nm* example
ejercer *v* exert, practise
ejército *nm* army
ejote *nm* green bean
él *pro* he
él mismo *pro* himself
elaborar *v* brew, make
elástico *adj* elastic
elección *nf* choice, election

electricidad *nf* electricity
electricista *nm* electrician
eléctrico *adj* electric
electrocutar *v* electrocute
electrónico *adj* electronic
elefante *nm* elephant
elegancia *nf* elegance
elegante *adj* elegant
elegible *adj* eligible
elegir *v* elect, pick
elemental *adj* elemental
elemento *nm* element
elevador *nm* elevator
elevar *v* raise, lift
eliminar *v* eliminate
élite *nf* elite
ella *pro* she
ellos *pro* they
ellos mismos *pro* themselves
elocuencia *nf* eloquence
elocuente *adj* eloquent
elogiar *v* praise
elogio *nm* praise
eludir *v* avoid
emanar *v* emanate
emancipar *v* emancipate
embadurnar *v* smear
embajada *nf* embassy
embajador *nm* ambassador
embalar *v* pack
embalsamar *v* embalm
embalse *nm* dam, reservoir

embarazada *adj* pregnant
embarazo *nm* pregnancy
embarcar *v* embark
embargar *v* impound, seize
embargo *nm* seizure
embarrado *adj* muddy
embaucar *v* fool, trick
embelesar *v* captivate
embellecer *v* beautify
embestida *nf* charge
embestir *v* charge
embobar *v* fascinate
embolsarse *v* pocket
emborrachar *v* get drunk
emboscar *v* ambush
emboscada *nf* ambush
embotellar *v* bottle
embrague *nm* clutch
embriagar *v* intoxicate
embriaguez *nf* intoxication
embrión *nm* embryo
embrollar *v* confuse
embrollo *nm* tangle, mess
embrujar *v* bewitch
embrujo *v* spell
embrutecer *v* brutalize
embrutecido *adj* brutalized
embudo *nm* funnel
embustero *nm* liar
emergencia *nf* emergency
emerger *v* emerge
emigrante *nm* emigrant

emigrar *v* emigrate
emisario *nm* emissary
emisión *n* emission
emitir *v* emit
emisora *nf* radio station
emoción *nf* emotion, thrill
emocionante *adj* exciting
emocionar *v* thrill
emotivo *adj* emotional
empalmar *v* join, connect
empalme *nm* connection
empantanado *adj* bogged down
empapar *v* soak
empapelar *v* paper
empaquetar *v* pack
emparejar *v* pair; make even
empastar *v* fill
empaste *nm* filling
empatar *v* tie
empate *nm* draw, tie
empedernido *adj* entrenched
empedrado *adj* paved
empeñado *adj* in debt
empeño *nm* determination
empeñar *v* pawn
empeorar *v* get worse
emperador *nm* emperor
emperatriz *nf* empress
empezar *v* begin, start
empinado *adj* steep
empleado *nm* employee
emplear *v* employ

empleo *nm* employment

empobrecer *v* impoverish

empotrado *adj* built-in

emprender *v* undertake

empresa *nf* enterprise

empresario *nm* entrepreneur

empujar *v* push, shove

empujón *nm* push, shove

empuñadura *nf* hilt

en *at* in, at

en algún lugar *adv* somewhere

en alta voz *adv* aloud

en el futuro *adv* hereafter

en lugar de *adv* instead

en medio de *pre* amid, midst

en ningún lugar *adv* nowhere

en otra parte *adv* elsewhere

en un rato *adv* in a while

enamorado *adj* in love

enamorarse *v* fall in love

enano *nm* dwarf

enarbolar *v* raise

encabezar *v* lead

encadenar *v* chain

encajar *v* fit

encaje *nm* lace

encallar *v* run aground

encaminarse *v* head for

encandilar *v* dazzle

encantador *adj* charming

encantar *v* charm

encanto *nm* charm

encapotado *adj* cloudy

encapuchado *adj* hooded

encaramarse *v* climb

encararse *v* face up

encarcelar *v* imprison, jail

encargado *nm* attendant

encargar *v* order

encargarse *v* take care

encargo *nm* errand

encariñarse *v* grow fond

encarnar *v* embody

encarnizado *adj* fierce

encarrilar *v* guide, direct

encauzar *v* channel

encender *iv* light, turn on

encerar *v* wax

encerrar *adj* lock, shut

encharcado *adj* flooded

enchufar *v* plug, connect

enchufe *nm* plug

encía *nf* gum

enciclopedia *nf* encyclopedia

encima *adv* above, over

encima de *pre* on top of

encina *nf* oak tree

encinta *adj* pregnant

enclave *nm* enclave

encogerse *v* shrink; shrug

encomendar *v* entrust

enconado *adj* heated

enconarse *v* fester

encontrar *v* find

encontrarse *v* meet
encrucijada *nf* crossroads
encuadernar *v* bind
encuadrar *v* center, fit
encubrimiento *nm* coverup
encubrir *v* hide, conceal
encuentro *nm* encounter
encuerarse *v* get naked
encuesta *nf* poll, survey
ende *adv* therefore
endeble *adj* delicate, weak
endemoniado *adj* possessed
enderezar *v* straighten out
enderezarse *v* straighten up
endeudarse *v* get into debt
endorsar *v* endorse
endrogarse *v* get into debt
endulzar *v* sweeten
endurecer *v* harden
enemigo *nm* enemy, foe
enemistad *nf* feud
energía *nf* energy
enérgico *adj* forceful
enero *nm* January
enfadar *v* annoy
enfado *nm* anger
énfasis *nm* emphasis
enfermar *v* get sick
enfermedad *nf* illness
enfermera *nf* nurse
enfermería *nf* infirmary
enfermo *nm* sick, ill

enflaquecer *v* lose weight
enfocar *v* focus
enfoque *nm* approach
enfrentamiento *nm* confrontation
enfrentarse *v* confront
enfrente *adv* opposite
enfriar *v* chill, cool
enfurecer *v* enrage
engalanar *v* decorate
engañar *v* deceive, fool
enganchar *v* hook, connect
engaño *nm* deceit
engañoso *adj* deceitful
engatusar *v* deceive
engendrar *v* breed; beget
engordar *v* fatten
engorroso *adj* complicated
engrasar *v* lubricate
engrase *nm* lubrication
engreído *adj* conceited
engrudo *nm* paste
engullir *v* swallow
enhebrar *v* thread
enigma *nm* puzzle, mystery
enjabonar *v* soap
enjambre *nm* swarm
enjaular *v* put in a cage
enjuagar *v* rinse
enjugar *v* wipe away
enjuiciar *v* prosecute
enlace *nm* liaison, link
enlazar *v* link, connect

enlatado *adj* canned
enlistarse *v* enlist
enloquecer *v* go crazy
enlutado *adj* in mourning
enmarañado *adj* tangled
enmascarado *adj* masked
enmendar *v* amend, rectify
enmienda *nf* amendment
enmohecerse *v* go moldy
enmudecer *v* fall silent
enojarse *v* get angry
enojo *nm* anger
enorgullecer *v* make proud
enorme *adj* huge
enredarse *v* entangle
enredo *nm* mess, tangle
enrevesado *adj* complicated
enriquecer *v* enrich
enrojecer *v* redden; blush
enrolar *v* enlist
enrollar *v* roll up, wind
enroscar *v* wind
ensalada *nf* salad
ensalzar *v* praise
ensanchar *v* widen
ensayar *v* test, rehearse
ensayo *nm* rehearsal; essay
enseguida *adv* shortly
ensenada *nf* cove
enseñar *v* teach
ensordecer *v* deafen
ensuciar *v* soil, litter

ensuciarse *v* get dirty
ensueño *nm* dream
entablar *v* start
ente *nm* being
entender *v* understand
enterarse *v* find out
entereza *nf* fortitude
enternecer *v* move, touch
entero *adj* entire, whole
enterrar *v* bury
entibiar *v* warm up
entierro *nm* burial
entonar *v* sing
entonces *adv* then
entorno *nm* enviroment
entorpecer *v* hinder
entrada *nf* entrance; deposit
entrañable *adj* dear
entrañas *nf* bowels
entrante *adj* coming, next
entrar *v* enter, go in
entre *pre* among, between
entreabierto *adj* ajar
entrega *nf* delivery
entregar *v* deliver, hand over
entregarse *v* devote to
entrelazar *v* intertwine
entremezclar *v* mix
entrenador *nm* trainer
entrenamiento *nm* training
entrenar *v* coach, train
entretanto *adv* meanwhile

E

entretener *v* entertain
entretenido *adj* amused
entrevista *nf* interview
entristecer *v* sadden
entrometerse *v* meddle
entrometido *adj* nosy
entumecerse *v* go numb
entumecido *adj* numb
enturbiar *v* blur
entusiasmar *v* enthuse
entusiasmarse *v* get excited
entusiasmo *nm* enthusiasm
entusiasta *adj* enthusiastic
enumerar *v* enumerate, list
envasar *v* can, pack
envase *nm* container
envejecer *v* grow old
envenenar *v* poison
enviado *nm* envoy
enviar *v* send, dispatch
envidia *nf* envy, jealousy
envidioso *adj* envious, jealous
envío *nm* shipment
envoltura *nf* wrapping
envolver *v* wrap; engulf
enyesar *v* plaster
enzarzarse *v* get involved
epidemic *nf* epidemia
epilepsia *nf* epilepsy
episodio *nm* episode
epístola *nf* epistle
epitafio *nm* epitaph

época *nf* epoch, time
equilibrar *v* balance
equilibrio *nm* balance
equipaje *nm* luggage
equipar *v* equip
equiparar *v* equate
equipo *nm* equipment; team
equivalente *adj* equivalent
equivocación *nf* mistake
equivocado *adj* mistaken
equivocarse *v* be wrong
erguido *adj* erect
erigir *v* erect
ermita *nf* chapel
ermitaño *nm* hermit
erosión *nf* erosion
erradicar *v* eradicate
errata *nf* misprint
erróneo *adj* erróneous
error *nm* error, mistake
erudito *adj* learned
erupción *nf* eruption; rash
erutar *v* burp
esbelto *adj* slender
esbozar *v* sketch
esbozo *nm* outline
escabroso *adj* rough, rugged
escabullirse *v* slip away
escala *nf* scale, stop over
escalar *v* climb, scale
escaldar *v* scald
escalera *nf* ladder, stairs

escalofriante *adj* frightening
escalofrío *nm* shiver
escalón *nm* step
escama *nf* flake
escamar *v* make weary
escandalizar *v* scandalize
escándalo *nm* scandal
escandaloso *adj* shocking
escaño *nm* seat
escaparse *v* escape
escaparate *nm* store window
escapatoria *nf* loophole, way out
escape *nm* leakage
escarabajo *nm* beetle
escaramuza *nf* skirmish
escarbar *v* scratch
escarcha *nf* frost
escardar *v* weed
escarmiento *nm* lesson
escarnio *nm* ridicule
escarpado *adj* steep
escasear *v* be scarce
escasez *nf* shortage
escaso *adj* scarce
escatimar *v* be stingy, save
escena *nf* scene
escenario *nm* stage
escéntrico *adj* eccentric
escéptico *adj* skeptic
esclarecer *v* clarify
esclavitud *nf* slavery
esclavo *nm* slave

escoba *nf* broom
escocer *v* sting
escoger *v* choose
escollo *nm* obstacle
escolta *nf* escort
escombros *nm* debris, rubble
esconder *v* hide, conceal
escondite *nm* hideout
escopeta *nf* shotgun
escoria *nf* slag, dregs
escorpión *nm* scorpion
escozor *nm* burning
escribir *v* write
escritor *nm* writer
escritorio *nm* desk
escritura *nf* writing
escrúpulos *nm* scruples
escrupuloso *adj* scrupulous
escuchar *v* listen
escudo *nm* shield
escuela *nf* school
esculcar *v* search
escultor *nm* sculptor
escultura *nf* sculpture
escupir *v* spit
escurrir *v* drain, wring out
escusado *nm* bathroom
ese *adj* that
esencia *nf* essence
esfera *nf* sphere; dial
esfinge *nf* sphinx
esforzarse *v* endeavor

esfuerzo *nm* effort

esfumarse *v* disappear

esgrima *nf* fencing

eslabón *nm* link

esmalte *nm* enamel

esmerado *adj* neat

esmeralda *nf* emerald

esmero *nm* care

eso *pro* that

esófago *nm* esophagus

esos *adj* those

espabilado *adj* smart, bright

espacio *nm* space

espacioso *adj* spacious

espada *nf* sword

espalda *nf* back

espantar *v* scare

espantarse *v* get scared

espanto *n* fright

espantoso *adj* frightening

España *nf* Spain

español *adj* Spanish

español *nm* Spaniard

esparcir *v* scatter

espárrago *nm* asparagus

espasmo *nm* spasm

especia *nf* spice

especial *adj* special

especialidad *nf* specialty

especializarse *v* specialize

especie *nf* species; kind

especificar *v* specify

específico *adj* specific

espectáculo *nm* spectacle

espectador *nm* spectator

especular *v* speculate

espejismo *nm* mirage

espejo *nm* mirror

espeluznante *adj* horrific

esperanza *nf* hope

esperar *v* wait, expect

espesar *v* thicken

espeso *adj* thick

espesor *nm* thickness

espía *nm* spy

espiar *v* spy

espiga *nf* ear

espina *nf* thorn

espina dorsal *nm* spine

espinazo *nm* backbone

espinilla *nf* shin; pimple

espinoso *adj* thorny

espionaje *nm* spying

espíritu *nm* spirit

espiritual *adj* spiritual

espléndido *adj* splendid

esplendor *nm* splendor

esponja *nf* sponge

espontaneidad *nf* spontaneity

espontáneo *adj* spontaneous

esporádico *adj* sporadic

esposa *nf* wife

esposas *nf* handcuffs

esposo *nm* husband

esprint *nm* sprint
espuela *nf* spur
espuma *nf* foam; lather
espumoso *adj* sparkling
esqueleto *nm* skeleton
esquema *nf* plan, sketch
esquiar *v* ski
esquilar *v* shear
esquina *nf* corner
esquivar *v* dodge, shun
esta *adj* this
estabilidad *nf* stability
estable *adj* stable
establecer *v* establish
establecerse *v* settle down
establo *nm* stable
estación *nf* season; station
estadio *nm* stadium
estadística *nf* statistic
estado *nm* state; condition
estafa *nf* swindle
estafador *nm* swindler
estafar *v* cheat, swindle
estallar *v* explode
estallido *nm* explosion
estampido *nm* stampede
estampilla *nf* stamp
estancamiento *nm* stagnation
estancarse *v* stagnate
estancia *nf* stay
estandarizar *v* standardize
estandarte *nm* banner

estaño *nm* tin
estanque *nm* pond
estante *nm* shelf
estantería *nf* bookcase
estantes *nm* shelves
estar *v* be
estar de pie *v* stand
estatua *nf* statue
estatuto *nm* statute
este *nm* east
este *adj* this
éste *pro* this one
estela *nf* trail
estera *nf* mat
estéril *adj* barren; sterile
esterilizar *v* sterilize
esternón *nm* breast bone
estética *nf* aesthetics
estético *adj* aesthetic
estiércol *nm* dung, manure
estilo *nm* style
estilográfica *nf* fountain pen
estima *nf* esteem
estimar *v* value, respect
estimulante *adj* stimulating
estimular *v* stimulate
estímulo *nm* incentive
estirar *v* stretch
estirón *nm* pull
estival *adj* summer
esto *pro* this
estofado *nm* stew

estoico *adj* stoic

estómago *nm* stomach

estorbar *v* bother, hinder

estornudar *v* sneeze

estos *adj* these

éstos *pro* these ones

estrafalario *adj* eccentric

estragos *nm* havoc

estrañarse *v* be surprised

estrangular *v* strangle

estrategia *nf* strategy

estrato *nm* layer

estrecho *adj* narrow

estrecho *nm* strait

estrecharse *v* become narrow

estrechez *v* tighness

estrecheces *nf* difficulties

estrella *nf* star

estrellarse *v* smash, crash

estremecer *v* shake

estremecerse *v* shake; shudder

estreñido *adj* constipated

estreñimiento *nm* constipation

estrépito *nm* big noise

estrés *nm* stress

estresante *adj* stressful

estribar *v* lie in

estricto *adj* strict

estropear *v* spoil, damage

estructura *nf* structure

estruendo *nm* roar

estrujar *v* squeeze

estuario *nm* estuary

estuche *nm* box

estudiante *nm* student

estudiar *v* study

estudio *nm* study

estufa *nf* stove

estupendo *adj* wonderful

estupidez *nf* stupidity

estúpido *adj* stupid

eternidad *nf* eternity

eterno *adj* eternal

ética *nf* ethics

etiqueta *nf* label, tag

étnico *adj* ethnic

euforia *nf* euphoria

eufórico *adj* elated

Europa *nf* Europe

europeo *adj* European

eutanasia *nf* euthanasia

evacuar *v* evacuate

evadir *v* evade, avoid

evaluación *nf* assessment

evaluar *v* evaluate, assess

evangelio *nm* gospel

evaporar *v* evaporate

evasión *nf* evasion

evasivo *adj* evasive

evento *nm* event

eventual *adj* possible

eventualidad *nf* eventuality

evidencia *nf* evidence

evidente *adj* obvious

evitable *adj* avoidable
evitar *v* avoid
evocar *v* evoke
evolución *nf* evolution
evolucionar *v* evolve
exactitud *nf* accuracy
exacto *adj* exact
exagerar *v* exaggerate
exaltar *v* exalt
exámen *nm* examination
examinar *v* examine
excavar *v* excavate
excedente *nm* surplus
exceder *v* exceed
excederse *v* overdo
excelencia *nf* excellence
excelente *adj* excellent
excepción *nf* exception
excepcional *adj* exceptional
excepto *pro* except
excesivo *adj* excessive
exceso *nm* excess
excitación *nf* excitement
excitar *v* excite, arouse
exclamar *v* exclaim
excluir *v* exclude
exclusivo *adj* exclusive
exculpar *v* exonerate
excursión *nf* excursion
excusa *nf* excuse
excusar *v* excuse
exento *adj* exempt

exhaustivo *adj* thorough
exhausto *adj* exhausted
exhibir *v* display, show
exhortar *v* exhort
exigente *adj* demanding
exigir *v* demand
eximir *v* exempt
existencia *nf* existence
existir *v* exist
éxito *nm* success, hit
exitoso *adj* successful
éxodo *nm* exodus
exorbitante *adj* exorbitant
exorcista *nm* exorcist
exótico *adj* exotic
expansión *nf* expansion
expectativa *nf* anticipation
expedición *nf* expedition
expediente *nm* dossier, file
expedir *v* issue
experiencia *nf* experience
experimento *nm* experiment
experto *adj* expert
expiación *nf* atonement
expiar *v* atone
expiración *nf* expiration
expirar *v* expire
expléndido *adj* explendid
explicar *v* explain
explícito *adj* explicit
explorador *nm* explorer
explorar *v* explore

**E
F**

explosión *nf* explosion
explosivo *adj* explosive
explotación *nf* explotation
explotar *v* exploit
exponer *v* expose; display
exportar *v* export
exposición *nf* exhibition
expresamente *adv* expressly
expresar *v* express
expresión *nf* expression
expreso *adj* express
exprimir *v* wring, squeeze
expropiar *v* expropriate
expulsar *v* expel, eject
expulsión *nf* expulsion
exquisito *adj* exquisite
éxtasis *nm* ecstasy
extático *adj* ecstatic
extender *v* extend, spread
extendido *adj* widespread
extensión *nf* extension
extenso *adj* vast
extenuar *v* weaken
exterior *adj* exterior, outer
exterminar *v* exterminate
externo *adj* external
extinción *nf* extinction
extinguido *adj* extinct
extinguir *v* extinguish
extirpar *v* remove
extorsión *nf* extortion
extracto *nm* excerpt

extradición *nf* extradition
extraer *v* extract, remove
extrañar *v* miss
extranjero *adj* foreign
extranjero *nm* foreigner
extraño *nm* stranger
extraño *adj* odd, strange
extravagante *adj* extravagant
extraviar *v* misplace
extraviarse *v* get lost
extremidades *nf* extremities
extremista *adj* extremist
extremo *adj* extreme
extrovertido *adj* outgoing

fábrica *nf* factory
fabricar *v* manufacture
fábula *nf* fable
fabuloso *adj* fabulous
faceta *nf* facet
facha *nf* look
fachada *nf* front
fácil *adj* easy
facilidad *nf* ease
facilitar *v* facilitate
fácilmente *adv* easily

factible *adj* feasible
factor *nf* factor
factura *nf* invoice
facultad *nf* faculty
facultar *v* authorize
faena *nf* work
faisán *nm* pheasant
faja *nf* sash; stretch
fajo *nm* bundle
falda *nf* skirt
fallar *v* backfire; falter
falla *nf* defect; mistake
fallecer *v* die, pass away
fallo *nm* verdict
falsear *v* falsify
falsedad *nf* falseness, lie
falsificación *nf* forgery
falsificar *v* forge, falsify
falso *adj* fake; untrue
falta *nf* lack; fault
faltar *v* be missing
fama *nf* fame
familia *nf* family
familiar *adj* familiar
familiares *nm* folks
famoso *adj* famous
fanático *adj* fanatic
fanfarronear *v* boast
fango *nm* mud
fantasía *nf* fantasy
fantasma *nm* ghost
fantástico *adj* fantastic

fardo *nm* bundle, bale
faringe *nf* pharinx
farmacéutico *nm* pharmacist
farmacia *nf* pharmacy
fármaco *nm* drug
faro *nm* lighthouse
farol *nm* streetlamp
farsa *nf* farce
fascinante *adj* intriguing
fascinar *v* fascinate
fase *nf* phase
fastidiar *v* bother, annoy
fastidio *nm* annoyance
fastidioso *adj* annoying
fastuoso *adj* lavish
fatal *adj* fatal
fatídico *adj* fateful
fatiga *nf* fatigue
fatigarse *v* get tired
fauna *nf* wildlife
favor *nm* favor
favorable *adj* favorable
favorito *adj* favorite
fe *nf* faith
fealdad *nf* ugliness
febrero *nm* February
fecha *nf* date
fecha tope *nf* deadline
fechado *adj* dated
fechoría *nf* misdeed
fecundo *adj* fertile
federal *adj* federal

F

felicidad *nf* happiness
felicitar *v* congratulate
feligrés *nm* parishioner
feliz *adj* happy
felonía *nf* felony
femenino *adj* feminine
fenómeno *nm* phenomenon
feo *adj* ugly
féretro *nm* coffin
feria *nf* fair
fermentar *v* ferment
ferocidad *nf* ferocity
feroz *adj* fierce
ferretería *nf* hardware
ferrocarril *nm* railroad
fértil *adj* fertile
fertilidad *nf* fertility
fertilizar *v* fertilize
ferviente *adj* fervent, pious
festejar *v* celebrate
festín *nm* banquet
festividad *nf* festivity
feto *nm* fetus
fiable *adj* reliable
fianza *nf* bail, bond
fiarse *v* trust
fiasco *nm* failure
fibra *nf* fiber
ficción *nf* fiction
ficha *nf* chip, token
fichero *nm* filing draw
ficticio *adj* fictitious

fidelidad *nf* fidelity
fideos *nm* noodles
fiebre *nf* fever
fiel *adj* faithful
fiera *nf* beast
fiero *adj* fierce
fiesta *nf* feast
figura *nf* figure, shape
figurarse *v* imagine
fijar *v* fix
fijarse *v* notice
fila *nf* row
filete *nm* steak, fillet
filo *nm* edge
filosofía *nf* philosophy
filósofo *nm* philosopher
filtro *nm* filter
fin *nm* end, purpose
final *adj* final
final *nm* ending
finalizar *v* finalize
financiar *v* finance, fund
finca *nf* estate, manor
fincar *v* build
fingir *v* feign, pretend
Finlandia *n* Finland
finlandés *adj* Finnish
fino *adj* fine; polite
fiordo *nm* fjord
firma *nf* signature; firm
firmamento *nm* sky
firmar *v* sign

firme *adj* firm, steady
firmeza *nf* firmness, strength
fiscal *nm* prosecutor
física *nf* physics
físico *adj* physical
fisura *nf* crack
flaco *adj* lean, skinny
flagelar *v* whip, scourge
flanquear *v* flank
flaqueza *nf* weakness
flauta *nf* flute
flecha *nf* arrow
flexible *adj* flexible
flirtear *v* flirt
flojedad *v* laziness; weakness
flojo *adj* loose; weak
flor *nf* flower
floreado *adj* floral
florecer *v* bloom, blosom
florero *nm* vase
flota *nf* fleet
flotar *v* float, hover
fluctuar *v* fluctuate
fluidez *nf* fluency; fluidity
fluído *nf* fluid; fluent
fluir *v* flow
flujo *nm* flow
fobia *nf* phobia
foca *nf* seal
foco *nm* focus; bulb
fogata *nf* bonfire
folleto *nm* brochure

follón *v* mess, fuss
fomentar *v* promote
fonda *nf* inn
fondo (a) *adv* in depth
fondo *nm* bottom; fund
fondos *nm* funds
fontanería *nf* plumbing
fontanero *nm* plumber
forastero *nm* outsider
forcejear *v* struggle
forjar *v* forge
forma *nf* form, shape
formación *nf* formation
formal *adj* formal
formalidad *nf* technicality
formalizar *v* formalize
formar *v* form
formato *nm* format
formidable *adj* awesome
fórmula *nf* formula
fornido *adj* very strong
forrar *v* line, cover
forro *nm* lining; cover
fortaleza *nf* fortress; strengh
fortificar *v* fortify
fortuna *nf* fortune
forzar *v* force, compel
fosa *nf* grave
fósforo *nm* match
fósil *nm* fossil
foso *nm* ditch
fotocopia *nf* photocopy

F.

fotografía *nf* photo
fotógrafo *nm* photographer
fracasar *v* fall through, fail
fracaso *nf* failure, flop
fracción *nf* fraction
fractura *nf* fracture
fracturar *v* fracture, break
fragancia *nf* fragrance
fragata *nf* frigate
frágil *adj* fragile
fragilidad *nf* frailty, weakness
fragmento *nm* fragment
fragua *nf* forge
fraile *nm* friar, monk
francés *adj* French
Francia *nf* France
franco *adj* blunt, frank
francotirador *nm* sniper
franqueza *nf* candor
franquicia *nf* franchise
frasco *nm* flask, jar
frase *nf* phrase, sentence
fraternal *adj* fraternal
fraternidad *nf* fraternity
fraude *nm* fraud
fraudulento *adj* fraudulent
frecuencia *nf* frequency
frecuente *adj* frequent
fregadero *nm* sink
fregar *v* wash, mop
freído *adj* fried
freír *v* fry

frenar *v* rein, curb
frenesí *nm* frenzy
frenético *adj* frenetic
freno *nm* brake
frente *nf* forehead
frente *nm* front
frente (de) *adv* head on
fresa *nf* strawberry
fresco *adj* cool, fresh
frescura *nf* freshness
frialdad *nf* coldness
fríamente *adv* coldly
fricción *nf* friction
frígido *adj* frigid
frijol *nm* bean
frío *nm* cold, chill
frío *adj* chilly, cold
frito *adj* fried
frivolidad *nf* frivolity
frívolo *adj* frivolous
frontera *nf* border, frontier
frotar *v* rub
frugal *adj* frugal
frugalidad *nf* frugality
fruncir *v* frown
frustrar *v* frustrate; foil
fruta *nf* fruit
fruto *nm* result
fuego *nm* fire
fuente *nf* fountain, font
fuera *adv* outside
fuerte *nm* fort

fuerte *adj* loud, strong
fuerza *nf* strength, force
fuga *nf* flight; leak
fugarse *v* escape
fugaz *adj* fleeting
fugitivo *nm* fugitive
fumador *nm* smoker
fumar *v* smoke
fumigar *v* fumigate
función *nf* function
funcionar *v* run, operate
funda *nf* pillowcase
fundación *nf* foundation
fundador *nm* founder
fundamental *adj* fundamental
fundamentos *nm* basics
fundar *v* found
fundir *v* melt; merge
funeral *nm* funeral
funeraria *nf* mortuary
funesto *adj* disastrous
furgoneta *nf* van, pick up
furia *nf* fury
furioso *adj* furious, mad
furor *nm* furor
fusible *nm* fuse
fusil *nm* rifle
fusilar *v* shoot
fusión *nf* fusion
fútbol *nm* football
futuro *adj* future

gabardina *nf* raincoat
gabinete *nm* office
gafas *nf* eyeglasses
galardón *nm* award
galacia *nf* galaxy
galería *nf* gallery
galgo *nm* greyhound
gallardía *nf* bravery
gallardo *adj* dashing
galleta *nf* biscuit, cookie
gallina *nf* hen
gallo *nm* rooster
galón *nm* gallon
galopar *v* gallop
gama *nf* range
gamba *nf* prawn
gamberro *nm* hooligan, thug
gana *nf* desire
ganado *nm* livestock, cattle
ganador *nm* winner
ganancia *nf* gain, profit
ganancias *nf* proceeds
ganar *v* earn, gain, win
gancho *nm* hook
ganga *nf* bargain
gangrena *nf* gangrene
gangster *nm* gangster
ganso *nm* goose
garaje *nm* garage

garantía *nf* guaranty

garantizar *v* guarantee

garbanzo *nm* chikpea

garbo *nm* grace

garganta *nf* throat

garra *nf* claw

garrote *nm* club, stick

gas *nm* gas

gasa *nf* gauze

gasolina *nf* gas

gastar *iv* spend

gasto *nm* expense

gastos *nm* expenditure

gástrico *adj* gastric

gatillo *nm* trigger

gatito *nm* kitten

gato *nm* cat

gaviota *nf* seagull

gaznate *nm* throat

géiser *nm* geyser

gelatina *nf* gelatin

gemelo *nm* cuff link; twin

gemido *nm* groan, moan

gemir *v* whine, moan

gen *nm* gene

genealogía *nf* genealogy

generación *nf* generation

generador *nm* generator

general *nm* general

general *adj* overall, general

general (en) *adv* generally

generalizar *v* generalize

generar *v* generate

genérico *adj* generic

género *nm* gender

generosidad *nf* generosity

genético *adj* genetic

genio *nm* genius

genocidio *nm* genocide

gente *nf* people

gentil *adj* charming

genuino *adj* genuine, real

geografía *nf* geography

geología *nf* geology

geometría *nf* geometry

gentileza *nf* cuurtesy

gentío *nm* crowd

geranio *nm* geranium

gerente *nm* manager

germen *nm* germ

gerundio *nm* gerund

gestación *nf* gestation

gestiones *v* procedure

gestionar *v* take care

gigante *nm* giant

gimnasia *nf* gymnastics

gimnasio *nm* gymnasium

ginebra *nf* gin

ginecología *nf* gynecology

generoso *adj* generous

genial *adj* bright

gesto *nm* gesture

gira *nf* tour, turn

girafa *nf* giraffe

girar *v* rotate, turn
giro *nm* money order; turn
gitano *nm* gypsy
glaciar *nm* glacier
gladiador *nm* gladiator
glándula *nf* gland
globo *nm* balloon; globe
glóbulo *nm* globule
gloria *nf* glory
glorificar *v* glorify
glorioso *adj* glorious
glotón *nm* glutton
glucosa *nf* glucose
gobernador *n* governor
gobernar *v* govern, rule
gobierno *nm* government
goce *nm* enjoyment
gol *nm* goal
golf *nm* golf
golfista *nm* golfer
golfo *nm* gulf
golosina *nf* candy
golpe *nm* blow; coup
golpeado *adj* beaten
golpear *v* hit, punch, beat
golpecito *nm* tap
goma *nf* eraser; glue
gordo *adj* obese, fat
gorila *nm* gorilla
gorra *nf* cap
gorrión *nm* sparrow
gota *nf* drop; gout

gotear *v* drip, leak
gotera *nf* leak
gozar *v* enjoy
gozo *nm* joy
grabado *nm* engraving
grabadora *nf* recorder
grabar *v* engrave, record
gracias *nf* thanks
gracioso *adj* cute, funny
grada *nf* step, row
grado *nm* degree
gradual *adj* gradual
graduarse *v* graduate
gráfico *adj* graphic
gramática *nf* grammar
gramo *nm* gram
granada *nf* hand grenade
grande *adj* big, large
grandeza *nf* greatness
grandioso *adj* grandiose
granero *nm* barn, granary
granito *nm* granite
granizar *v* hail
granizo *nm* hail
granja *nf* farm
granjearse *v* earn, win
grano *nm* grain; pimple
granuja *nm* rascal
grapa *nf* staple
grapadora *nf* stapler
grapar *v* staple
grasa *nf* fat, grease

G

grasiento *adj* greasy, oily
grasoso *adj* fatty, greasy
gratificación *nf* reward
gratificar *v* gratify
gratis *adv* free
gratitud *nf* gratitude
grato *adj* pleasant
gratuito *adj* free
gravar *v* tax
grave *adj* serious
gravedad *nf* seriousness
gravitar *v* gravitate
Grecia *nf* Greece
gremio *nm* guild
griego *adj* Greek
grieta *nf* crack, crevise
grifo *nm* faucet
grillo *nm* cricket
grillos *nm* shackles
gripe *nf* influenza, flu
gris *adj* gray
gritar *v* cry out, shout
griterío *nm* shouting
grosería *nf* rudness
grosero *adj* crass, gross
grosor *nm* thickness
grotesco *adj* grotesque
grúa *nf* crane
grueso *adj* thick
gruñir *v* growl; grumble
grupo *nm* group
gruta *nf* grotto

guajolote *nm* turkey
guantazo *nm* slap
guante *nm* glove
guapo *adj* handsome
guardameta *nm* goalkeeper
guardar *v* keep
guardería *nf* nursery
guardia *nm* policeman
guardián *nm* guardian
guarida *nf* den
guarnición *nf* garrison
guarro *adj* sucio
guasa *nf* joke
guerra *nf* war
guerrero *nm* warrior
guerrillero *nm* guerrilla
guía *nm* guide
guiar *v* guide, lead
guijarro *nm* pebble
guillotina *nf* guillotine
guinda *nf* cherry
guiñar *v* wink at
guiño *nm* wink
guión *nm* hyphen; script
guirnalda *nf* garland
guisado *nm* stew
guisante *nm* pea
guisar *v* cook
guitarra *nf* guitar
gusano *nm* worm
gustar *v* taste; like
gusto *nm* flavor, taste

hábil *adj* capable, skilful
habilidad *nf* ability, skill
hábilmente *adv* ably
habitable *adj* habitable
habitación *nf* room
habitante *nm* inhabitant
habitar *v* dwell, inhabit
hábito *nm* habit, custom
hablador *adj* talkative
hablar *v* speak, talk
hacer *v* do, make
hacer añicos *v* shatter
hacer campaña *v* campaign
hacer caso *v* heed
hacer cola *v* line up
hacer cosquillas *v* tickle
hacer cumplir *v* enforce
hacer ejercicios *v* exercise
hacer énfasis *v* emphasize
hacer frente *v* cope
hacer garabatos *v* scribble
hacer gárgaras *v* gargle
hacer gestos *v* gesticulate
hacer reverencia *v* bow
hacer señas *v* beckon
hacer una oferta *iv* bid
hacerse *v* become
hacerse amigo *v* befriend
hacha *nm* ax, hatchet

hacia *pre* towards
hacia adelante *adv* onwards
hacia arriba *adv* upwards
hacia atrás *adv* backwards
hacia dentro *adv* inwards
hacia el este *adv* eastbound
hacia el norte *adv* northbound
hacia el oeste *adv* westbound
hacia el sur *adv* southbound
hacienda *nf* ranch, estate
halagar *v* flatter
halago *nm* flattery
halcón *nm* hawk
halucinar *v* hallucinate
hamaca *nf* hammock
hambre *nm* hunger, famine
hambriento *adj* hungry
hamburguesa *nf* hamburger
harapiento *adj* ragged
harapo *nm* rag
harén *nm* harem
harina *nf* flour
harto *adj* fed up; full
hasta *adv* till, until
hastiado *adj* fed up; full
hastío *nm* weariness
haz *nm* bundle
hazaña *nf* accomplishment
hebilla *nf* buckle
hebra *nf* thread
hechicería *nf* sorcery
hechicero *nm* sorcerer

hechizar *v* bewitch
hechizo *nm* spell
hecho *nm* deed; fact
heder *v* stink
hediondo *adj* stinking
hedor *nm* stench, stink
helada *nf* frost
helado *adj* frozen
helado *nm* ice cream
helar *v* freeze
helecho *nm* fern
helicóptero *nm* helicopter
hembra *nf* female
hemisferio *nm* hemisphere
hemorragia *nf* hemorrhage
hendidura *nf* crack
heno *nm* hay
heraldo *nm* herald
heredar *v* inherit
heredera *nf* heiress
heredero *nm* heir
hereditario *adj* hereditary
herejía *nf* heresy
herencia *nf* inheritance
herético *adj* heretic
herida *nf* injury, wound
herido *adj* wounded
herir *v* injure, wound
hermana *nf* sister
hermanastra *nf* stepsister
hermanastro *nm* stepbrother
hermandad *nf* brotherhood

hermano *nm* brother
hermanos *nm* brethren
hermético *adj* airtight
hermoso *adj* beautiful
hermosura *nf* beauty
hernia *nf* hernia
héroe *nm* hero
heróico *adj* heroic
heroína *nf* heroine; heroin
heroísmo *nm* heroism
herradura *nf* horseshoe
herramienta *nf* tool
herrero *nm* blacksmith
herrumbre *nf* rust
hervir *v* boil, simmer
hevilla *nf* buckle
hez *nf* dregs
hidratar *v* moisturise
hidráulico *adj* hydraulic
hidrógeno *nm* hydrogen
hiedra *nf* ivy
hiel *nf* gall, bile
hielo *nm* ice
hiena *nf* hyena
hierba *nf* grass, herb
hierro *nm* iron
hígado *nm* liver
higiene *nf* hygiene
higiénico *adj* hygienic
higo *nm* fig
hija *nf* daughter
hijastra *nf* stepdaughter

hijastro *nm* stepson
hijo *nm* son
hilar *v* spin
hilera *nf* row; string
hilo *nm* yarn; thread
himno *nm* anthem, hymn
hincar *v* stick into
hincarse *v* kneel down
hinchado *adj* swollen
hinchar *v* swell
hinchazón *nm* swelling
hipertensión *nf* hypertension
hipnosis *nf* hypnosis
hipnotizar *v* hypnotize
hipo *nm* hiccups
hipocresía *nf* hypocrisy
hipócrita *nm* hypocrite
hipódromo *nm* racetrack
hipopótamo *nm* hippopotamus
hipoteca *nf* mortgage
hipótesis *nf* hypothesis
hipotético *adj* hypothetical
hiriente *adj* offensive, hurting
hispano *adj* Hispanic
histeria *nf* hysteria
histérico *adj* hysterical
historia *nf* history, story
historiador *nm* historian
historial *nm* record
histórico *adj* historical, historic
hito *nm* milestone
hogar *nm* home

hoguera *nf* bonfire
hoja *nf* leaf; sheet; blade
hojear *v* browse
hola *e* hello
Holanda *nf* Holland
holandés *adj* Dutch
holgado *adj* baggy, rich
holgazán *adj* lazy
holocausto *nm* holocaust
hombre *nm* man
hombres *nm* men
hombro *nm* shoulder
homenaje *nm* homage
homicida *nm* murderer
homicidio *nm* homocide
homólogo *nm* counterpart
homogéneo *adj* homogenous
hondo *adj* deep
honestidad *nf* honesty
honesto *adj* honest
hongo *nm* mushroom
honor *nm* honor
honorarios *nm* fee
honra *nf* honor
honradez *nf* honesty
hora *nf* hour
horario *nm* schedule
horca *nf* gallows
horda *nf* horde
horizontal *adj* horizontal
horizonte *nm* horizon
hormiga *nf* ant

H

hormigón *nm* concrete
hormona *nf* hormone
horno *nm* furnace, oven
horóscopo *nm* horoscope
horrendo *adj* horrendous
horrible *adj* awful, horrible
horripilante *adj* spooky
horror *nm* horror
horrorizado *adj* appalled
horrorizar *v* appall, horrify
horroroso *adj* dreadful
hosco *adj* sullen
hospedarse *v* stay
hospicio *nm* orphanage
hospital *nm* hospital
hospitalidad *nf* hospitality
hospitalizar *v* hospitalize
hostia *nf* host
hostigar *v* harass
hostil *adj* hostile
hostilidad *nf* hostility
hotel *nm* hotel
hoy *adv* today
hoyo *nm* hole, pit
hoz *nf* sickle
hucha *nf* money box
hueco *adj* hollow, empty
hueco *nm* hole, gap
huelga *nf* strike, walk out
huella *nf* fingerprint; track
huérfano *nm* orphan
huero *adj* blond

huerta *nf* garden
huerto *nm* orchard
hueso *nm* bone
huésped *nm* guest
huevo *nm* egg
huida *nf* flight
huir *v* flee, escape
humanidad *nf* mankind
humanidades *nf* humanities
humanizar *v* humanize
humano *adj* human, humane
humedad *nf* humidity
humedecer *v* moisten
húmedo *adj* damp, humid
humildad *nf* humility
humilde *adj* humble, lowly
humillar *v* humiliate
humo *nm* smoke
humor *nm* humor, mood
hundir *v* sink, scuttle
hundirse *v* collapse; sink
húngaro *adj* Hungarian
Hungría *nf* Hungary
huracán *nm* hurricane
huraño *adj* unfriendly
hurgar *v* poke
hurtar *v* steal

I

iceberg *nm* iceberg
ida *nf* departure
idea *nf* idea
ideal *adj* ideal
idéntico *adj* identical
identidad *nf* identity
identificar *v* identify
ideología *nf* ideology
idílico *adj* idyllic
idilio *nm* romance
idiota *nm* idiot
idiotez *nf* idiocy, nonsense
idolatrar *v* worship
idolatría *nf* idolatry
ídolo *nm* idol
idóneo *adj* suitable
iglesia *nf* church
ignorancia *nf* ignorance
ignorar *v* ignore
igual *adj* equal
igualar *v* match; level off
igualdad *nf* equality
ilegal *adj* illegal
ilegible *adj* illegible
ilegítimo *adj* illegitimate
ileso *adj* unhurt
ilícito *adj* illicit
ilimitado *adj* unlimited
ilógico *adj* illogical

iluminar *v* illuminate
ilusionarse *v* get excited
ilusión *nf* illusion
ilusionado *adj* excited
iluso *nm* dreamer
ilustrar *v* illustrate; teach
ilustre *adj* famous
imagen *nf* image
imaginación *nf* imagination
imaginar(se) *v* imagine
imán *nm* magnet
imbécil *adj* stupid
imbécil *nm* idiot
imitar *v* imitate, mimic
impaciencia *nf* impatience
impacientarse *v* lose patience
impaciente *adj* impatient
impactar *v* impact; move
impacto *nm* impact
impar *adj* odd
imparcial *adj* impartial
impartir *v* give
impasible *adj* impassive
impecable *adj* impeccable
imperdible *nm* safety pin
impedimento *nm* obstacle
impedir *v* prevent
imperante *adj* prevailing
imperar *v* rule
imperativo *adj* imperative
imperfección *nf* imperfection
imperial *adj* imperial

imperialismo *nm* imperialism
imperio *nm* empire
impermeable *nm* raincoat
impermeable *adj* waterproof
impersonal *adj* impersonal
impertérrito *adj* unperturbed
impertinencia *nf* impertinence
impertinente *adj* impertinent
impetuoso *adj* impetuous
implacable *adj* relentless
implantar *v* implant
implementar *v* implement
implicar *v* imply, involve
implícito *adj* implicit
implorar *v* implore
imponente *adj* stunning
imponer *v* impose
imponerse *v* prevail
impopular *adj* unpopular
importación *nf* importation
importancia *nf* importance
importante *adj* important
importar *v* import; mind
importe *nm* amount
importunar *v* bother
importuno *adj* inopportune
imposibilidad *nf* impossibility
imposible *adj* impossible
imposición *nf* imposition
impotente *adj* powerless
impreciso *adj* vague
impredecible *adj* unpredictable

imprenta *nf* printing
imprescindible *adj* essential
impresión *nf* impression
impresionante *adj* impressive
impresionar *v* impress
impreso *adj* printed
impresor *nm* printer
imprevisto *adj* unforeseen
imprimir *v* print
improbable *adj* unlikely
impropio *adj* inappropiate
improvisar *v* improvise
imprudente *adj* unwise
impuesto *nm* levy, tax
impulsar *v* propel; urge
impulsivo *adj* impulsive
impulso *nm* impulse, urge
impune *adj* unpunished
impunidad *nf* impunity
impureza *nf* impurity
impuro *adj* impure
inacesible *adj* inaccessible
inadaptado *adj* misfit
inadmisible *adj* inadmissible
inaguantable *adj* unbearable
inalámbrico *adj* cordless
inapropiado *adj* inappropriate
inasequible *adj* unattainable
inaudito *adj* unheard-of
inaugurar *v* inaugurate
incalculable *adj* incalculable
incansable *adj* tireless

incapacidad *nf* inability
incapacitado *adj* helpless
incapacitar *v* incapacitate
incapaz *adj* incapable
incautarse *v* seize
incendiar *v* set fire
incendiarse *v* burn
incendio *nm* arson, fire
incentivo *nm* incentive
incertidumbre *nf* suspense
incidente *nm* incident
incienso *nm* incense
incierto *adj* uncertain
incinerar *v* cremate
incisión *nf* incision
incitar *v* incite
inclinación *nf* leaning
inclinar *v* tilt, incline
inclinarse *v* bow, bend
incluír *v* include
incoherente *adj* incoherent
incoloro *adj* colorless
incomodidad *nf* discomfort
incómodo *adj* uncomfortable
incompatible *adj* incompatible
incompetente *adj* incompetent
incompleto *adj* incomplete
inconcebible *adj* unthinkable
inconfundible *adj* unmistakable
incongruente *adj* inconsistent
inconsciente *adj* unconcious
inconstante *adj* fickle

incontable *adj* countless
incontinencia *nf* incontinence
inconveniente *nm* inconvenient
incorporar *v* incorporate
incorrecto *adj* inaccurate
incorregible *adj* incorrigible
incredulidad *nf* disbelief
increíble *adj* incredible
incrementar *v* increase
incremento *nm* increment
incruento *adj* bloodless
incubar *v* incubate
incumbencia *nf* responsibility
inculcar *v* instill
inculto *adj* uneducated
incurable *adj* incurable
incurrir *v* incur
indagar *v* investigate
indecencia *nm* indecency
indecible *adj* unspeakable
indecisión *nf* indecision
indeciso *adj* undecided
indefenso *adj* defenceless
indefinido *adv* indefinite
indemnización *nf* indemnitiation
indemnizar *v* indemnify
independiente *adj* independent
indeseable *adj* undesirable
indicación *nf* sign
indicar *v* indicate
índice *nm* index
indicio *nm* sign, clue

indiferencia *nf* indifference

indiferente *adj* indifferent

indigente *adj* indigent, poor

indigestión *nf* indigestion

indignación *nf* outrage

indignado *adj* outraged

indignar *v* anger

indigno *adj* unworthy

indirecta *nf* innuendo

indiscreto *adj* indiscreet

indispensable *adj* indispensable

indispuesto *adj* not well

indivisible *adj* indivisible

inducir *v* induce

indulgente *adj* lenient

indulto *nm* pardon

indumentaria *nf* clothing

industria *nf* industry

ineficacia *nf* inefficiency

ineficaz *adj* inefficient

ineludible *adj* unavoidable

inepto *adj* inept

inesperado *adj* unexpected

inestable *adj* unstable

inevitable *adj* unavoidable

inexcusable *adj* inexcusable

inexperto *adj* inexperience

inexplicable *adj* inexplicable

infalible *adj* infallible

infame *adj* infamous

infancia *nf* infancy

infantería *nf* infantry

infantil *adj* childish

infarto *nm* heart attack

infección *nf* infection

infectar *v* infect

infectarse *v* get infected

infeliz *adj* unhappy

inferior *adj* inferior

inferioridad *nf* inferiority

inferir *v* infer

infertilidad *nf* infertility

infestar *v* infest

infidelidad *nf* infidelity

infiel *adj* unfaithful

infierno *nm* hell, inferno

infiltrar *v* infiltrate

infinito *adj* infinite

inflamar *v* inflame

inflamable *adj* flammable

inflamación *nf* swelling

inflar *v* inflate

inflexible *adj* inflexible

infligir *v* inflict

influencia *nf* influence

influir *v* influence

influyente *adj* influential

información *nf* information

informal *adj* informal

informalidad *nf* informality

informar *v* brief, inform

informe *nm* report

infracción *nf* infraction

infrarrojo *adj* infrared

infrecuente *adj* infrequent
infundado *adj* unfounded
infundir *v* instil, inspire
ingeniarse *v* manage
ingeniero *nm* engineer
ingenio *nm* wit
ingenioso *adj* witty
ingenuo *adj* naive
ingerir *v* swallow
Inglaterra *nf* England
ingle *nf* groin
inglés *adj* English
ingratitud *nf* ingratitude
ingrato *adj* ungrateful
ingrediente *nm* ingredient
ingresar *v* enter
ingresos *nm* income, revenue
inhalar *v* inhale
inherente *adj* inherent
inhumano *adj* inhuman
inicial *adj* initial
iniciales *nf* initials
iniciar *v* start
iniciativa *nf* initiative
injertar *v* graft
injerto *nm* graft
injuria *nf* offence
injuriar *v* offend, insult
injusticia *nf* injustice
injustificado *adj* unjustified
injusto *adj* unfair, unjust
inmaculado *adj* immaculate

inmadurez *nf* immaturity
inmaduro *adj* immature
inmediato *adj* immediate
inmejorable *adj* excellent
inmensidad *nf* magnitude
inmenso *adj* huge
inmersión *nf* immersion
inmigración *nf* immigration
inmigrante *nm* immigrant
inmigrar *v* immigrate
inminente *adj* imminent
inmiscuirse *v* meddle
inmobilizar *v* immobilize
inmoral *adj* immoral
inmoralidad *nf* immorality
inmortal *adj* immortal
inmortalidad *nf* immortality
inmóvil *adj* still
inmune *adj* immune
inmundo *adj* filthy
inmunidad *nf* immunity
inmunizar *v* immunize
innecesario *adj* unnecessary
innegable *adj* undeniable
innumerable *adj* countless
inocente *adj* innocent
inofensivo *adj* harmless
inolvidable *adj* unforgetable
inoportuno *adj* untimely
inoxidable *adj* stainless
inquietar *v* worry
inquieto *adj* restless

I

inquilino *nm* tenant
inquisición *nf* inquisition
insaciable *adj* insatiable
insatisfecho *adj* dissatisfied
inscribir *v* enroll
inscripción *nf* inscription
insecto *nm* insect
inseguridad *nf* insecurity
inseguro *adj* uneasy
insensato *adj* foolish
insensible *adj* insensitive
inseparable *adj* inseparable
insertar *v* insert
inservible *adj* useless
insignificante *adj* insignificant
insinceridad *nf* insincerity
insinuación *nf* hint
insinuar *v* insinuate
insípido *adj* insipid, tasteless
insistencia *nf* insistence
insistente *adj* pushy
insistir *v* insist
insolación *nf* sunstroke
insólito *adj* unusual
insolvente *adj* bankrupt
insomnio *nm* insomnia
insoportable *adj* unbearable
inspeccionar *v* inspect
inspiración *nf* inspiration
instalar *v* install
instantáneo *adj* instantaneous
instante *nm* instant

instar *v* urge
instigar *v* instigate
instinto *nm* instinct
institución *nf* institution
instructor *nm* instructor
instruir *v* teach
insuficiente *adj* insufficient
insulso *adj* insipid
insultar *v* insult
insulto *nm* insult
insurgencia *nf* insurgency
insurrección *nf* insurrection
intachable *adj* blameless
intacto *adj* intact
integrar *v* integrate
integridad *nf* integrity
integro *adj* entire
inteligente *adj* intelligent
intemperie *nf* open air
intención *nf* intention
intencionado *adj* deliberate
intensidad *nf* intensity
intensificar *v* intensify
intensivo *adj* intensive
intenso *adj* intense
intentar *v* try
intercalar *v* insert
intercambiar *v* swap
intercambio *nm* exchange
interceder *v* intercede
interceptar *v* intercept
interés *nm* interest

interesado *adj* interested
interesante *adj* interesting
interferir *v* interfere
interior *adj* inner, interior
intermediario *nm* intermediary
interminable *adj* endless
interno *adj* internal
interpretar *v* interpret
intérprete *v* interpreter
interrogar *v* question
interrumpir *v* interrupt
interruptor *nm* switch
intervalo *nm* gap, interval
intervenir *v* intervene
intestino *nm* intestine
intimidad *nf* intimacy
intimidar *v* intimidate
íntimo *adj* intimate
intocable *adj* untouchable
intolerable *adj* intolerable
intolerancia *nf* intolerance
intranquilo *adj* restive, worried
intravenoso *adj* intravenous
intrépido *adj* intrepid
intriga *nf* intrigue, plot
intrincado *adj* complicated
intrínsico *adj* intrinsic
introducir *v* introduce
introvertido *adj* introvert
intruso *nm* intruder
inundación *nf* flooding
inundar *v* flood

inusitado *adj* unusual
inútil *adj* useless
invadir *v* invade
invalidar *v* override
inválido *adj* disable
invasión *nf* invasion
invasor *nm* invader
invencible *adj* invincible
invención *nf* invention
inventar *v* invent, devise
inventario *nm* inventory
invento *nm* invention
inverosímil *adj* unlikely
invernadero *nm* greenhouse
inversión *nf* investment
invertebrado *adj* invertebrate
invertir *v* invest
investigación *nf* inquiry, probe
investigar *v* investigate
invierno *nm* winter
invisible *adj* invisible
invitado *nm* guest
invitar *v* invite
invocar *v* invoke
inyección *nf* injection
inyectar *v* inject
ir *v* go
ira *nf* anger
ironía *nf* irony
irracional *adj* irrational
irrazonable *adj* unreasonable
irreal *adj* unreal

irrefutable *adj* irrefutable
irregular *adj* irregular
irrelevante *adj* irrelevant
irreparable *adj* irreparable
irresistible *adj* irresistible
irreverente *adj* irreverent
irreversible *adj* irreversible
irrevocable *adj* irrevocable
irritación *nf* exasperation
irritar *v* irritate, annoy
irrompible *adj* unbreakable
isla *nf* island, isle
islámico *adj* Islamic
Italia *nf* Italy
italiano *adj* Italian
itinerario *nm* itinerary
izar *v* hoist
izquierdo *adj* left

J

jabalí *nm* boar
jabón *nm* soap
jactarse *v* brag, boast
jadeante *adj* breathless
jadear *v* pant
jaguar *nm* jaguar
jalar *v* pull
jamás *adv* never

jamón *nm* ham
Japón *nm* Japan
japonés *adj* Japanese
jaque *nm* check
jaqueca *nf* migraine
jarabe *nm* syrup
jardín *nm* garden
jardinero *nm* gardener
jarra *nf* jug, pitcher
jarrón *nm* vase
jaula *nf* cage
jazmín *nm* jasmine
jefe *nm* leader, chief
jenjibre *nm* ginger
jerarquía *nf* hierarchy
jerez *nm* sherry
jeringa *nf* syringe
jinete *nm* rider
jirafa *nf* giraffe
jornal *nm* wages
jornalero *nm* day laborer
joroba *nf* hump
jorobado *adj* hunchbacked
jorobar *v* ruin
joven *adj* young
jovial *adj* cheerful
joya *nf* jewel
joyería *nf* jewelry store
joyero *nm* jeweler
juanete *nm* bunion
jubilación *nf* retirement
jubilarse *v* retire

júbilo *nm* joy
jubiloso *adj* jubilant
Judaísmo *nm* Judaism
judía *nf* bean
judío *nm* Jew
judío *adj* Jewish
juego *nm* set, game
juerga *nf* party
jueves *nm* Thursday
juez *nm* judge
jugada *nf* move
jugador *nm* player
jugar *v* play
jugarse *v* risk, gamble
jugo *nm* juice
jugoso *adj* juicy
juguete *nm* toy
juguetón *adj* playful
juicio *nm* judgment; trial
juicioso *adj* wise
julio *nm* July
junco *nm* reed
jungla *nf* jungle
junio *nm* June
junta *nf* council
juntar *v* join; gather
juntarse *v* get together
junto *adj* adjacent
juntos *adv* together
jurado *nm* jury
juramento *nm* oath
jurar *v* swear, vow

justicia *nf* justice
justificar *v* justify
justo *adj* just, fair
juvenil *adj* youthful
juventud *nf* youth
juzgado *nm* courthouse
juzgar *v* judge

karate *nm* karate
kilogramo *nm* kilogram
kilómetro *nm* kilometer
kilovatio *nm* kilowatt
kiosco *nm* newsstand

laberinto *nm* maze, labyrinth
labio *nm* lip
labor *nf* work
laborable *adj* working day
laboratorio *nm* laboratory
labrar *v* carve

J
K
L

labriego *nm* peasant
lacio *adj* straight
lácteo *adj* milky
ladearse *v* tilt, lean
ladera *nf* hillside, slope
ladrar *v* bark
ladrillo *nm* brick
ladrón *nm* burglar, thief
lagarto *nm* lizard
lago *nm* lake
lágrima *nf* tear
laguna *nf* lagoon
laico *nm* lay
lamentable *adj* regrettable
lamentar *v* regret, lament
lamer *v* lick
laminar *v* laminate
lámpara *nf* lamp
lana *nf* wool
lana (de) *adj* woolen
lancha *nf* small boat
langosta *nf* lobster, locust
languidecer *v* languish
lánguido *adj* languid
lanza *nf* spear, lance
lanzar *v* launch; throw
lanzarse *v* plunge
lápida *nf* tombstone
lápiz *nm* pencil
lapso *nm* interval, span
largo *adj* lengthy, long
laringe *nf* larynx

lascivo *adj* lewd
láser *nm* laser
lástima *nf* pity
lastimar *v* hurt
lastimoso *adj* pitiful
lustre *nm* burden
lata *nf* can, tin
latente *adj* latent
lateral *adj* lateral
latido *nm* heartbeat
latigazo *nm* lash
látigo *nm* whip
latir *v* throb, beat
latitud *nf* latitude
latón *nm* brash
lavabo *nm* toilet
lavandería *nf* laundry
lavadora *nf* washing machine
lavaplatos *nm* dishwasher
lavar *v* wash
laxante *adj* laxative
laxo *adj* lax
lazo *nm* ribbon; bond
leal *adj* loyal
lealtad *nf* loyalty
lección *nf* lesson
leche *nf* milk
lechería *nf* dairy
lechero *nm* milkman
lecho *nf* bed
lechoso *adj* milky
lechuga *nf* lettuce

L

lechuza *nf* owl
lector *nm* reader
lectura *nf* reading
leer *v* read
legal *adj* legal
legalizar *v* legalize
legar *v* bequeath
legión *nf* legion
legislación *nf* legislation
legislador *nm* lawmaker
legislar *v* legislate
legislatura *nf* legislature
legitimar *v* legitimate
legítimo *adj* authentic
legua *nf* league
legumbre *nf* vegetables
lejanía *nf* distance
lejano *adj* faraway
lejía *nf* bleach
lejos *adv* far, away
lema *nm* motto, slogan
lencería *nf* lingerie
lengua *nf* language; tongue
lenteja *nf* lentil
lentitud *nf* slowness
lento *adj* slow
leña *nf* firewood
leñador *nm* woodcutter
leño *nm* log
león *nm* lion
leona *nf* lioness
leopardo *nm* leopard

lepra *nf* leprosy
leproso *nm* leper
lerdo *adj* clumsy, slow
lesión *nf* injury
lesionar *v* injure
letal *adj* lethal
letanía *nf* litany
letargo *nm* lethargy
letrero *nm* placard, sign
leucemia *nf* leukemia
levadura *nf* leaven, yeast
levantar *v* raise, lift
levantarse *v* get up, rise
leve *adj* light, feint
ley *nf* law
leyenda *nf* legend
liarse *v* get involved
liberación *nf* liberation
liberal *adj* broadminded
liberar *v* free, liberate
libertad *nf* freedom, leeway
libertino *adj* dissolute
libidinoso *adj* lustful
libra *nf* pound
librar *v* spare, save
libre *adj* free; vacant
librería *nf* bookstore
librero *nm* bookseller
librito *nm* booklet
libro *nm* book
licencia *nf* license, permit
licenciado *adj* graduated

L

licenciarse *v* graduate

lícito *adj* lawful, legal

licor *nm* liqueur

licuado *nm* milkshake

licuadora *nf* blender

líder *nm* leader

liderazgo *nm* leadership

lidiar *v* fight

liebre *nf* hare

lienzo *nm* canvas

liga *nf* league; rubber band

ligamento *nm* ligament

ligero *adj* light; fast

lija *nf* sandpaper

lima *nf* file

limar *v* file

limitación *nf* limitation

limitar *v* limit

límite *nm* boundary, limit

límites *nm* confines, limits

limón *nm* lemon

limonada *nf* lemonade

limosna *nf* alm, handout

limosnero *nm* beggar

limpiar *v* clean, cleanse

limpieza *nf* cleaning

limpio *adj* clean

linaje *nm* descent

lince *nm* lynx

linchar *v* lynch

lindar *v* adjoin

lindo *adj* pretty

línea *nf* line

lino *nm* linen

linterna *nf* flashlight

lío *nm* tangle, mess

liquidación *nf* sellout

liquidar *v* liquidate

líquido *nm* liquid, fluid

lirio *nm* lily

lisiado *adj* crippled, injured

lisiar *v* maim

liso *adj* smooth, even

lisonja *nf* compliment

lista *nf* list

listo *adj* clever, ready

litera *nf* berth

literalmente *adv* literally

literatura *nf* literature

litigar *v* litigate

litigio *nm* lawsuit

litoral *nm* coastline

litro *nm* liter

liturgia *nf* liturgy

liviano *adj* light

lívido *adj* livid

llaga *nf* sore, wound

llama *nf* flame

llamada *nf* call

llamar *v* call

llamarada *nf* flare

llamas (en) *adv* alight

llamativo *adj* loud, striking

llano *adj* even, flat

llanta *nf* rim
llanto *nm* sobbing
llanura *nf* plain
llave *nf* key
llave inglesa *nf* wrench
llavero *nm* key ring
llegada *nf* arrival
llegar *v* arrive
llenar *v* fill
lleno *adj* full
llevadero *adj* bearable
llevar *v* carry; wear
llevar a cabo *v* carry out
llevar consigo *v* entail
llevarse bien *v* get along
llorar *v* cry, weep
llorar la muerte *v* mourn
lloriquear *v* whine
lloro *nm* crying
llover *v* rain
lloviznar *v* drizzle
lluvia *nf* rain
lluvioso *adj* rainy
lo que *adj* whatever
loable *adj* praiseworthy
lobo *nm* wolf
lóbrego *adj* gloomy
lóbulo *nm* lobe
local *nm* premises
localidad *nf* locality
localizar *v* locate
loción *nf* lotion

loco *adj* crazy, insane
locuaz *adj* talkative
locura *nf* madness, folly
locutor *nm* announcer
lodo *nm* mud
lógica *nf* logic
lógico *adj* logical
lograr *v* accomplish
logro *nm* achievement
loma *nf* hill
lombriz *nf* worm
lomo *nm* loin
lona *nf* canvas
longitud *nf* length
loro *nm* parrot
losa *nf* gravestone
lote *nm* batch
lotería *nf* lottery
loza *nf* china set
lubina *nf* sea bass
lucha *nf* struggle, fight
lucha libre *nf* wrestling
luchador *nm* wrestler
luchar *v* fight, struggle
lúcido *adj* lucid
lucir *v* shine
lucirse *v* show off
lucrativo *adj* lucrative
lucro *nm* gain, profit
luego *adv* afterwards, then
lugar *nm* spot, place
lugarteniente *nm* deputy

L

lúgubre *adj* gloomy
lujo *nm* luxury
lujoso *adj* luxurious
lujuria *nf* lust
lumbre *nf* fire
luminoso *adj* bright
luna *nf* moon
luna de miel *nf* honeymoon
lunes *nm* Monday
lupa *nf* magnifying glass
lustrar *v* polish
luto *nm* mourning
luz *nf* light

L
M

maceta *nf* flower pot
machacar *v* mash, crush
machista *adj* chauvinist
macho *nm* male
machucar *v* bruise
macizo *adj* solid
madera *nf* lumber, wood
madera (de) *adj* wooden
maderería *nf* lumberyard
madero *nm* log
madrastra *nf* stepmother
madre *nf* mother, mom

madriguera *nf* burrow
madrugada *nf* dawn
madrugar *v* get up early
madurar *v* ripen, mature
madurez *nf* maturity
maduro *adj* mature, ripe
maestro *nm* teacher
magia *nf* magic
magistrado *nm* magistrate, judge
magistral *adj* masterful
magnate *nm* tycoon
magnético *adj* magnetic
magnetismo *nm* magnetism
magnífico *adj* wonderful
magnitud *nf* magnitude
mago *nm* magician
magullar *v* bruise
mahometano *adj* islamic
maíz *nm* corn
majadero *adj* silly, stupid
majestad *nf* majesty
majestuoso *adj* majestic
majo *adj* nice
mal *adv* badly
mal *nm* evil
malabarista *nm* juggler
malaria *nf* malaria
malcriar *v* spoil
maldad *nf* wickedness
maldecir *v* damn, curse
maldición *nf* curse
maldito *adj* damned

maleante *adj* criminal
maleante *nm* crook
maleducado *adj* rude
malentendido *nm* misunderstanding
malestar *nm* discomfort
maleta *nf* suitcase
maletero *nm* porter
maletín *nm* briefcase
malévolo *adj* malevolent
maleza *nf* weeds
malgastar *v* waste
malhechor *nm* delinquent
malhumorado *adj* sullen
malicia *nf* malice
malicioso *adj* malicious
maligno *adj* malignant
malla *nf* mesh
malo *adj* bad
malogrado *adj* untimely death
malograr *v* spoil, ruin, waste
maloliente *adj* smelly
malsano *adj* unhealthy
maltratar *v* mistreat
maltrato *nm* mistreatment
malvado *adj* wicked
malversar *v* embezzle
mamar *v* suck
manada *nf* herd, pack
mancha *nf* blemish, stain
manchar *v* stain, defile
manco *adj* one-armed
mandado *nm* errand

mandar *v* command
mandarina *nf* tangerine
mandato *nm* precept, order
mandíbula *nf* jaw
mandíl *nm* apron
mando *nm* command
mandón *adj* bossy
manejable *adj* manageable
manejar *v* manage; operar
manejarse *v* get by
manejo *nm* handling
manera *nf* way
maneras *nf* manners
manga *nf* sleeve
mango *nm* handle
mangonear *v* boss around
manguera *nf* hose
manía *nf* habit
maniatar *v* tie
maniático *adj* maniac
manicomio *nm* madhouse
manifestar *v* declare, show
manifiesto *nm* manifesto
manifiesto *adj* evident, clear
maniobra *nf* maneuver
maniobrar *v* maneuver
manipular *v* manipulate
manirroto *adj* extravagant
manivela *nf* crank, handle
mano *nf* hand
mano de obra *nf* manpower
manojo *nm* bunch

M

manosear *v* touch, fondle
manotazo *nm* slap
mansedumbre *nf* meekness
mansión *nf* mansion
manso *adj* meek, docile
manta *nf* blanket
manteca *nf* lard, fat
mantel *nm* tablecloth
mantener *v* maintain, keep
mantenimiento *nm* upkeep
mantequilla *nf* butter
manto *nm* cloak
manual *mn* handbook
manual *adj* manual
manuscrito *nm* manuscript
manzana *nf* apple
manzano *nm* apple tree
maña *nf* skill
mañana *nf* morning
mañana *adv* tomorrow
mañoso *adj* skilful
mapa *nm* map
maqueta *nf* model
maquillaje *nm* makeup
maquillar *v* make up
máquina *nf* machine
mar *nm* sea
maravilla *nf* marvel, wonder
maravillar *v* amaze
maravilloso *adj* wonderful
maratón *nm* marathon
marca *nf* brand; mark

marcador *nm* marker
marcapasos *nm* pacemaker
marcar *v* mark, dial
marcha *nf* departure; gear
marchar *v* march
marcharse *v* go, leave
marchitarse *v* wither
marco *nm* frame; setting
marea *nf* tide
mareado *adj* dizzy, seasick
maremoto *nm* tidal wave
mareo *nm* dizziness
marfil *nm* ivory
margarita *nf* daisy
márgen *nm* margin
marginal *adj* marginal
marido *nm* husband
marina *nf* navy
marinero *nm* sailor
marino *adj* marine
marioneta *nf* puppet
mariposa *nf* butterfly
mariscal *nm* marshal
marisco *nm* shellfish
mármol *nm* marble
marqués *nm* marquis
marrano *nm* pig
marrano *adj* dirty
marrón *adj* brown
Marruecos *nm* Marocco
marte *nm* Mars
martes *nm* Tuesday

M

martillar *v* hammer
martillo *nm* hammer
mártir *nm* martyr
martirio *nm* martyrdom
marxista *adj* marxist
marzo *nm* March
más *adj* more
más (de) *adv* extra
más allá *adv* beyond
más bien *adv* rather
más o menos *adv* so-and-so
masa *nf* dough; mass
masacre *nm* massacre
masaje *nm* massage
masajista *nm* masseur
mascar *v* chew, munch
máscara *nf* mask
masculino *adj* masculine, male
masilla *nf* putty
masivo *adj* massive
masón *nm* mason
masoquismo *nm* masochism
masticar *v* chew
mástil *nm* mast
mata *nf* bush
matanza *nf* slaughter
matar *v* kill, slaughter
matasellos *nm* postmark
matemáticas *nf* math
materia *nf* matter; subject
material *nm* material
materialismo *nm* materialism

maternal *adj* maternal
maternidad *nf* motherhood
matiz *nm* nuance, shade
matón *adj* bully
matorral *nm* bushes
matrícula *nf* registration
matricularse *v* register, enrol
matrimonio *nm* marriage
maullar *v* miaow
máxima *nf* maxim
máximo *adj* maximum
mayo *nm* May
mayonesa *nf* mayonnaise
mayor *adj* senior, older
mayordomo *nm* butler
mayoría *nf* majority
mayorista *nm* wholesaler
mayúscula *nf* capital letter
mazapán *nm* marzipan
mecánico *nm* mechanic
mecanismo *nm* mechanism
mecanizar *v* mechanize
mecedora *nf* rocking chair
mecer *v* rock
mecha *nf* wick, fuse
mechero *nm* lighter
medalla *nf* medal
medallón *nm* medallion
media *nf* stocking
mediano *adj* medium
medianoche *nf* midnight
mediador *nm* mediator

M

mediar *v* mediate
medicina *nf* medicine
médico *nm* doctor
medida *nf* measure
medida (a) *adv* custom-made
medieval *adj* medieval
medio *nm* center
mediocre *adj* mediocre
mediocridad *nf* mediocrity
mediodía *nf* midday, noon
medios *nm* means
medir *v* measure
meditación *nf* meditation
meditar *v* meditate
médula *nf* marrow
medusa *nf* jellyfish
mejilla *nf* cheek
mejor *adj* better
mejora *nf* improvement
mejorar *v* improve
mejunje *nm* concoction
melancolía *nf* melancholy
melena *nf* long hair
mellizo *nm* twin
melocotón *nm* peach
melodía *nf* melody
melódico *adj* melodic
melón *nm* melon
membrana *nf* membrane
membrecía *nf* membership
membrillo *nm* quince
memorable *adj* memorable

memoria *nf* memory
memorias *nf* memoirs
memorizar *v* memorize
mención *nf* mention
mencionar *v* mention
mendigar *v* beg
mendigo *nm* beggar
menear *v* stir, move
menguante *adj* decreasing
menguar *v* decrease, wane
meningitis *nf* meningitis
menisco *nm* cartilage
menopausia *nf* menopause
menor *adj* younger
menos *adj* less, minus
menoscabar *v* diminish
menospreciar *v* belittle, despise
menosprecio *nm* scorn
mensaje *nm* message
mensajero *nm* messenger
menstruación *nf* menstruation
mensual *adj* monthly
menta *nf* mint
mentalidad *nf* mentality
mentalmente *adv* mentally
mente *nf* mind
mentecato *nm* fool
mentir *v* lie
mentira *nf* lie
mentirilla *nf* white lie
mentiroso *adj* liar
mentón *nm* chin

M

menú *nm* menu
menudo (a) *adv* often
meollo *nm* marrow
mercadillo *nm* street market
mercado *nm* market
mercancía *nf* merchandise
mercurio *nm* mercury
merecer *v* deserve
mercenario *nm* mercenary
merienda *nf* snack
mérito *nm* merit
meritorio *adj* deserving
merluza *nf* hake
mermelada *nf* marmalade
mero *adj* mere, simple
merodear *v* prowl
mes *nm* month
mesa *nf* table
mesera *nf* barmaid
mesero *nm* barman
meseta *nf* plateau
Mesías *nm* Messiah
mesón *nm* inn
mestizo *adj* mixed race
mesura *nf* moderation
meta *nf* goal
metáfora *nf* metaphor
metálico *adj* metallic
meteoro *nm* meteor
meter la pata *v* goof
meter miedo *v* intimidate
meterse en líos *v* embroil

meticuloso *adj* meticulous
metido *adj* involved
metódico *adj* methodical
método *nm* method
metralla *nf* shrapnel
métrico *adj* metric
metro *nm* meter; subway
mexicano *adj* Mexican
mezcla *nf* blend, mixture
mezclar *v* blend, mix
mezclarse *v* mingle, mix
mezquindad *nf* pettiness
mezquino *adj* petty, mean
mezquita *nf* mosque
mi *adj* my
microbio *nm* germ
micrófono *nm* microphone
microondas *nm* microwave
microscopio *nm* microscope
miedo *nm* fear
miedo (de) *adj* scary
miedoso *adj* timid
miel *nf* honey
miembro *nm* member
mientras *c* as, while
mientras tanto *adv* meanwhile
miércoles *nm* Wednesday
miga *nf* crumb
migraña *nf* migraine
migratorio *adj* migratory
mil *adj* thousand
milagro *nm* miracle

M

milagroso *adj* miraculous
milenio *nm* millennium
milicia *nf* militia
miligramo *nm* milligram
milímetro *nm* millimeter
militante *adj* militant
militar *nm* soldier
milla *nf* mile
millaje *nm* mileage
millón *nm* million
millonario *adj* millionaire
mimar *v* pamper, spoil
mimo *nm* caress
mina *nf* mine
minar *v* mine, undermine
mineral *nm* mineral, ore
minero *nm* miner
miniatura *nf* miniature
minifalda *nf* miniskirt
mínimo *nm* minimum
ministerio *nm* ministry
ministro *nm* minister
minoría *nf* minority
minucioso *adj* meticulous
minusválido *adj* disabled
minuto *nm* minute
mío *pro* mine
miope *adj* short-sighted
miopía *nf* near-sightedness
mirada *nf* look
miramiento *nm* consideration
mirador *nm* viewpoint

mirar *v* look
mirar fijo *v* stare, gaze
mirilla *nf* peephole
misa *nf* mass
miserable *adj* miserable
miseria *nf* misery
misericordia *nf* mercy
misil *nm* missile
misión *nf* mission
misionero *nm* missionary
mismo *adj* same
misterio *nm* mystery
misterioso *adj* mysterious
místico *adj* mystic
mitad *nf* half
mitigar *v* mitigate
mitin *nm* rally, meeting
mito *nm* myth
mitología *nf* mythology
mixto *adj* mixed
mobiliario *nm* furniture
mobilizar *v* mobilize
mochila *nf* backpack
moción *nf* motion, vote
moco *nm* mucus
mocoso *adj* brat
moda *nf* vogue, fashion
moda (de) *adj* fashionable
modelar *v* model
modales *nm* manners
modelo *nm* model
moderación *nf* restraint

M

moderado *adj* moderate
moderar *v* moderate
modernizar *v* modernize
moderno *adj* modern
modestia *nf* modesty
modesto *adj* modest
modificar *v* modify
modismo *nm* idiom
modista *nf* dressmaker
modo *nm* way, manner
modorra *nf* drowsiness
mofarse *v* make fun
moho *nm* mildew, mold
mojado *adj* wet
mojar *v* moisten, dip
mojarse *v* get wet
molde *nm* mold
moldear *v* mold
moldura *v* molding
molécula *nf* molecule
moler *v* grind
molestar *v* bother, annoy
molestarse *v* get upset
molestia *nf* discomfort
molido *adj* exhausted; ground
molino *nm* mill
momento *nm* moment
momia *nf* mummy
momificar *v* mummify
monarca *nm* monarch
monarquía *nf* monarchy
monasterio *nm* monastery

monástico *adj* monastic
moneda *nf* coin, currency
monedero *nm* purse
monigote *nm* idiot
monja *nf* nun
monje *nm* monk
mono *nm* monkey
mono *adj* pretty, cute
monogamia *nf* monogamy
monólogo *nm* monologue
monopolio *nm* monopoly
monopolizar *v* monopolize
monotonía *nf* monotony
monótono *adj* monotonous
monstruo *nm* monster
monstruoso *adj* monstrous
montaña *nf* mountain
montañoso *adj* mountainous
montar *v* mount, ride
monte *nm* mount, mountain
montón *nm* heap, stack, pile
montura *nf* frame
monumento *nm* monument
mora *nf* blackberry
morada *nm* dwelling
morado *adj* purple
moral *adj* moral
moraleja *nf* moral
moralidad *nf* morality
moralizar *v* moralize
morboso *adj* morbid
mordaz *adj* biting

M

mordaza *nf* gag	**motocicleta** *nf* motorcycle
mordedura *nf* bite	**motor** *nm* engine, motor
morder *v* bite	**motora** *nf* motorboat
mordisco *nm* bite, nibble	**mover** *v* move
morena *nf* brunette	**movible** *adj* movable
moreno *adj* brown; tanned	**móvil** *adj* mobile
moretón *nm* bruise	**móvil** *nm* motif; cellphone
morfina *nf* morphine	**movilizar** *v* mobilize
moribundo *adj* dying	**movimiento** *nm* movement
morir *v* die	**mozo** *nm* young boy
moro *adj* moorish	**muchacho** *nm* boy, lad
morriña *nf* homesickness	**muchacha** *nf* girl
morro *nm* nose	**muchedumbre** *nf* crowd
morsa *nf* walrus	**mucho** *adj* much, a lot of
mortaja *nf* shroud	**muchos** *adj* many
mortal *adj* deadly, lethal	**muda** *nf* change of clothes
mortalidad *nf* mortality	**mudanza** *nf* moving
mortífero *adj* deadly	**mudar** *v* change
mortificar *v* mortify	**mudarse** *v* relocate; change
mosaico *nm* mosaic	**mudo** *adj* dumb; silent
mosca *nf* fly	**muebles** *nm* furniture
mosquito *nm* mosquito	**mueca** *nf* grimace
mostaza *nf* mustard	**muela** *nf* molar
mostrador *nm* counter	**muelle** *nm* wharf; spring
mostrar *v* show	**muerte** *nf* death
mota *nf* speck	**muerto** *adj* dead, deceased
mote *nm* nickname	**muestra** *nf* sample, token
motel *nm* motel	**mugre** *nf* dirt, filth
motín *nm* mutiny, riot	**mugriento** *adj* dirty, filthy
motivar *v* motivate	**mujer** *nf* woman
motivo *nm* motive	**mujeres** *nf* women
moto *nf* scooter	**mujeriego** *adj* womanizer

M

mula *nf* mule
muleta *nf* crutch
multa *nf* fine, penalty
multar *v* fine
múltiple *adj* multiple, many
multiplicar *v* multiply
multitud *nf* multitude
mundano *adj* worldly
mundial *adj* worldwide
mundo *nm* world
muñeca *nf* wrist; doll
municiones *nf* ammunition
municipio *nm* borough
muralla *nf* wall
murciélago *nm* bat
murmullo *nm* murmur
murmurar *v* murmur
muro *nm* wall
músculo *nm* muscle
museo *nm* museum
musgo *nm* moss
música *nf* music
músico *nm* musician
muslo *nm* thigh
mustio *adj* withered
musulmán *nm* Muslim
mutilar *v* mutilate, maim
mutuo *adj* mutual
muy *adv* very

nabo *nm* turnip
nacer *v* be born
nacido *adj* born
nacimiento *nm* birth
nación *nf* nation
nacional *adj* national
nacionalidad *nf* nationality
nacionalizar *v* nationalize
nada *nf* nothing
nadador *nm* swimmer
nadar *v* swim
nadie *pro* nobody
naranja *nf* orange
narcótico *nm* narcotic
nardo *nm* lilly
nariz *nf* nose
narrar *v* narrate, tell
nata *nf* cream
natillas *nf* custard
nativo *adj* native
natural *adj* natural
naufragar *v* sink
naufragio *nm* shipwreck
náufrago *nm* castaway
náusea *nf* nausea
nauseabundo *adj* sickening
navaja *nf* knife
nave *nf* nave; ship
navegador *nm* browser

navegar *v* navigate, sail
Navidad *nf* Christmas
navío *nm* ship
neblina *nf* haze, mist
necesario *adj* necessary
necesidad *nf* need
necesitado *adj* needy
necesitar *v* need
necio *adj* foolish
nectarina *nf* nectarine
nefasto *adj* disastrous
negación *nf* denial
negar *v* deny
negativa *nf* refusal
negativo *adj* negative
negligencia *nf* negligence
negligente *adj* negligent
negociante *nm* businessman
negociar *v* negotiate
negocio *nm* business
negro *adj* black
nervio *nm* nerve
nervioso *adj* nervous
neto *adj* net
neurótico *adj* neurotic
neutral *adj* neutral
neutralizar *v* neutralize
nevada *nf* snowfall
nevar *v* snow
nevera *nf* icebox
nexo *nm* link
ni *c* nor, neither

nicotina *nf* nicotine
nido *nm* nest
niebla *nf* fog
nieto *nm* grandson
nieve *nf* snow
nilón *nm* nylon
ninfa *nf* nymph
ninguno *pro* no one
niñera *nf* babysitter
niñez *nf* childhood
niño *nm* baby, child
niño pequeño *nm* toddler
niños *nm* children
nitrógeno *n* nitrogen
nivel *nm* level
no *adv* not
no obstante *c* nonetheless
noble *adj* noble
nobleza *nm* nobility
noche *nf* night
noche (de) *adv* nightly
noción *nf* notion
nocivo *adj* harmful
nocturno *adj* nocturnal
nogal *nm* walnut tree
nombrar *v* appoint, name
nombre *nm* noun; name
nómina *nf* payroll
noria *nf* waterwheel
norma *nf* norm, rule
normal *adj* normal
normalizar *v* normalize

normas *nf* guidelines
noroeste *nm* northeast
norte *nm* north
norteño *adj* northerner
Noruega *nf* Norway
noruego *adj* Norwegian
nosotros *pro* we
nostalgia *nf* nostalgia
nostálgico *adj* homesick
nota *nf* footnote; grade
notable *adj* remarkable
notar *v* notice
notario *nm* notary
noticias *nf* news
noticiero *nm* newscast
notificación *nf* notification
notificar *v* notify
notorio *adj* notorious
novato *adj* inexperienced
novedad *nf* novelty
novela *nf* novel
novelista *nm* novelist
noveno *adj* ninth
noventa *adj* ninety
novia *nf* bride
noviazgo *nm* courtship
novicio *nm* novice
noviembre *nm* November
novio *nm* fiancé
nubarrón *nm* storm cloud
nube *nf* cloud
nublado *adj* cloudy

nuclear *adj* nuclear
núcleo *nm* core
nudista *nm* nudist
nudo *nm* knot
nuera *nf* daughter-in-law
nuestro *adj* our
nuestro *pro* ours
nueve *adj* nine
nuevo *adj* new
nuevo (de) *adv* again
nuez *nf* walnut
nulo *adj* null, void
numerar *v* number
número *nm* number
numeroso *adj* numerous
nunca *adv* never
nutria *nf* otter
nutrición *nf* nutrition
nutrir *v* nourish
nutritivo *adj* nutritious

o *c* or
obedecer *v* obey
obediencia *nf* obedience
obeso *adj* obese
obispo *nm* bishop

N
O

objeción *nf* objection

objetar *v* object

objetivo *nm* objective

objeto *nm* object; aim

oblicuo *adj* oblique

obligación *nf* obligation

obligar *v* bind, compel

obligatorio *adj* compulsory

obra *nf* work; play

obra maestra *nf* masterpiece

obrero *nm* worker

obscenidad *nf* obscenity

obsceno *adj* lewd, obscene

obscuridad *nf* darkness

obsequiar *v* give a present

obsequio *nm* gift, present

observar *v* notice, observe

observatorio *nm* observatory

obsesión *nf* obsession

obsesionar *v* obsess

obstaculizar *v* hinder, obstruct

obstáculo *nm* obstacle

obstáculos *nm* red tape

obstante (no) *adv* however

obstinado *adj* obstinate

obstinarse *v* insist on

obstrucción *nf* obstruction

obstruir *v* obstruct

obtener *v* get, obtain

obturar *v* plug, block

obvio *adj* obvious

ocasión *nf* occasion

ocasionar *v* cause

ocaso *nm* decline; sunset

occidental *adj* western

océano *nm* ocean

ochenta *adj* eighty

ocho *adj* eight

ocio *nm* leisure

ocioso *adj* idle

octavo *adj* eighth

octubre *nm* October

ocultar *v* conceal, hide

oculto *adj* hidden

ocupación *nf* occupation

ocupado *adj* busy

ocupar *v* occupy

ocurrencia *nf* idea

ocurrir *v* occur

odiar *v* hate

odio *nm* hatred

odioso *adj* hateful

odisea *nf* odyssey

odómetro *nm* odometer

oeste *nm* west

ofender *v* offend

ofensa *nf* offense

ofensiva *nf* offensive

ofensivo *adj* offensive

oferta *nf* bid, offer

oficial *adj* official

oficiar *v* officiate, preside

oficina *nf* office, bureau

oficio *nm* craft, job

O

ofrecer *v* offer
ofrecerse *v* volunteer
ofrenda *nf* offering
ofuscar *v* confuse
oído *nm* hearing
oír *v* hear
ojal *nm* buttonhole
ojeada *nf* glance, peek
ojear *v* glance, have a look
ojo *nm* eye
ola *nf* wave
oleada *nf* big wave
oleoducto *nm* pipeline
oler *v* smell
olfatear *v* sniff
olimpiada *nf* olympics
oliva *nf* olive
olivo *nm* olive tree
olla *nf* pot
olmo *nm* elm
olor *nm* odor, smell
oloroso *adj* fragrant
olvidar *v* forget
olvido *nm* oblivion
ombligo *nm* navel, belly button
omisión *nf* omission
omitir *v* omit
once *adj* eleven
onceavo *adj* eleventh
onda *nf* wave, ripple
ondulado *adj* wavy
onza *nf* ounce

opaco *adj* opaque
opción *nf* option
opcional *adj* optional
ópera *nf* opera
operación *nf* operation
operar *v* operate
opinar *v* think
opinión *nf* opinion
opio *nm* opium
oponerse *v* oppose, object
oportunidad *nf* opportunity
oportuno *adj* timely
oposición *nf* opposition
opresión *nf* oppression
oprimir *v* oppress
optar *v* opt for, choose
óptico *adj* optical
optimismo *nm* optimism
optimista *adj* optimistic
optometrista *nm* optician
opuesto *adj* opposite
opulencia *nf* opulence
oración *nf* prayer; sentence
oral *adj* oral
orangután *nm* orangutan
órbita *nf* orbit
orden *nm* order
ordenación *nf* ordination
ordenado *adj* neat
ordenador *nm* computer
ordenar *v* ordain
ordeñar *v* milk

O

ordinario *adj* common
oreja *nf* ear
orfanato *nm* orphanage
organismo *nm* organism
organista *nm* organist
organización *nf* organization
organizar *v* organize
órgano *nm* organ
orgullo *nm* pride
orgulloso *adj* proud
orientación *nf* orientation
oriental *adj* eastern, oriental
oriente *nm* orient, east
orificio *nm* orifice
origen *nm* origin
original *adj* original
originar *v* cause
originarse *v* originate
orilla *nf* shore; edge
orina *nf* urine
orinar *v* urinate
oriundo *adj* native
ornamentar *v* decorate
oro *nm* gold
orquesta *nf* orchestra
ortodoxo *adj* orthodox
ortografía *nf* spelling
oruga *nf* caterpillar
osar *v* dare
oscilar *v* fluctuate, swing
oscurecer *v* darken
oscuridad *nf* darkness

oscuro *adj* dark, obscure
oso *nm* bear
ostentoso *adj* ostentatious
ostra *nf* oyster
otoño *nm* autumn, fall
otorgar *v* bestow, award
otro *adj* another, other
ovación *nf* cheer, ovation
ovalado *adj* oval
ovario *nm* ovary
oveja *nf* sheep
ovular *v* ovulate
óvulo *nm* ovule
oxidado *adj* rusty
oxidar *v* rust
oxígeno *nm* oxygen
oyente *nm* listener

pacer *v* graze
paciencia *nf* patience
paciente *adj* patient
pacificar *v* pacify
pacífico *adj* peaceful
pacotilla (de) *adj* shoddy
pactar *v* agree
pacto *nm* pact, deal

O
P

padecer *v* suffer
padrastro *nm* stepfather
padre *nm* father; priest
padres *nm* parents
padrino *nm* godfather
paga *nf* pay, wages
pagadero *adj* payable
pagano *adj* pagan
pagar *v* pay
página *nf* page
pago *nm* payment, fee
país *nm* country
paisaje *nm* landscape
paisano *nm* countryman
paja *nf* straw
pajar *nm* haystack
pájaro *nm* bird
paje *nm* page
pala *nf* shovel, spade
palabra *nf* word
palabra (de) *adv* verbally
paladar *nm* palate
palacio *nm* palace
palanca *nf* lever
palco *nm* box
palidez *nf* paleness
pálido *adj* pale
paliza *nf* beating
palma *nf* palm
palmada *nf* pat
palmera *nf* palm tree
palo *nm* stick

paloma *nf* dove, pigeon
palomitas *nf* popcorn
palpar *v* touch, feel
palpitación *nf* palpitation
palpitar *v* beat, throb
pan *nm* bread
panadería *nf* bakery
panadero *nm* baker
pañal *nm* diaper
pancarta *nf* banner
páncreas *nm* pancreas
pandilla *nf* gang
pánico *nm* panic
panorama *nm* panorama
pantalla *nf* screen; lampshade
pantalón corto *nm* shorts
pantalones *nm* trousers, pants
pantano *nm* reservoir
pantera *nf* panther
paño *nm* cloth
pañuelo *nm* handkerchief
panza *nf* belly
Papa *nm* Pope
papá *nm* dad
Papado *nm* papacy
papas fritas *nf* fries
papel *nm* paper
papeleo *nm* paperwork
papelera *nf* wastebasket
paperas *nf* mumps
paquete *nm* package
parejo *adj* even

P

par *nm* pair
para *pre* for
parábola *nf* parable
parabrisas *nm* windshield
paracaídas *nm* parachute
parachoque *nm* fender
parada *nf* stop
paradero *nm* whereabouts
parado *adj* idle
paradoja *nf* paradox
paraguas *nf* umbrella
paraíso *nm* paradise
paralelo *adj* parallel
parálisis *nf* paralysis
paralizado *adj* standstill
paralizar *v* paralyze
paranoico *adj* paranoid
parar *v* halt, stop
parásito *nm* parasite
parcial *adj* partial, biased
parecer *v* seem
parecerse *v* resemble
parecido *nm* likeness
parecido *adj* alike, similar
pared *nf* wall
pareja *nf* couple; mate
parentesco *nm* relationship
paréntesis *nm* parenthesis
paridad *nf* parity
pariente *nm* relative
parir *v* give birth
parlamento *nm* parliament

paro *nm* unemployment
parpadear *v* blink
párpado *nm* eyelid
parque *nm* park
parra *nf* grapevine
párrafo *nm* paragraph
parrilla *nf* grill
párroco *nm* pastor, vicar
parroquia *nf* parish
parroquiano *nm* parishioner
parte *nf* part
parte (en) *adv* partly
participación *nf* involvement
participar *v* participate
participio *nm* participle
partícula *nf* particle
particular *adj* particular
partida *nf* departure
partidario *nm* follower
partido *nm* party; game
partir *v* leave; break
parto *nm* birth
pasa *nf* raisin
pasado *adj* past, last
pasaje *nm* fare; crossing
pasajero *nm* passenger
pasaporte *nm* passport
pasar *v* elapse, pass
pasatiempo *nm* pastime
Pascua *nf* Easter
pasear *v* stroll
pasillo *nm* aisle, corridor

P

pasión *nf* passion
pasivo *adj* passive
pasmar *v* astound
pasmoso *adj* astounding
paso *nm* pace, step
pasta *nf* paste
pastar *v* graze
pastel *nm* cake
pasteles *nm* pastry
pastilla *nf* pill, tablet
pastor *nm* shepherd
pata *nf* leg; paw
patata *nf* potato
patear *v* kick
patente *nf* patent
patente *adj* obvious
paternal *adj* paternal
paternidad *nf* paternity
patético *adj* pathetic
patíbulo *nm* gallows
patillas *nf* sideburns
patín *nm* skate
patinar *v* skate
patio *nm* courtyard, patio
pato *nm* duck
patria *nf* homeland
patriarca *nm* patriarch
patrimonio *nm* patrimony
patriota *nm* patriot
patriótico *adj* patriotic
patrocinador *nm* sponsor
patrocinar *v* patronize

patrón *nm* patron
patrono *nm* employer
patrulla *nf* patrol
paulatino *adj* slow
pausa *nf* pause
pausado *adj* slow
pausterizar *v* pasteurize
pavimento *nm* pavement
pavo *nm* turkey
pavo real *nm* peacock
pavor *nm* terror
payaso *nm* clown
paz *nf* peace
peaje *nm* toll
peatón *nm* pedestrian
peca *nf* freckle
pecado *nm* sin
pecador *nm* sinner
pecaminoso *adj* sinful
pecar *v* sin
pecho *nm* chest, breast
peculariedad *nf* mannerism
peculiar *adj* peculiar
pedagogía *nf* pedagogy
pedal *nm* pedal
pedante *adj* pedantic
pedazo *nm* piece, bit
pediatra *nm* pediatrician
pegajoso *adj* sticky
pegamento *nm* glue
pegar *v* hit; glue, stick
peinado *nm* hairdo

P

peinar *v* comb
peine *nm* comb
pelar *v* peel
peldaño *nm* step
pelear *v* scuffle, fight
pelele *nm* puppet
peliagudo *adj* difficult
pelícano *nm* pelican
película *nf* film, movie
peligrar *v* be in danger
peligro *nm* danger, peril
peligroso *adj* dangerous
pellejo *nm* skin
pellizcar *v* nip, pinch
pellizco *nm* nip, pinch
pelo *nm* hair
pelota *nf* ball
pelotón *nm* platoon, squad
peluca *nf* hairpiece, wig
peludo *adj* hairy
peluquera *nf* hairdresser
peluquero *nm* barber
pena *nf* grief, regret
penal *adj* penal
penalizar *v* penalize
pendiente *nm* earring
pendiente *adj* pending
penetrar *v* penetrate
penicilina *nf* penicillin
península *nf* peninsula
penique *nm* penny
penitencia *nf* penance

penitente *nm* penitent
penoso *adj* laborious
pensamiento *nm* thought
pensar *v* think
pensión *nf* pension
pentágono *nm* pentagon
penuria *nf* shortage
peña *nf* rock
peñasco *nm* boulder
peón *nm* laborer; pawn
peor *adj* worse
pepino *nm* cucumber
pequeño *adj* petite, small
pera *nf* pear
percance *nm* setback
percatarse *v* realize
percepción *nf* perception
percha *nf* hanger
percibir *v* perceive, receive
perdedor *nm* loser
perder *v* lose
perdición *nf* ruin, disgrace
pérdida *nf* loss
perdido *adj* missing, lost
perdigón *nm* pellet
perdiz *nf* partridge
perdón *nm* forgiveness
perdonable *adj* forgivable
perdonar *v* forgive, pardon
perdurar *v* last
perecedero *adj* perishable
perecer *v* perish

peregrinación *nf* pilgrimage
peregrino *nm* pilgrim
perejil *nm* parsley
perenne *adj* everlasting
pereza *nf* laziness
perezoso *adj* lazy
perfección *nf* perfection
perfecto *adj* perfect
perfil *nm* profile
perforación *nf* perforation
perforar *v* perforate, drill
perfume *nm* perfume
pergamino *nm* parchment
pericia *nf* skill
perico *nm* parrot, parakeet
periferia *nf* outskirts
perímetro *nm* perimeter
periódico *nm* newspaper
periódico *adj* periodic
periodista *nm* reporter
periodo *nm* period, term
perjudicar *v* harm, damage
perjudicial *adj* damaging
perjuicio *nm* damage
perjurio *nm* perjury
perla *nf* pearl
permanecer *v* remain
permanente *adj* permanent
permiso *nm* permission
permitir *v* permit, allow
pernicioso *adj* harmful
pero *c* but

perpetrar *v* perpetrate
perpetuo *adj* permanent
perplejo *adj* bewildered
perrera *nf* kennel
perro *nm* dog
persecución *nf* chase, persecution
perseguir *v* chase, persecute
perseverar *v* persevere
persiana *nf* blind
persistencia *nf* persistence
persistente *adj* persistent
persistir *v* persist
persona *nf* person
personal *adj* personal
personal *nm* staff, personnel
personalidad *nf* personality
personificar *v* personify
perspectiva *nf* viewpoint
perspicaz *adj* shrewd
persuadir *v* persuade
persuasión *nf* persuasion
persuasivo *adj* persuasive
pertenecer *v* belong, pertain
pertenencias *nf* belongings
pertinente *adj* relevant
perturbar *v* disturb, perturb
pertrechar *v* supply
peruano *adj* Peruvian
perverso *adj* perverse
pervertido *adj* pervert
pervertir *v* pervert

P

pesa *nf* scale
pesadez *nf* heaviness
pesadilla *nf* nightmare
pesado *adj* heavy
pésame *nm* condolence
pesar *v* weigh
pescado *nm* seafood, fish
pescador *nm* fisherman
pescuezo *nm* neck
pesebre *nm* manger
pesimismo *nm* pessimism
pesimista *adj* pessimistic
pésimo *adj* awful
peso *nm* weight
pestaña *nf* eyelash
pestañear *v* blink
pestillo *nm* bolt
pez *nm* fish
piadoso *adj* pious, kind
picar *v* bite, sting, mince
picado *adj* minced
picado (en) *adv* nosedive
picadura *nf* bite, sting
picazón *nm* itching
pie *nm* foot
pie (de) *adv* standing
pierna *nf* leg
pies *nm* feet
pieza *nf* piece
pigmeo *nm* pygmy
pijamas *nm* pajama
pila *nf* battery

pilar *nm* pillar
píldora *nf* pill
pillar *v* catch
piloto *nm* pilot
pimienta *nf* pepper
pimiento *nm* bell pepper
pinchar *v* puncture; prick
pinchazo *nm* puncture; prickle
pinguino *nm* penguin
pino *nm* pine tree
pinta *nf* pint
pintar *v* paint
pintor *nm* painter
pintoresco *adj* picturesque
pintura *nf* paint; painting
pinza *nf* clothes pin
piña *nf* pineapple
piojo *nm* louse
pionero *nm* pioneer
pipa *nf* pipe
piragua *nf* canoe
pirámide *nf* pyramid
piraña *nf* piranha
pirata *nm* pirate
piratería *nf* piracy
pirómano *nm* arsonist
piropo *nm* flattery
pisada *nf* footprint
pisar *v* tread, step on
piscina *nf* pool
piso *nm* floor, apartment
pisotear *v* trample

pista *nf* clue
pistola *nf* gun, pistol
pistolero *nm* gunman
pistón *nm* piston
pitar *v* honk, referee
pizarra *nf* blackboard
pizca *nf* bit, pinch
placa *nf* badge, plate
placentero *adj* delightful
placer *nm* pleasure
plaga *nf* plague
plagado *adj* infested
plan *nm* plan
planchar *v* iron
planear *v* glide; plan
planeta *nm* planet
planicie *nf* plain
plano *nm* blueprint
plano *adj* flat
planta *nf* plant
plantar *v* plant
plantear *v* pose
plástico *nm* plastic
plastificar *v* laminate
plata *nf* silver
plataforma *nf* platform
plátano *nm* banana
platero *nm* silversmith
platicar *v* chat
platillo *nm* saucer
platino *nm* platinum
plato *nm* dish, plate

playa *nf* beach
plaza *nf* square
plazo *nm* period
plegar *v* fold
plegaria *nf* prayer
pleito *nm* lawsuit
pleno *adj* full
pliegue *nm* crease, pleat
plomero *nm* plumber
plomo *nm* lead
pluma *nf* feather; pen
plural *adj* plural
plusvalía *nf* capital gain
población *nf* population
poblar *v* populate
pobre *nm* poor
pobreza *nf* poverty
poco *adj* little
pocos *adj* few
podar *v* prune
poder *v* can, may
poder *nm* power
poderoso *adj* powerful
podredumbre *nf* rot
podrido *adj* rotten
poema *nm* poem
poesía *nf* poetry
poeta *nm* poet
polaco *adj* Polish
polar *adj* polar
polea *nf* pulley
polémica *nf* controversy

P

polémico *adj* controversial

polen *nm* pollen

policía *nm* policeman, cop

policía *nf* police

poligamia *nf* polygamy

polígamo *adj* polygamist

polilla *nf* moth

polio *nm* polio

política *nf* politics

político *nm* politician

póliza *nf* policy

pollito *nm* chick

pollo *nm* chicken

Polonia *nf* Poland

polo *nm* pole

polución *nf* pollution

polvo *nm* dust, powder

pólvora *nf* gunpowder

polvoriento *adj* dusty

pomada *nf* cream

pomelo *nm* grapefruit

pompa *nf* pomp

pomposidad *nf* pomposity

pómulo *nm* cheekbone

ponderar *v* ponder

poner *v* set, put; lay

pontífice *nm* pontiff

ponzoña *nf* poison

popular *adj* popular

popularizar *v* popularize

por *pre* along, by

por ciento *adv* percent

por eso *c* therefore

por la borda *adv* overboard

por la presente *adv* hereby

por lo tanto *adv* therefore

por lo visto *adv* apparently

por partes *adv* piecemeal

por poderes *adv* proxy

por qué *adv* why

por razón de *pre* because of

porcelana *nf* porcelain

porcentage *nm* percentage

porción *nf* portion

pordiosero *adj* downtrodden

porfiar *v* insist

pormenor *nm* detail

poro *nm* pore

poroso *adj* porous

porque *c* because

porqué *nm* reason

porquería *nf* crap, mess

porra *nf* stick, club

porrazo *nm* blow

portada *nf* cover

portador *nm* bearer

portátil *adj* portable

portavoz *nf* spokesman

portazo *nm* slam

portero *nm* doorman

pórtico *nm* porch

Portugal *nf* Portugal

portugués *adj* Portuguese

posada *nf* inn

posar *v* pose
poseer *v* own, possess
posesión *nf* ownership
posesivo *adj* possessive
posibilidad *nf* possibility
posible *adj* possible
posición *nf* position
positivo *adj* positive
posponer *v* postpone
postal *nf* postcard
poste *nm* pole
posteridad *nf* posterity
posterior *adj* posterior
postizo *adj* fake
postre *nm* dessert
póstumo *adj* posthumous
postura *nf* pose, attitude
potable *adj* drinkable
potaje *nm* stew, soup
potencial *adj* potential
potente *adj* powerful
potestad *nf* authority
potro *nm* colt, pony
pozo *nm* well
práctica *nf* practice
practicar *v* practice
práctico *adj* practical
pradera *nf* meadow, prairie
pragmático *adj* pragmatist
preámbulo *nm* preamble
precario *adj* precarious
precaución *nf* precaution

precavido *adj* wary
precedente *nm* precedent
preceder *v* precede
precepto *nm* commandment
precintar *v* seal
precio *nm* price, cost, fare
precioso *adj* precious
precipicio *nm* precipice
precipitarse *v* rash
precisar *v* specify
precisión *nf* precision
preciso *adj* accurate
precoz *adj* precocious
precursor *nm* forerunner
predecir *v* prophesy
predicador *nm* preacher
predicar *v* preach
predicción *nf* prediction
predilección *nf* predilection
predilecto *adj* favorite
predisponer *v* predispose
predispuesto *adj* predisposed
predominar *v* predominate
predominio *nm* prevalence
prefabricar *v* prefabricate
prefacio *nm* preface
preferencia *nf* preference
preferible *adj* preferable
preferir *v* prefer
prefijo *nm* prefix
pregonar *v* announce
pregunta *nf* question

P

preguntar _v_ ask, question
preguntarse _v_ wonder
prehistórico _adj_ prehistoric
prejuicio _nm_ prejudice
preliminar _adj_ preliminary
preludio _nm_ prelude
prematuro _adj_ premature
premeditar _v_ premeditate
premiar _v_ reward
premio _nm_ award, prize
premisa _nf_ premise
premonición _nf_ premonition
prenda _nf_ garment
prender _v_ catch fire
prensa _nf_ press
prensar _v_ press
preñada _adj_ pregnant
preocupación _nf_ worry, concern
preocupado _adj_ uneasy
preocupante _adj_ worring
preocupar(se) _v_ worry
preparación _nf_ preparation
preparado _adj_ ready
preparar _v_ prepare
preparativos _nm_ arrangements
preparatorio _adj_ preparatory
preposición _nf_ preposition
prerequisito _nm_ prerequisite
prerrogativa _nf_ prerogative
presa _nf_ prey; dam
presagiar _v_ foreshadow
presagio _nm_ omen

prescindir _v_ disregard
prescribir _v_ prescribe
prescripción _nf_ prescription
presencia _nf_ presence
presenciar _v_ be present
presentación _nf_ presentation
presentar _v_ introduce
presentarse _v_ show up
presente _adj_ present
presentimiento _nm_ feeling
presentir _v_ have a feeling
preservar _v_ preserve
presidencia _nf_ presidency
presidente _nm_ president
presidio _nm_ carcel
presidir _v_ preside
presión _nf_ pressure
presionar _v_ pressure
preso _nm_ prisoner
prestado _adj_ borrowed
prestamista _nm_ pawnbroker
préstamo _nm_ loan
prestar _v_ lend, loan
presteza _nf_ promptness
prestigio _nm_ prestige
presumido _adj_ conceited
presumir _v_ show off
presunción _nm_ presumption
presunto _adj_ presumed
presuponer _v_ presuppose
presuposición _nf_ presumption
presupuesto _nm_ budget

pretender *v* pretend
pretensión *nf* pretension
pretesto *nm* excuse, pretext
prevalecer *v* prevail
prevalente *adj* prevalent
prevención *nf* prevention
prevenir *v* prevent
preventivo *adj* preventive
prever *v* foresee
previo *adj* previous
previsión *nf* foresight
primacía *nf* primacy
primado *nm* primate
primavera *nf* spring
primero *adj* first
primitivo *adj* primitive
primo *nm* cousin
primordial *adj* paramount
princesa *nf* princess
principal *adj* main
príncipe *nm* prince
principiante *nm* beginner
principio *nm* beginning
prioridad *nf* priority
prisa *nf* haste, rash
prisa (de) *adv* hastely
prisión *nf* prison
prisionero *nm* prisoner
prisma *nm* prism
privación *nf* deprivation
privado *adj* private
privar *v* deprive

privilegio *nm* privilege
probabilidad *nf* probability
probabilidades *nf* odds
probable *adj* probable
probar *v* prove; test; taste
problema *nm* problem
problemático *adj* problematic
procedencia *nf* origin
proceder *v* proceed
procedimiento *nm* procedure
procesar *v* prosecute
procesión *nf* procession
proceso *nm* process
proclamar *v* proclaim
procreate *v* procrear
procurar *v* try; get
prodigio *nm* prodigy
prodigioso *adj* prodigious
producción *nf* production
producir *v* produce
producto *nm* product
productor *nm* producer
proeza *nf* feat, deed
profanar *v* desecrate
profano *adj* profane
profecía *nf* prophecy
proferir *v* utter
profesar *v* profess
profesión *nf* profession
profesional *adj* professional
profesor *nm* professor
profeta *nm* prophet

P

prófugo *adj* fugitive
profundidad *n* depth
profundizar *v* deepen
profundo *adj* deep
programa *nm* program
programador *nm* programmer
programar *v* program
progresista *adj* progressive
progreso *nm* progress
progresar *v* progress
prohibición *nf* prohibition
prohibir *v* prohibit, forbid
projectil *nm* missile
prójimo *nm* fellow man
prole *nf* offspring
proliferar *v* proliferate
prólogo *nm* prologue
prolongado *adj* protracted
prolongar *v* prolong
promedio *nm* average
promesa *nf* pledge, promise
prometedor *adj* promising
prometer *v* pledge, promise
promiscuo *adj* promiscuous
promoción *nf* promotion
promover *v* promote
pronombre *nm* pronoun
pronosticar *v* predict
pronóstico *nm* forecast
pronto *adv* soon
pronunciar *v* pronounce
pronunciar mal *v* mispronounce

propaganda *nf* propaganda
propagar *v* propagate
propensión *nf* propensity
propenso *adj* prone
propicio *adj* favorable
propiedad *nf* property
propietario *nm* owner
propina *nf* gratuity, tip
propio *adj* own
proponer *v* propose
proporción *nf* proportion
proposición *nf* proposition
propósito *nm* purpose
propósito (a) *adv* on purpode
propuesta *nf* proposal
propulsar *v* stimulate
prórroga *nf* extension
prorrogar *v* extend
prosa *nf* prose
proscribir *v* outlaw, ban
prosperar *v* thrive
prosperidad *nf* prosperity
próspero *adj* prosperous
próstata *n* prostate
prostitución *nf* prostitution
protección *nf* protection
proteger *v* protect
protesta *nf* protest
protestar *v* protest
provecho *nm* benefit
provechoso *adj* fruitful, useful
proveer *v* provide

provenir *v* come from
proverbio *nm* proverb
providencia *nf* providence
provincia *nf* province
provisional *adj* provisional
provocación *nf* provocation
provocar *v* provoke
proximidad *nf* proximity
próximo *adj* next
proyectar *v* project
proyectil *nm* projectile
proyecto *nm* project
prudencia *nf* prudence
prudente *adj* prudent
prueba *nf* proof, test
psicología *nf* psychology
psiquiatra *nm* psychiatrist
psiquiatría *nf* psychiatry
psíquico *adj* psychic
púa *nf* prickle
pubertad *nf* puberty
publicación *nf* publication
publicar *v* publish
publicidad *nf* publicity
público *adj* public
puchero *nm* cooking pot
pudín *nm* pudding
pudor *nm* modesty
pudrir *v* rot, decay
pueblo *nm* village
puente *nm* bridge
puerco *adj* filthy

pueril *adj* childish
puerta *nf* door, gate
puerto *nm* harbor, port
pues *c* then
puesta *nf* sunset
puesto *nm* post, stall
pulga *nf* flea
pulgada *nf* inch
pulir *v* polish
pulmón *nm* lung
pulmonía *nf* pneumonia
pulpa *nf* pulp
púlpito *nm* pulpit
pulpo *nm* octopus
pulsación *nf* beat
pulsar *v* pulsate
pulsera *nf* bracelet
pulso *nm* pulse
pulverizar *v* pulverize
puño *nm* cuff; fist
punta *nf* tip
puntada *nf* stitch
puntapié *nm* kick
puntiagudo *adj* pointed
puntillas (de) *adv* tiptoe
punto *nm* dot; point
punto culminante *nm* highlight
punto de vista *nm* viewpoint
puntuación *nf* score; grade
puntual *adj* punctual
punzada *nf* prick, beat
punzante *adj* sharp

P

puñal *nf* dagger
puñalada *nf* stab
puñetazo *nm* punch
pupitre *nm* desk
puré *nm* puree
pureza *nf* purity
purga *nf* purge
purgar *v* purge
purgatorio *nm* purgatory
purificación *nf* purification
purificar *v* purify
puritano *adj* puritan
puro *adj* pure
púrpura *nf* purple
pus *nf* pus
pútrido *adj* rotten

Q

que *adj* what, which
quebrado *adj* broken
quebrantar *v* transgress
quebrar *v* go bankrupt; break
quedarse *v* stay, remain
queja *nf* complaint
quejarse *v* complain
quejón *adj* grumpy
quemadura *nf* burn

quemar *v* burn
quemarropa (a) *adv* point-blank
querella *nf* dispute
querer *v* wish, want
querido *adj* dear, beloved
queso *nm* cheese
quiebra *nf* bankruptcy
quiebra (en) *adj* bankrupt
quien *pro* who
quienquiera *pro* whoever
quieto *adj* quiet
quilate *nm* carat
quimera *nf* dream
química *nf* chemistry
químico *adj* chemical
quince *adj* fifteen
quinientos *adj* five hundred
quinto *adj* fifth
quiosco *nm* kiosk
quirúrjico *adj* surgical
quisquilloso *adj* fuzzy
quiste *nm* cyst
quitamanchas *nm* cleaner
quitar *v* remove
quizá *adv* maybe, perhaps

R

rábano *nm* radish
rabia *nf* rabies; anger
rabieta *nf* tantrum
rabioso *adj* furious
rabo *nm* tail
racimo *nm* bunch
ración *nf* allotment, portion
racional *adj* rational
racionalizar *v* rationalize
racionar *v* ration
racismo *nm* racism
racista *adj* racist
racún *nm* raccoon
radiación *nf* radiation
radiador *nm* radiator
radiante *adj* radiant
radiar *v* radiate
radical *adj* radical
radicar *v* originate
radio *nf* radio
radiografía *nf* X-ray
ráfaga *nf* gust, burst
raído *adj* shabby
raíz *nf* root
raja *nf* slice; crack
rajar *v* slit
rajatable (a) *adv* strictly
ralámpago *nm* flash
rallar *v* grate

rama *nf* bough, branch
ramificación *nf* ramification
ramo *nm* bouquet, bunch
rampa *nf* chute, ramp
rana *nf* frog
rancho *nm* ranch
rancio *adj* stale
rango *nm* rank, class
ranura *nf* groove, slot
rapar *v* shave
rápidamente *adv* quickly
rapidez *nf* speed
rápido *adj* quick, fast
raptar *v* kidnap
raqueta *nf* racquet
raramente *adv* seldom
rareza *nf* oddity, quirk
raro *adj* rare, weird, odd
rascacielos *nm* skyscraper
rascar *v* scratch
rasgar *v* tear, slash
rasgo *nm* trait, feature
rasguñar *v* scratch
rasguño *nm* scratch
raso *adj* flat, leveled
raspadura *nf* scratch, scrape
raspar *v* scrape
rastrear *v* trail, track
rastrillo *nm* rake
rastro *nm* trace
rasurarse *v* shave
rata *nf* rat

R

ratero *nm* pickpocket
ratificar *v* ratify
rato *nm* a while
ratón *nm* mouse
ratones *nm* mice
raudal *nm* torrent
raya *nf* stripe, line
rayado *adj* striped
rayar *v* cross out; verge on
rayo *nm* beam, ray
raza *nf* breed, race
razón *nf* reason
razonable *adj* reasonable
razonar *v* reason
razones *nf* grounds
reacción *nf* reaction
reaccionar *v* react
reacio *adj* reluctant
reactivar *v* reactivate
readmitir *v* reinstate
reajustar *v* readjust, reset
reajuste *nm* readjustment
real *adj* real, royal
realeza *nf* royalty
realidad *nf* reality
realidad (en) *adv* actually
realismo *nm* realism
realización *nf* fulfillment
realizar *v* fulfill, achieve
realzar *v* enhance
reanimar *v* revive
reanudación *nf* resumption

reanudar *v* resume
reaparecer *v* reappear
rearme *nm* rearmament
rebaja *nf* reduction
rebajar *v* reduce, lower
rebanada *nf* slice
rebaño *nm* flock, herd
rebasar *v* overtake, exceed
rebatir *v* rebut, refute
rebelarse *v* rebel
rebelde *nm* rebel
rebelión *nf* rebellion
rebosar *v* overflow
rebotar *v* bounce
recado *nm* errand
recaída *nf* relapse
recalcar *v* stress, emphasize
recalcitrante *adj* recalcitrant
recámara *n* bedroom
recambio *nm* spare part
recapacitar *v* reflect
recapitular *v* recap
recargar *v* recharge
recargo *nm* surcharge
recatado *adj* modest
recato *nf* modesty
recaudar *v* collect
recelo *nm* mistrust
recepción *n* reception
recesión *nf* recession
receta *nf* recipe
recetar *v* prescribe

redada

rechazar *v* reject, repulse
rechazo *nm* rejection
rechinar *v* creak, squeak
rechistar *v* protest
rechoncho *adj* plump
recibimiento *nm* welcome
recibir *v* receive
recibo *nm* receipt
reciclar *v* recycle
reciente *adj* recent
recinto *nm* enclosure
recio *adj* strong
recipiente *nm* container
recíproco *adj* reciprocal
recitar *v* recite
reclamación *nf* claim
reclamar *v* claim
reclamo *nm* claim
reclinar *v* recline
recluir *v* confine
recluso *nm* inmate
recluta *nm* recruit
reclutar *v* recruit
recobrar *v* recover
recogedor *nm* dustpan
recoger *v* gather, pick up
recolectar *v* harvest
recomendar *v* recommend
recompensa *nf* reward
recompensar *v* reward
reconciliar *v* reconcile
reconocer *v* recognize

reconquistar *v* recapture
reconsiderar *v* reconsider
reconstruir *v* rebuild
recopilación *nf* compilation
recopilar *v* compile
recordar *v* recall, remind
recordatorio *nm* reminder
recorrer *v* travel
recorrido *nm* route
recortar *v* cut out; trim
recorte *nm* clipping
recostar *v* lean
recreación *nf* recreation
recrear *v* recreate
recreo *v* recreation
recriminar *v* reproach
recrudecer *v* worsen
recrutamiento *nm* recruitment
rectangular *adj* oblong
rectángulo *nm* rectangle
rectificar *v* rectify, correct
recto *nm* rectum
recto *adj* straight, honest
rector *nm* director
recuento *nm* recount
recuerdo *nm* memory
recuperación *nf* recovery
recuperar *v* recover
recurrir *v* resort, turn to
recurso *nm* recourse
red *nf* net, network
redada *nf* roundup

R

redención *nf* redemption

redil *nm* sheepfold

redimir *v* redeem

réditos *nm* yield

redoblar *v* redouble

redondear *v* round

redondel *nm* circle

redondo *adj* round

reducción *nf* reduction

reducir *v* reduce

reelegir *v* reelect

reembolsar *v* reimburse

reembolso *nm* reimbursement

reemplazar *v* replace

referencia *nf* reference

referente *adj* referring to

referirse *v* refer to

refinanciar *v* refinance

refinar *v* refine

refinería *nf* refinery

reflejar *v* reflect, mirror

reflejo *nm* reflex, reflection

reflexionar *v* ponder

reflexión *nf* reflection

reflexivo *adj* reflexive

reforma *nf* reform

reformar *v* reform

reforzar *v* reinforce

refrán *nm* proverb, saying

refrenar *v* curb

refrendar *v* endorse

refrescante *adj* refreshing

refrescar *v* refresh

refresco *nm* refreshment

refriega *nf* skirmish, brawl

refrigerar *v* refrigerate

refuerzo *nm* reinforcement

refugiado *nm* refugee

refugiarse *v* take refuge

refugio *nm* haven, shelter

refunfuñar *v* grumble

refutar *v* refute

regalar *v* give away

regalo *nm* gift, present

regañar *v* scold, chide

regaño *nm* scolding

regar *v* irrigate, water

regatear *v* haggle, bargain

regazo *nm* lap

regeneración *nf* regeneration

regente *nm* regent

régimen *nm* regime

regimiento *nm* regiment

regio *adj* regal

región *nf* region

regional *adj* regional

regir *v* govern

registrarse *v* register

regla *nf* ruler

regocijarse *v* rejoice

regocijo *nm* joy

regordete *adj* chubby

regresar *v* return

regreso *nm* return

regularizar *v* regulate
regularmente *adv* regularly
rehabilitar *v* rehabilitate
rehacer *v* redo, remake
rehén *nm* hostage
rehusar *v* refuse
reimprimir *v* reprint
reina *nf* queen
reinar *v* reign, rule
reincidir *v* relapse
reino *nm* kingdom
reinoceronte *nm* rhinoceros
reír *v* laugh
reiterar *v* reiterate
reja *nf* grille
rejuvenecer *v* rejuvenate
relación *nf* relationship
relajación *nf* relaxation
relajarse *v* relax
relámpago *nm* lightning
relatar *v* tell, recount
relativo *adj* relative
relato *nm* tale
relegar *v* relegate
relevante *adj* relevant
relevar *v* replace
relevo *nm* replacement
religión *nf* religion
religioso *adj* religious
reliquia *nf* relic
rellenar *v* refill; stuff
relleno *nm* padding

reloj *nm* watch, clock
relojero *nm* watchmaker
relucir *v* glitter, shine
reluciente *adj* bright
remachar *v* hammer
remar *v* row
remarcar *v* stress
rematar *v* finish off
remedar *v* mimic
remediar *v* remedy
remedio *nm* remedy
remendar *v* repair, mend
remiendo *nm* patch, mend
remisión *nf* remission
remitir *v* remit
remo *nm* oar
remodelar *v* remodel
remojar *v* soak
remolacha *nf* beet
remolcar *v* tow, tug
remolino *nm* whirlpool
remontarse *v* soar; go back
remordimiento *nm* remorse
remoto *adj* remote
remunerar *v* remunerate
renacimiento *nm* rebirth
rencilla *nf* quarrel
rencor *nm* grudge, resentment
rencoroso *adj* resentful
rendición *nf* surrender
rendido *adj* exhausted
rendija *nf* crack, gap

R

rendimiento *nm* output
rendirse *v* surrender
renglón *nm* printed line
reno *nm* reindeer
renovación *nf* renewal
renovar *v* renew, revamp
renta *nf* rent
rentable *adj* profitable
rentar *v* rent
renuncia *nf* resignation
renunciar *v* renounce, resign
reñir *v* quarrel
reorganizar *v* reorganize
reparación *nf* reparation
reparar *v* mend, repair
reparo *n* qualm, problem
repartir *v* share
repasar *v* review, revise
repatriar *v* repatriate
repelente *adj* repulsive
repente (de) *adv* suddenly
repentino *adj* sudden
repetición *nf* repetition
repetir *v* repeat
repetirse *v* recur
repicar *v* toll
replegarse *v* withdraw
repleto *adj* replete, full
repollo *nm* cabbage
reponer *v* replenish
reponerse *v* recover
reportar *v* report

reporte *nm* report
reposo *nm* repose, rest
reposar *v* rest
repostar *v* refuel
repostería *nf* pastry
reprender *v* rebuke
represalia *nf* reprisal
representar *v* represent
represión *nf* repression
reprimenda *nf* rebuke
reprimir *v* repress
reprochar *v* reproach
reproche *nm* reproach
reproducción *nf* replica
reproducir *v* reproduce
reptil *nm* reptile
república *nf* republic
repudiar *v* repudiate
repuesto *nm* spare part
repugnancia *nf* disgust
repugnante *adj* disgusting
repulsión *nf* repulsion
reputación *nf* reputation
requerir *v* require
requisito *nm* requirement
resaltar *v* highlight, stress
resbaladizo *adj* slippery
resbalar *v* slide, slip
resbalón *nm* slip
rescatar *v* ramson, rescue
rescate *nm* rescue, ransom
rescindir *v* cancel, rescind

resentimiento *nm* resentment
resentirse *v* resent
reservación *nf* reservation
reservado *adj* aloof, reserved
reservar *v* reserve
resfriado *nm* cold
resfriarse *v* catch a cold
residencia *nm* residence
resident *adj* residente
residir *v* reside
residuo *nm* residue, waste
resignar *v* resign
resignarse *v* resign oneself
resistencia *nf* resistance
resistente *adj* strong
resistir *v* resist, withstand
resolución *nf* resolution
resolver *v* resolve, settle
resonar *v* resound
resorte *nm* spring
respaldar *v* back, support
respaldo *nm* support
respectivo *adj* respective
respetar *v* respect
respeto *nm* respect
respetuoso *adj* respectful
respiración *nf* breathing
respiradero *nm* vent
respirar *v* breathe
respiro *nm* respite, breath
resplandecer *v* shine
resplandor *nm* brilliance

responder *v* answer, reply
responsable *adj* responsible
respuesta *nf* answer, reply
resquicio *nm* crack, opening
resta *nf* subtraction
restante *adj* remaining
restar *v* subtract
restaurante *nm* restaurant
restaurar *v* restore
restitución *nf* restitution
restituir *v* return
resto *nm* remainder
restos *nm* remains
restregar *v* scrub
restricción *nf* constraint
restringir *v* restrict, curtail
resucitar *v* revive
resuelto *adj* determined; solved
resultado *nm* outcome, result
resultar *v* result, happen
resumen *nm* summary
resumen (en) *adv* briefly
resumir *v* summarize
resurgir *v* come back
resurrección *nf* resurrection
retaguardia *nf* rearguard
retaliar *v* retaliate
retar *v* challenge
retardar *v* delay, retard
retención *nf* retention
retener *v* retain, withhold
retirada *nf* withdrawal

R

retirado *adj* secluded
retirar *v* withdraw, remove
retirarse *v* retreat
retiro *nm* retreat
retocar *v* retouch
retornar *v* return
retractarse *v* retract
retraído *adj* loner, shy
retrasado *adj* late; retarded
retrasar *v* postpone, delay
retrasarse *v* be late
retraso *nm* delay
retratar *v* take a picture
retrato *nm* portrait
retrete *nm* toilet, bathroom
retroactivo *adj* retroactive
retroceder *v* recede, go back
retroceso *nm* step backwards
retrógado *adj* retrograde
retrospectiva *nf* hindsight
retumbar *v* rumble, resound
retumbe *nm* rumble
reuma *nm* rheumatism
reumatismo *nm* rheumatism
reunión *nf* reunion, meeting
reunir *v* convene, gather
reunirse *v* meet
revancha *nf* revenge
revelación *nf* revelation
revelar *v* reveal, disclose
reventa *nf* resale
reventar *v* burst, pop

reventón *nm* blowout
reverencia *nf* bow
reverenciar *v* revere
reversible *adj* reversible
revés *nm* setback
revisar *v* revise, check
revisión *nf* revision, check
revista *nf* magazine
revivir *v* revive; relive
revocación *nf* repeal
revocar *v* repeal, revoke
revolcarse *v* roll around
revolotear *v* flutter
revoltoso *adj* naughty
revólver *v* revolver, gun
revuelo *nm* commotion
revuelta *nf* revolt
revuelto *adj* mixed
rey *nm* king
reyerta *nf* brawl
rezagarse *v* lag behind
rezar *v* pray
ría *nf* estuary
riachuelo *nm* creek
riada *nf* flood
ribera *nf* bank
rico *adj* wealthy, rich
ridículo *adj* ridiculous
riego *nm* watering
rienda *nf* rein
riesgo *nm* risk
rifa *nf* raffle

R

rigidez *nf* stiffness
rígido *adj* rigid, terse, stiff
rigor *nm* rigor
riguroso *adj* strict
rima *nf* rhyme
riña *nf* quarrel
rincón *nm* corner
riñón *nm* kidney
río *nm* river
riqueza *nf* wealth
risa *nf* laughter
risible *adj* laughable
risueño *adj* cheerful
ritmo *nm* rhythm
rito *nm* rite
rival *nm* rival
rivalidad *nf* rivalry
rizado *adj* curly
rizar *v* curl
rizo *nm* curl
robar *v* steal, rob
roble *nm* oak
robo *nm* theft, robbery
robustecer *v* strenghen
robusto *adj* robust
roca *nf* boulder, rock
roce *nm* friction
rociar *v* sprinkle, spray
rocío *nm* dew
rocoso *adj* rocky
rodaja *nf* slice
rodear *v* surround

rodilla *nf* knee
rodillo *nm* roller
roedor *nm* rodent
roer *v* gnaw
rogar *v* beg, plead
rojo *adj* red
rollo *nm* scroll, reel
romance *nm* romance
romería *nf* pilgrimage
rompecabezas *nm* puzzle
romper *v* break
ron *nm* rum
roña *nf* dirt, grime
roncar *v* snore
ronco *adj* hoarse
ronquido *nm* snore
ropa *nf* clothing
ropa blanca *nf* linen
ropa de cama *nf* bedding
ropa interior *nf* underware
ropero *nm* wardrobe
rosa *nf* rose
rosado *adj* pink
rosal *nm* rosebush
rosario *nm* rosary
rosca *nf* thread; cake
rostro *nm* face
rotación *nf* rotation
roto *adj* broken, torn
rótula *nf* kneecap
rótulo *nm* title, inscription
rotundo *adj* outright

R

rotura *nf* fracture
rozar *v* rub
rubí *nm* ruby
rubio *adj* blond
rubor *nm* blush
ruborizarse *v* blush
rudimentario *adj* rudimentary
rudo *adj* rude
rueda *nf* wheel
ruedo *nm* bullring
rugido *nm* roar
rugir *v* roar
ruido *nm* noise
ruidoso *adj* noisy
ruina *nf* ruin
ruiseñor *nm* nightingale
ruleta *nf* roulette
Rumania *nf* Romania
rumano *adj* Romanian
rumiar *v* chew; ponder
rumor *nm* rumor, hearsay
ruptura *nf* break
rural *adj* rural
Rusia *nf* Russia
ruso *adj* Russian
rústico *adj* rustic
ruta *nf* route
rutina *nf* routine

S

sábado *nm* Saturday
sábana *nf* sheet
saber *v* know
saber (a) *adv* namely
sabiduría *nf* wisdom
sabiendas (a) *adv* knowingly
sabio *adj* wise
sabor *nf* taste
saborear *v* relish, savor
sabotaje *nf* sabotage
sabotear *v* sabotage
sabroso *adj* tasty
sacar *v* take out
sacapuntas *nm* sharpener
sacerdocio *nm* priesthood
sacerdote *nm* priest
sacerdotisa *nf* priestess
saciar *v* satisfy
saco *nm* sack
sacramento *nm* sacrament
sacrificio *nm* sacrifice
sacrilegio *nm* sacrilege
sacudida *nf* jerk, jolt
sacudir *v* jolt, shake
sádico *adj* sadist
saeta *nf* arrow
sagaz *adj* shrewd
sagrado *adj* sacred
sal *nf* salt

sala *nf* room

salado *adj* salty

salario *nm* salary, pay

salchicha *nf* sausage

saldar *v* pay off; settle

salida *nf* exit, departure

salir *v* depart, go out

saliva *nf* saliva

saldo *nm* balance

salmo *nm* psalm

salmón *nm* salmon

salón *nm* lounge, parlor

salpicar *v* splash

salsa *nf* sauce, gravy

saltamontes *nm* grasshopper

saltar *v* jump, leap

saltarse *v* skip

salto *nm* leap, jump

salubridad *nf* sanidad

salud *nf* health

saludar *v* greet, nod

saludos *nm* greetings

salvación *nf* salvation

salvado *nm* bran

salvado *adj* saved

salvador *nm* savior

salvaguardar *adj* safeguard

salvaje *adj* savage, wild

salvajismo *nm* savagery

salvar *v* save

salvavidas *nm* lifejacket

salvo *adj* safe

sanar *v* heal

sanción *nf* sanction

sancionar *v* sanction

sandalia *nf* sandal

sandez *nf* stupidity

sandía *nf* watermelon

sangrar *v* bleed

sangre *nf* blood

sangriento *adj* bloody, gory

sanguijuela *nf* leech

sanguinario *adj* bloodthirsty

sanidad *adj* health; sanity

sano *adj* healthy

santidad *nf* holiness

santificar *v* sanctify

santo *nm* saint

santo *adj* holy

santuario *nm* sanctuary

saña *nf* rage

sapo *nm* toad

saque *nm* kickoff

saquear *v* loot, plunder

saqueo *nm* loot, plunder

sarampión *nm* measles

sarcasmo *nm* sarcasm

sarcástico *adj* sarcastic

sardina *nf* sardine

sargento *nm* sergeant

sarro *nm* tartar, plaque

sartén *nf* pan, frying pan

sastre *nm* tailor

satánico *adj* satanic

S

satélite *nm* satellite

sátira *nf* satire

satisfacción *nf* satisfaction

satisfacer *v* satisfy

satisfactorio *adj* satisfactory

saturar *v* saturate

sauce *nm* willow

savia *nf* sap

sazonar *v* flavor, season

sebo *nm* grease

secadora *nf* dryer

secar *v* dry

sección *nf* section

secesión *nf* secession

seco *adj* dried, dry

secretario *nm* secretary

secreto *nm* secret

secreto *adj* secret

secreto (en) *adv* secretly

secta *nf* sect

sector *nm* sector

secuencia *nf* sequence

secuestrador *nm* kidnapper

secuestrar *v* abduct, kidnap

secuestro *nm* abduction

secundario *adj* secondary

sed *nf* thirst

seda *nf* silk

sedación *nf* sedation

sedado *adj* sedated

sede *nf* seat

sediento *adj* thirsty

seducción *nf* seduction

seducir *v* seduce

segar *v* cut, mow

seglar *adj* layman

segmento *nm* segment

segregación *nf* segregation

segregar *v* segregate

seguir *v* follow

según *pre* according to

según dicen *adv* reportedly

segundo *nm* second

segundo *adj* second

seguramente *adv* surely

seguridad *nf* safety

seguro *adj* safe, sure

seguro *nm* insurance

seis *adj* six

selección *nf* selection

seleccionar *v* select

sellar *v* stamp

sello *nm* postage; seal

selva *nf* forest

semáforo *nm* traffic light

semana *nf* week

semblante *nm* countenance, look

sembrar *v* sow

semejante *adj* similar

semejanza *nf* similarity

semestre *nm* semester

semilla *nf* seed

seminario *nm* seminary

senado *nm* senate

senador *nm* senator

senda *nf* path

sendero *nm* trail

seno *nm* bossom

sensación *nf* sensation

sensato *adj* sensible

sensual *adj* sensual

sentarse *v* sit

sentencia *nf* sentence

sentenciar *v* sentence

sentido *nm* meaning; sense

sentimental *adj* sentimental

sentimiento *nm* feeling

sentir *v* feel

seña *nf* gesture

señal *nf* signal

señalar *v* point, indicate

señor *nm* lord, mister, sir

señora *nf* lady, madam

señorita *nf* miss

separación *nf* separation

separar *v* separate

separarse *v* part, secede

septiembre *nm* September

séptimo *adj* seventh

sepulcro *v* tomb, grave

sepultar *v* bury

sequedad *nf* dryness

sequía *nf* drought

séquito *nm* entourage

ser *nm* being

ser *v* be

serenarse *v* calm down

serenata *nf* serenade

serenidad *nf* serenity

sereno *adj* serene

serie *nf* series

seriedad *nf* seriousness

serio *adj* serious

serio (en) *adv* seriously

sermón *nm* sermon

serpiente *nf* serpent, snake

serrar *v* saw

servicio *nm* service

servidumbre *nf* servitude

servilleta *nf* napkin

servir *v* serve

sesenta *adj* sixty

sesión *nf* session, sitting

sesos *nm* brain

seta *nf* mushroom

setenta *adj* seventy

severidad *nf* severity

severo *adj* harsh, severe

sexo *nm* sex

sexto *adj* sixth

sexualidad *nf* sexuality

si *c* if, whether

sí *adv* yes

sicario *nm* assasin

sidra *nf* cider

siembra *nf* sowing

siempre *adv* always

sien *nf* temple

S

sierra *nf* saw; mountain range

sierra eléctrica *n* chainsaw

siervo *nm* servant

siesta *nf* nap

siete *adj* seven

sífilis *nf* syphilis

sifón *nm* syphon

sigiloso *adj* stealthy

siglo *nm* century

significado *nm* meaning

significar *v* mean, signify

significativo *adj* significant

signo *nm* sign

siguiente *adj* next

sílaba *nf* syllable

silbar *v* hiss, whistle

silbato *nm* whistle

silenciador *nm* muffler

silenciar *v* silence

silencio *nm* silence

silla *nf* chair

silla de montar *nf* saddle

silla de ruedas *nf* wheelchair

sillón *nm* armchair

silueta *nf* silhouette

silvestre *adj* wild

sima *adj* chasm

símbolo *nm* symbol

simetría *nf* symmetry

simiente *nf* seed

simio *nm* ape

simpatía *nf* sympathy

simpático *adj* likable, nice

simpatizar *v* sympathize

simple *adj* simple

simplicidad *nf* simplicity

simplificar *v* simplify

simultáneo *adj* simultaneous

sin *pre* without

sin brillo *adv* mate

sin cesar *adv* ceaselessly

sin confirmar *adv* unofficially

sin control *adj* rampant

sin defectos *adj* flawless

sin dolor *adj* painless

sin embargo *c* however, yet

sin empleo *adj* unemployed

sin entrañas *adj* cold-blooded

sin éxito *adj* unsuccessful

sin fondo *adj* bottomless

sin fundamento *adj* groundless

sin hijos *adj* childless

sin hogar *adj* homeless

sin junturas *adj* seamless

sin límites *adj* boundless

sin mangas *adj* sleeveless

sin nubes *adj* cloudless

sin parar *adv* nonstop

sin pepitas *adj* seedless

sin plomo *adj* unleaded

sin recursos *adj* stranded

sin remedio *adj* hopeless

sin reparar *adv* regardless

sin sentido *adj* unconscious

sin un centavo *adj* penniless

sin valor *adj* worthless

sin vida *adj* lifeless

sinagoga *nf* synagogue

sincerarse *v* level with

sinceridad *nf* sincerity

sincero *adj* sincere

sincronizar *v* synchronize

síndrome *nm* syndrome

sinfín *adj* endless

sinfonía *nf* symphony

singular *adj* singular

siniestro *adj* sinister

sínodo *nm* synod

sintasis *nf* syntax

síntesis *nf* synthesis

síntoma *nm* symptom

sintonizar *v* tune

siquiera *adv* at least

sirena *nf* mermaid

sirvienta *nf* housekeeper

sísmico *adj* seismic

sistema *nm* system

sitiar *v* besiege

sitio *nm* place, site

situación *nf* situation

situado *adj* situated

sobaco *nm* armpit

soberanía *nf* sovereignty

soberano *adj* sovereign

soberbia *nf* pride

soberbio *adj* proud

sobornar *v* bribe

soborno *nm* bribery

sobrante *adj* remaining

sobras *nf* leftovers

sobre *nm* envelope

sobre *pre* over, upon, on

sobre todo *adv* above all

sobrecargar *v* overcharge

sobrecogido *adj* startled

sobredosis *nf* overdose

sobreestimar *v* overestimate

sobrellevar *v* endure

sobrenombre *nm* nickname

sobrepasarse *v* go too far

sobrepesar *v* outweigh

sobreponerse *v* overcome

sobresaliente *adj* outstanding

sobresaltarse *v* jump, startle

sobresalir *v* excel; stick out

sobrevivir *v* survive

sobriedad *nf* sobriety

sobrina *nf* niece

sobrino *nm* nephew

sobrio *adj* moderate

socarrón *nm* sarcastic

socavar *v* undermine

sociable *adj* sociable

socialismo *nm* socialism

socialista *adj* socialist

sociedad *nf* society

socio *nm* partner

socorrer *v* help

S

socorrista *nm* lifeguard

soez *adj* vulgar, obscene

sofá *nm* couch, sofa

sofocante *adj* stifling

sofocar *v* suffocate

soga *nf* rope

sol *nm* sun

solamente *adv* only, solely

solapa *nf* lapel

solar *adj* solar

soldado *nm* soldier

soldador *nm* welder

soldar *v* solder, weld

soleado *adj* sunny

soledad *nf* solitude

solemne *adj* solemn

soler *v* use to

solicitante *v* applicant

solicitar *v* request

solidaridad *nf* solidarity

sólido *adj* solid

solitario *adj* solitary; lonely

sollozar *v* sob

sollozo *nm* sob

solo *adv* alone, lonely

solomillo *nm* sirloin

soltar *v* release; loose

soltero *nm* single, bachelor

solterona *nf* spinster

soluble *adj* soluble

solución *nf* solution

solucionar *v* solve

solvente *adj* solvent

sombra *nf* shadow

sombrero *nm* hat

sombrío *adj* grim, somber

someter *v* subject, submit

somnoliento *adj* drowsy

sonar *v* ring, sound

soñar *v* dream

soneto *nm* sonnet

sonido *nm* sound

sonreír *v* smile

sonrisa *nf* smile

sonrojarse *v* blush

sopa *nf* soup

soplar *v* blow

soplo *nm* puff

sopor *nm* drowsiness

soportar *v* bear

soporte *nm* support

sorber *v* sip

sorbito *nm* sip

sordera *nf* deafness

sordo *adj* deaf

sorprendente *adj* amazing

sorprender *v* surprise

sorpresa *nf* surprise

sortear *v* dodge, raffle

sorteo *nm* raffle

sortija *nf* ring

sosegar *v* calm

soso *adj* tasteless

sospecha *nf* suspicion

sospechar *v* suspect
sospechoso *adj* suspect
sostener *v* hold, sustain
sotana *nf* cassock
sótano *nm* basement
su *adj* her, his
suave *adj* soft, smooth
suavidad *nf* softness
subasta *nf* auction
subastador *nm* auctioneer
subastar *v* auction
súbdito *nm* subject
subdividir *v* subdivide
subir *v* go up
súbitamente *adj* suddenly
sublevación *nf* uprising
sublevarse *v* revolt
sublime *adj* sublime
subrayar *v* underline
subscripción *nf* subscription
subsidio *nm* allowance
subsistir *v* subsist, survive
substituir *v* substitute
subtítulo *nm* subtitle
substraer *n* substract
subterráneo *adj* underground
suburbio *nm* suburb
subvención *nf* subsidy
subvencionar *v* subsidize
subyugar *v* subdue
suceder *v* happen, occur
suceso *nm* event

sucesor *nm* successor
suciedad *nf* dirt
sucio *adj* dirty, messy
suculento *adj* succulent
sucumbir *v* succumb
sudar *v* perspire, sweat
sudario *nm* shroud
sudor *nm* sweat
Suecia *nf* Sweden
sueco *adj* Swedish
suegra *nf* mother-in-law
suegro *nm* father-in-law
suegros *nm* in-laws
suela *nf* sole
sueldo *nm* wage
suelo *nm* floor
suelto *adj* loose
sueño *nm* dream
suero *nm* serum
suerte *nf* luck, lot
suéter *nm* sweater
suficiente *adj* sufficient
sufragar *v* pay for
sufrimiento *v* suffering
sufrir *v* suffer
sugerencia *nf* suggestion
sugerir *v* suggest
sugestión *nf* suggestion
sugestivo *adj* suggestive
suicidio *nm* suicide
Suiza *adj* Switzerland
suizo *adj* Swiss

S

sujetapapeles *nm* paperclip
sujetar *v* fasten
suma *nf* addition, sum
sumar *v* add
sumario *nm* summary
sumergir *v* immerse
sumergirse *v* submerge
suministrar *v* supply
suministro *nm* provision
suministros *nm* supplies
sumir *adj* submerge, plunge
sumiso *v* submissive
sumo *adj* cuidado
suntuoso *adj* sumptuous
superar *v* overcome
superficial *adj* shallow
superficie *nf* surface
superfluo *adj* superfluous
superior *adj* superior; upper
superioridad *nf* superiority
supermercado *nm* supermarket
superpoblado *adj* overcrowded
superpotencia *nf* superpower
superstición *nf* superstition
supervisar *v* supervise
supervivencia *nf* survival
superviviente *nm* survivor
suplantar *v* replace
suplente *adj* substitute
súplica *nf* plea
suplicar *v* beg, plead
suplicio *nm* torture

suplir *v* replace
suponer *v* suppose
suponiendo *c* supposing
suposición *nf* assumption
supremo *adj* supreme
supresión *nf* suppression
suprimir *v* abolish
supuestamente *adv* allegedly
supuesto *adj* alleged
sur *nm* south
surco *nm* furrow
sureño *adj* southern
sureste *nm* southeast
surgir *v* emerge, spring
suroeste *nm* southwest
surtido *nm* assortment
surtir *v* provide
susceptible *adj* susceptible
suscitar *v* arouse
suscribir *v* subscribe
suspender *v* suspend, fail
suspensión *nf* suspension
suspicacia *nf* suspicion
suspicaz *adj* suspicious
suspirar *v* sigh, long for
suspiro *nm* sigh
sustancia *nf* substance
sustancial *adj* substantial
sustentar *v* sustain
sustento *nm* livelihood
sustituir *v* substitute
sustituto *nm* substitute

susto *nm* scare, fright
sustracción *nf* substraction
sustraer *v* take away
susurrar *v* whisper
susurro *nm* whisper
sutil *adj* subtle
sutilmente *adv* subtly
suyo *pro* his, hers

T

tabaco *nm* tobacco
taberna *nf* tavern, bar
tabernáculo *nm* tabernacle
tabique *nm* partition, wall
tablero *nm* board
tableta *nf* tablet
taburete *nm* stool
tacaño *adj* stingy
tachar *v* cross out
tachuela *nf* tack
taciturno *adj* somber
tacón *nm* heel
táctica *nf* tactics
táctico *adj* tactical
tacto *nm* tact, touch
tajada *nf* slice
tajo *nm* cut

tal *adj* such
taladrar *v* drill
talante *nm* mood
talento *nm* talent
talla *nf* size
tallar *v* carve
taller *nm* workshop
tallo *nm* stalk, stem
talón *nm* heel
tamaño *nm* size
tambalearse *v* stagger, totter
también *adv* also, too
tambor *nm* drum
tampoco *adv* nor, neither
tanda *nf* shift
tangente *nf* tangent
tangible *adj* tangible
tanque *nm* tank
tantear *v* test, feel
tanto *adj* so much
tañido *nm* peal
tapadera *nf* lid, cover, cap
tapar *v* plug, cover
tapia *nf* wall, fence
tapicería *nf* upholstery
tapiz *nm* tapestry
tapón *nm* plug
taponar *v* block
taquigrafía *nf* shorthand
taquilla *nf* box office
tarántula *nf* tarantula
tararear *v* hum

tardanza *nf* delay
tardar(se) *v* be late
tarde *adv* late, tardy
tarde *nf* afternoon, evening
tardío *adj* slow; late
tarea *nf* assignment, task
tareas *nf* homework
tarifa *nf* tariff, price
tarima *nf* platform
tarjeta *nf* card
tarro *nm* jar
tarta *nf* tart, pie
tartamudear *v* stutter, stammer
tartamudo *adj* stutterer
tasa *nf* rate, tax
tasar *v* value, assess
tasca *nf* cantina, bar
tatuaje *nm* tattoo
taxi *nm* cab
taza *nf* cup, mug
tazón *nm* bawl
té *nm* tea
teatro *nm* theater
techo *nm* ceiling
tecla *nf* key
teclado *nm* keyboard
técnica *nf* technique
técnico *adj* technical
técnico *nm* technician
tecnología *nf* technology
tedio *nm* boredom
teja *nf* tile

tejado *nm* roof
tejer *v* knit, weave
tejido *nm* fabric; tissue
tela *nf* fabric, material
telaraña *nf* web
teléfono *nm* telephone
telegrama *nm* telegram
telepatía *nf* telepathy
telescopio *nm* telescope
televisar *v* televise
televisión *nf* television
telón *nm* curtain
tema *nm* theme, topic
temblar *v* tremble
temblor *nm* tremor
temer *v* fear, be afraid
temerario *adj* reckless
temeroso *adj* afraid, fearful
temible *adj* terrifying
temor *nm* fear
temperatura *nf* temperature
tempestad *nf* storm
tempestuoso *adj* stormy
templado *adj* warm
templo *nm* temple
temporada *nf* season
temporal *adj* temporary
temprano *adv* early
tenacidad *nf* tenacity
tenaz *adj* tenacious
tenazas *nf* pliers, tongs
tendedero *nm* clothes line**

tendencia *nf* tendency
tendón *nm* tendon
tenebroso *adj* gloomy
tenedor *nm* fork
tener *v* have
tener antipatía *v* dislike
tener cuidado *v* beware
tener éxito *v* succeed
tener horror *v* dread
tener intención *v* intend
tener que *v* have to, must
tener sed *v* thirst
teniente *nm* lieutenant
teñir *v* dye
tenis *nm* tennis
tensar *v* tighten, flex
tensión *nf* tension
tenso *adj* uptight, tense
tentación *nf* temptation
tentáculo *nm* tentacle
tentador *adj* tempting
tentar *v* tempt
tenue *adj* tenuous, faint
teología *nf* theology
teólogo *nm* theologian
teoría *nf* theory
teórico *adj* theoretical
terapeutico *adj* therapeutic
terapia *nf* therapy
tercero *adj* third
terciar *v* mediate
terciopelo *nm* velvet

terco *adj* obstinate
tergiversar *v* distort
terminación *nf* completion
terminar *v* finish
terminología *nf* terminology
termita *nf* termite
termómetro *nm* thermometer
termostato *nm* thermostat
ternera *nf* veal
ternero *nm* calf
ternura *nf* tenderness
terquedad *nf* obstinacy
terraza *nf* terrace
terremoto *nm* earthquake
terrenal *adj* earthly
terreno *nm* land
terrestre *adj* terrestrial
terrible *adj* terrible
territorio *nm* territory
terror *nm* terror, fright
terrorismo *nm* terrorism
terrorista *nm* terrorist
tesis *nf* thesis
tesón *nm* tenacity
tesorero *nm* treasurer
tesoro *nm* treasure
testamento *nm* testament
testarudo *adj* stubborn
testificar *v* testify
testigo *nm* witness
testimonio *nm* testimony
tetera *nf* teapot

T

tétrico *adj* gloomy

texto *nm* text

textura *nf* texture

tez *nf* complexion

tía *nf* aunt

tibio *adj* lukewarm

tiburón *nm* shark

tiempo *nm* time; weather

tienda *nf* shop, store

tierno *adj* tender

tierra *nf* earth, soil

tierra (en) *adv* ashore

tieso *adj* stiff

tiesto *nm* flowerpot

tifón *nm* typhoon

tigre *nm* tiger

tijeras *nf* scissors

timar *v* swindle, cheat

timbre *nm* bell

timidez *nf* shyness

tímido *adj* bashful, shy

timo *nm* scam

timón *nm* helm, rudder

tímpano *nm* eardrum

tinieblas *nf* darkness

tino *nm* skill, aim

tinta *nf* ink

tinte *nm* dye

tinto *adj* red

tintorería *nf* dry cleaners

típico *adj* typical

tipo *nm* guy, type

tipográfico *adj* printed

tira *nf* strip

tirada *nf* run

tirador *nm* marksman; knob

tiranía *nf* tyranny

tirano *nm* tyrant

tirante *adj* tight

tirar *v* pull, throw

tiritar *v* shiver

tiro *nm* shot

tirón *nm* pull

tiroteo *nm* shooting, firing

títere *nm* puppet

titubear *v* hesitate

título *nm* heading, title

tiza *nf* chalk, crayon

toalla *nf* towel

tobillo *nm* ankle

tocado *adj* nutty

tocante *pre* with regard to

tocar *v* touch; play

tocino *nm* bacon

todavía *adv* still

todos *adj* all

toldo *nm* awning

tolerable *adj* tolerable

tolerancia *nf* tolerance

tolerar *v* tolerate

tomar *v* take

tomar el pelo *v* tease

tomar el sol *v* bask

tomar prestado *v* borrow

tomate *nm* tomato

tomo *nm* volume

tonel *nm* barrel

tonelada *nf* ton

tónica *nf* tonic

tono *nm* tone

tontería *nf* foolishness

tonto *adj* fool, silly

topar con *v* encounter

tope *nm* limit, end

topo *nm* mole

toque *nm* touch

torbellino *nm* whirlwind

torcer *v* twist

torcerse *v* sprain

torcido *adj* crooked, twisted

torear *v* avoid

torero *nm* bullfighter

tormenta *nf* storm

tormento *nm* torment

tornado *nm* twister

tornarse *v* become

torneo *nm* tournament

tornillo *nm* screw

toro *nm* bull

toronja *nf* grapefruit

torpe *adj* clumsy

torpedear *v* torpedo

torpedo *nm* torpedo

torpeza *nf* clumsiness

torre *nf* tower

torrente *nm* avalanche, stream

torreón *nm* turret

tórrido *adj* torrid

torta *nf* cake

tortículis *nf* stiff neck

tortilla *nf* omelette

tortuga *nf* tortoise, turtle

tortuoso *adj* winding

tortura *nf* torture

torturar *v* torture

tos *nf* cough

tosco *adj* rough

toser *v* cough

tostador *nm* toaster

tostar *v* toast

total *adj* total

totalidad *n* totality

totalitario *adj* totalitarian

totalmente *adv* entirely

tóxico *adj* toxic

toxina *nf* toxin

tozudo *adj* stubborn

trabajador *nm* worker

trabajar *v* work

trabajo *nm* job, work

trabajoso *adj* hard

tradición *nf* tradition

traducir *v* translate

traductor *nm* translator

traer *v* bring

traficante *nm* dealer

traficar *v* trade

tráfico *nm* traffic

T

tragar *v* swallow

tragedia *nf* tragedy

trágico *adj* tragic

trago *nm* drink

traición *nf* betrayal

traicionar *v* betray

traidor *nm* traitor

traje *nm* suit

trajectoria *nf* trajectory

tramar *v* plot

tramitar *v* transact

trámite *nm* formality, step

tramo *nm* section

trampa *nf* trap; scam

trampear *v* cheat

trampolín *nm* springboard

tramposo *adj* crooked

tramposo *nm* cheater

trance *nm* trance

tranquilidad *nf* tranquility

tranquilizar *v* reassure

transacción *nf* transaction

transbordar *v* transfer

transcender *v* transcend

transcribir *v* transcribe

transcurrir *v* lapse

transeunte *nm* passerby

transferir *v* transfer

transformar *v* transform

transformarse *v* become

tránsfuga *nm* defector

transfusión *nf* transfusion

transición *nf* transition

transigir *v* compromise

tránsito *nm* transit

transitorio *adj* transient

transladar *v* transfer

translado *nm* transfer

transmitir *v* transmit

transparente *adj* transparent

transplantar *v* transplant

transportar *v* transport

transtornado *adj* deranged

tranvía *nm* tram, trolley

trapear *v* mop

trapecio *nm* trapeze

trapo *nm* cloth, rag

tráquea *nf* windpipe

traquetear *v* rattle

trascender *v* transcend

trasero *adj* back, rear

traslado *nm* transfer

traslucir *v* reveal, show

trasnochar *v* stay up late

traspasar *v* go through

traspié *nm* stumble, trip

trasquilar *v* shear

trasplantar *v* transplant

trastero *nm* backroom

trastienda *nf* back room

trastornar *v* disrupt

trastorno *nm* disruption

trastos *nm* junk, old dishes

tratado *nm* treaty

tratamiento *nm* treatment

tratar *v* try; treat

tratar de *v* deal

trato *nm* treatment

traumático *adj* traumatic

traumatizar *v* traumatize

travesía *nf* crossing

travesura *nf* mischief, prank

travieso *adj* naughty

trayecto *nm* journey

trayectoria *nf* path, course

trazado *nm* layout

trazar *v* draw, outline

trébol *nm* shamrock

trece *adj* thirteen

trecho *nm* distance, stretch

tregua *nf* truce

treinta *adj* thirty

tremendo *adj* tremendous

tren *nm* train

trenza *nf* braid

trepar *v* climb

trepidar *v* shake, vibrate

tres *adj* three

treta *nf* trick

triángulo *nm* triangle

tribu *nf* tribe

tribulación *nf* tribulation

tribuna *nf* grandstand

tribunal *nm* tribunal

tributo *nm* tribute; tax

trigo *nm* wheat

trillar *v* thresh

trimestral *adj* quarterly

trimestre *nm* trimester

trinchar *v* carve

trinchera *nf* trench

trineo *nm* sleigh

tripa *nf* belly, gut

triple *adj* triple

triplicar *v* triple

tripulación *nf* crew

tripular *v* man

triste *adj* sad

tristeza *nf* sadness

triturar *v* grind; shred

triunfante *adj* triumphant

triunfar *v* win

triunfo *nm* triumph

trivial *adj* trivial

trivializar *v* trivialize

triza *nf* shred, fragment

trofeo *nm* trophy

tromba *nf* downpour

trombosis *nf* thrombosis

trompeta *nf* trumpet

tronco *nm* log

trono *nm* throne

tropa *nf* troop

tropezar *v* stumble, trip

tropezarse con *v* bump into

tropezón *nm* trip, stumble

tropical *adj* tropical

trópico *nm* tropic

T

tropiezo *nm* setback; slip
trozo *nm* bit, chunk, slice
trucha *nf* trout
truco *nm* gimmick, trick
trueno *nm* thunder
tu *adj* your
tú *pro* you
tú mismo *pro* yourself
tuberculosis *nf* tuberculosis
tubería *nf* pipe
tubo *nm* pipe
tuerca *nf* nut
tuerto *adj* with one-eye
tufo *nm* stench; vapour
tulipán *nm* tulip
tullido *adj* crippled
tumba *nf* tomb
tumbar *v* knock down
tumbarse *v* lie down
tumor *nm* tumor
tumulto *nm* commotion, uproar
tumultuoso *adj* tumultuous
tunante *adj* rascal
túnel *nm* tunnel
túnica *nf* tunic
tupido *adj* thick, dense
turba *nf* crowd
turbar *v* upset
turbio *adj* murky
turbulencia *nf* turbulence
turco *adj* Turk
turismo *nm* tourism

turista *nm* tourist
turnarse *v* take turns
turno *nm* turn, shift
Turquía *nf* Turkey
turrón *nm* nougat
tutela *nf* protection
tutor *nm* tutor, guardian
tuyo *pro* yours

uango *adj* baggy
ubicar *v* locate
ufano *adj* proud
ujier *nm* usher
úlcera *nf* ulcer
ulterior *adj* further
últimamente *adv* lately
ultimar *v* finalize
ultimatum *nm* ultimatum
último *adj* last
ultrajar *v* insult
ultraje *nm* outrage, insult
ultratumba *nf* next life
umbral *nm* threshold
un poco *adv* slightly
un(a) *art* a, an
una vez *adv* once

una vez que *c* once
unánime *adj* unanimous
unanimidad *nf* unanimity
undécimo *adj* eleventh
ungir *v* anoint
unguento *nm* ointment
unicamente *adv* only
único *adj* sole, unique
unidad *nf* unit, unity
unificación *nf* unification
unificar *v* unify
uniformar *v* estandardize
uniforme *nm* uniform
uniformidad *nf* uniformity
unilateral *adj* unilateral
unión *nf* union
unir *v* link, join
unirse *v* unite
universal *adj* universal
universidad *nf* university
universo *nm* universe
uno *adj* one
uno mismo *pro* oneself
untar *v* spread
uña *nf* nail, claw
uña del pie *nf* toenail
urbano *adj* urban
urdir *v* plot
urgencia *nf* urgency
urgente *adj* urgent
urgir *v* be urgent
urna *nf* ballot box; urn

usar *v* use, wear
uso *nm* use, wear
usted *pro* you
usuario *nm* user
usura *nf* usury
usurpar *v* usurp, sieze
utensilio *nm* utensil
útero *nm* uterus, womb
útil *adj* useful
utilidad *nf* usefulness
utilizar *v* use
uva *nf* grape

vaca *n* cow
vacación *nf* vacation
vacante *adj* vacant
vaciar *v* empty
vacilante *adj* hesitant
vacilar *v* hesitate
vacío *nm* emptiness
vacío *adj* empty
vacuna *nf* vaccine
vacunar *v* vaccinate
vagabundo *nm* vagrant
vagamente *adv* vaguely
vagancia *v* laziness

vagar *v* loiter, roam

vago *adj* vague, lazy

vagón *nm* wagon, carriage

vagoneta *nf* van

vaina *nf* green bean

vajilla *nf* dishes

vale *nm* voucher

valer *v* be worth; be valid

valedero *adj* valid

valentía *nf* bravery

valeroso *adj* brave

valerse *v* fend, manage

validar *v* validate

válido *adj* valid

valiente *adj* bold, brave

valija *nf* bag

valioso *adj* worthwhile

valla *nf* fence

valle *nm* valley

valor *nm* value, worth

valoración *nf* appraisal

valorar *v* appraise; appreciate

vals *nm* waltz

válvula *nf* valve

vampiro *nm* vampire

vanagloriarse *v* boast

vandalismo *nm* vandalism

vándalo *nm* vandal

vanguardia *nm* vanguard

vanidad *nf* vanity

vanidoso *adj* conceited

vano *adj* vain, futile

vano (en) *adv* in vain

vapor *nm* steam; vapor

vaporizar *v* vaporize

vaquero *nm* cowboy

vaqueros *nm* jeans

vara *nf* stick, rod

variable *adj* variable

variación *nf* variation

variado *adj* assorted, varied

variar *v* vary

variedad *nf* variety

varios *adj* several

varón *nm* male

varonil *adj* manly

vasallo *nm* vassal

vasija *nf* container

vaso *nm* glass

vasto *adj* huge, vast

vaticinar *v* predict

vaticinio *nm* prediction

vatio *nm* watt

veces *nf* times

veces (a) *adv* sometimes

vecindad *nf* neighborhood

vecino *nm* neighbor

vecino *adj* neighboring

vedar *v* ban

vegetación *nf* vegetation

vegetal *nm* vegetable

vegetales *nm* produce

vegetariano *adj* vegetarian

vehículo *nm* vehicle

veinte *adj* twenty
veintiuno *adj* twenty-one
vejación *nf* humilation
vejez *nf* old age
vejiga *nf* bladder
vela *nf* candle, sail
velar *v* look after
velero *nm* sailboat
vello *nm* hair
velloso *adj* hairy
velo *nm* veil
velocidad *nf* velocity
veloz *adj* speedy, fast
vena *nf* vein
venado *nm* deer, elk
vencedor *nm* victor, winner
vencer *v* beat, defeat
venda *nf* bandage
vendar *v* dress, bandage
vendaval *nm* gale
vendedor *nm* seller
vender *v* sell
vendimia *nf* grape harvest
veneno *nm* poison, venom
venenoso *adj* poisonous
venerable *adj* venerable
venerar *v* venerate
venganza *nf* revenge
vengar *v* avenge
vengarse *v* take revenge
vengativo *adj* vindictive
venial *adj* venial

venida *nf* coming
venidero *adj* coming
venir *v* come
venta *nf* sale
ventaja *nf* advantage
ventajoso *adj* advantageous
ventana *nf* window
ventilación *nf* ventilation
ventilador *nm* fan
ventilar *v* air
ventisca *nf* blizzard
ventoso *adj* windy
ver *v* see
veraneante *nm* vacationer
verano *nm* summer
veraz *adj* truthful
verbena *nf* festival
verbo *nm* verb
verdad *nf* truth
verdadero *adj* actual, true
verde *adj* green
verdugo *nm* executioner
verdura *nf* vegetable
veredicto *nm* verdict
vergonzoso *adj* shameful; shy
verguenza *nf* shame
verificación *nf* verification
verificar *v* verify
verosímil *adj* plausible
verruga *nf* wart
versátil *adj* versatile
versión *nf* version

verso *nm* verse

vértebra *nf* vertebra

vertedero *nm* landfill

verter *v* spill, dump

vertiente *nf* slope

vértigo *nm* vertigo

vesícula *nf* gallbladder

vestíbulo *nm* lobby

vestido *nm* dress, garment

vestigio *nm* trace, vestige

vestir *v* wear, clothe

vestirse *v* get dressed

vetar *v* veto

veterano *adj* veteran

veterinario *nm* veterinarian

veto *nm* veto

vez *nf* time

vía *nf* rail

viable *adj* feasible

viaducto *nm* viaduct

viajar *v* travel

viaje *nm* tour, trip

viaje por mar *n* voyage

viajero *nm* traveler

víbora *nf* viper

vibración *nf* vibration

vibrante *adj* vibrant, exciting

vibrar *v* vibrate

viceversa *adv* vice versa

viciado *adj* corrupt

vicio *nm* vice

vicisitudes *adj* ups and downs

víctima *nf* victim

victoria *nf* victory

victorioso *adj* victorious

vid *nf* grapevine

vida *nf* life

vidrio *nm* glass

viejo *adj* old, outdated

viento *nm* wind

vientre *nm* womb

viernes *nm* Friday

viga *nf* beam

vigente *adj* valid

vigésimo *adj* twentieth

vigilancia *nf* surveillance

vigilar *v* watch

vigilia *nf* vigil

vigor *adv* vigor, energy

vil *adj* vile

villancico *nm* carol

villano *nm* villain

vilo *nm* suspense

viña *nf* vineyard

vinagre *nm* vinegar

vincular *v* link

vínculo *nm* bond

vino *nm* wine

violación *nf* rape

violador *nm* rapist

violar *v* rape

violencia *nf* violence

violento *adj* violent

violeta *nf* violet

violín *nm* violin

violinista *nm* violinist

viraje *nm* turn

virar *v* turn, swerve

virgen *adj* virgin

virginidad *nf* virginity

virilidad *nf* virility

virrey *nm* viceroy

virtual *adj* virtual

virtud *nf* virtue

virtuoso *adj* virtuous

viruela *nf* smallpox

virulento *adj* virulent

virus *nm* virus

visado *nm* visa

visibilidad *nf* visibility

visible *adj* visible

visión *nf* vision

visita *nf* visit

visitante *nm* visitor

visitar *v* visit

vislumbrar *v* glimpse

víspera *nf* eve

vista *nf* sight, view

vista general *n* overview

vistazo *v* glimpse, look

vistoso *adj* colorful

visual *adj* visual

visualizar *v* visualize

vital *adj* vital

vitalidad *nf* vitality

vitamina *nf* vitamin

vitorear *v* cheer

vituperar *v* insult

viuda *nf* widow

viudo *nm* widower

vivaz *adj* vivacious

víveres *nm* supplies

vivero *nm* nursery

vivienda *nf* dwelling, house

viviente *adj* living

vivir *v* live

vivo *adj* alive

vocabulario *nm* vocabulary

vocación *nf* vocation

vocal *nf* vowel

volar *v* fly

volante *nm* steering wheel

volátil *adj* volatile

volcán *nm* volcano

volcar *v* overturn

vólibol *nm* volleyball

voltaje *nm* voltage

voltear *v* turn over

voluble *adj* fickle

volumen *nm* volume

voluminoso *adj* bulky

voluntad *nf* will

voluntario *adj* volunteer

volver *v* return, go back

vomitar *v* vomit

vómito *nm* vomit

voraz *adj* voracious

vosotros *pro* you (pl)

votación *nf* ballot
votante *nm* voter
votar *v* vote
voto *nm* vote; vow
voz *nf* voice
vuelo *nm* flight
vuelta *nf* return, turn
vuelta (de) *adv* back
vuestro *adj* your (pl)
vulgar *adj* vulgar
vulgaridad *nf* vulgarity
vulnerable *adj* vulnerable
vulnerar *v* harm, hurt

Y

y *c* and
ya *adv* already
ya que *c* since
yacer *v* lie
yacimiento *nm* deposit
yarda *nf* yard
yate *nm* yacht
yedra *nf* ivy
yegua *nf* mare
yema *nf* yolk; fingertip
yerno *nm* son-in-law
yeso *nm* plaster

yo *pro* I
yo mismo *pro* myself
yodo *nm* iodine
yugo *nm* yoke
yunque *nm* anvil

Z

zafiro *nm* sapphire
zalamero *adj* flattering
zambullida *nf* plunge
zambullirse *v* dive
zanahoria *nf* carrot
zancudo *nm* mosquito
zanja *nf* ditch
zapatería *nf* shoe store
zapatero *nm* shoemaker
zapato *nm* shoe
zar *nm* czar
zarandear *v* shake
zarpa *nf* claw
zarzamora *nf* blackberry
zinc *nm* zinc
zona *nf* zone
zoología *nf* zoology
zoológico *nm* zoo
zorra *nf* fox
zumbar *v* buzz

zumbido *nm* buzz
zumo *nm* juice
zurcir *v* darn

zurdo *adj* left-handed
zurrar *v* spank

Z

Word to Word® Bilingual Dictionary Series

Language - Item Code - Pages ISBN #

Albanian - 500X - 345 pgs
ISBN - 978-0-933146-49-5

Amharic - 820X - 362 pgs
ISBN - 978-0-933146-59-4

Arabic - 650X - 378 pgs
ISBN - 978-0-933146-41-9

Bengali - 700X - 372 pgs
ISBN - 978-0-933146-30-3

Burmese - 705X - 310 pgs
ISBN - 978-0-933146-50-1

Cambodian - 710X - 376 pgs
ISBN - 978-0-933146-40-2

Chinese - 715X - 374 pgs
ISBN - 978-0-933146-22-8

Farsi - 660X - 372 pgs
ISBN - 978-0-933146-33-4

French - 530X - 358 pgs
ISBN - 978-0-933146-36-5

German - 535X - 352 pgs
ISBN - 978-0-933146-93-8

Gujarati - 720X - 334 pgs
ISBN - 978-0-933146-98-3

Haitian-Creole - 545X - 362 pgs
ISBN - 978-0-933146-23-5

Hebrew - 665X - 316 pgs
ISBN - 978-0-933146-58-7

Hindi - 725X - 362 pgs
ISBN - 978-0-933146-31-0

Hmong - 728X - 294 pgs
ISBN - 978-0-933146-31-0

Italian - 555X - 362 pgs
ISBN - 978-0-933146-51-8

Japanese - 730X - 372 pgs
ISBN - 978-0-933146-42-6

Korean - 735X - 374 pgs
ISBN - 978-0-933146-97-6

Lao - 740X - 319 pgs
ISBN - 978-0-933146-54-9

Pashto - 760X - 348 pgs
ISBN - 978-0-933146-34-1

Polish - 575X - 358 pgs
ISBN - 978-0-933146-64-8

Portuguese - 580X - 362 pgs
ISBN - 978-0-933146-94-5

Punjabi - 765X - 358 pgs
ISBN - 978-0-933146-32-7

Romanian - 585X - 354 pgs
ISBN - 978-0-933146-91-4

Russian - 590X - 334 pgs
ISBN - 978-0-933146-92-1

Somali - 830X - 320 pgs
ISBN- 978-0-933146-52-5

Spanish - 600X - 400 pgs
ISBN - 978-0-933146-99-0

Swahili - 835X - 308 pgs
ISBN - 978-0-933146-55-6

Tagalog - 770X - 332 pgs
ISBN - 978-0-933146-37-2

Thai - 780X - 354 pgs
ISBN - 978-0-933146-35-8

Turkish - 615X - 348 pgs
ISBN - 978-0-933146-95-2

Ukrainian - 620X - 337 pgs
ISBN - 978-0-933146-25-9

Urdu - 790X - 360 pgs
ISBN - 978-0-933146-39-6

Vietnamese - 795X - 366 pgs
ISBN - 978-0-933146-96-9

All languages are two-way: English-Language / Language-English. More languages in planning and production.

Order Information

To order our Word to Word® Bilingual Dictionaries or any other products from Bilingual Dictionaries, Inc., please contact us at (951) 296-2445 or visit us at **www.BilingualDictionaries.com**. Visit our website to download our current Catalog/Order Form, view our products, and find information regarding Bilingual Dictionaries, Inc.

 Bilingual Dictionaries, Inc.

PO Box 1154 • Murrieta, CA 92562 • Tel: (951) 296-2445 • Fax: (951) 461-3092
www.BilingualDictionaries.com